JOHNATHAN THURSTON

THE AUTOBIOGRAPHY

JOHNATHAN THURSTON

THE AUTOBIOGRAPHY

WITH JAMES PHELPS

HarperCollins*Publishers*

HarperCollins*Publishers*

First published in Australia in 2018
by HarperCollins*Publishers* Australia Pty Limited
ABN 36 009 913 517
harpercollins.com.au

Copyright © Thurston Promotions Pty Ltd 2018

The right of Johnathan Thurston to be identified as the author of this work has been
asserted by him in accordance with the *Copyright Amendment (Moral Rights) Act 2000*.

HarperCollins*Publishers*
Level 13, 201 Elizabeth Street, Sydney NSW 2000, Australia
Unit D1, 63 Apollo Drive, Rosedale, Auckland 0632, New Zealand
A 53, Sector 57, Noida, UP, India
1 London Bridge Street, London, SE1 9GF, United Kingdom
Bay Adelaide Centre, East Tower, 22 Adelaide Street West, 41st floor, Toronto,
Ontario M5H 4E3, Canada
195 Broadway, New York NY 10007, USA

A catalogue record for this book is available from the National Library of Australia

ISBN 978 1 4607 5260 9 (hardback)
ISBN 978 1 4607 0741 8 (ebook)

Cover and internal design by Hazel Lam, HarperCollins Design Studio
Front cover photo by Mark Evans/Newspix (NP1222643)
Back cover photo by Grant Trouville/National Rugby League (SOO 2016 RD02)
Internal photos: p14, Thurston Family Collection; p82, Daniel Berehulak/Getty;
p184, Cameron Spencer/Getty; p318, Grant Trouville/NRL Photos;
p370, Scott Davis/NRL Photos.
'JT' poem © Rupert McCall, 2018
Typeset in Sabon LT Std by Kirby Jones
Printed and bound in Australia by McPherson's Printing Group
The papers used by HarperCollins in the manufacture of this book are a natural, recyclable
product made from wood grown in sustainable plantation forests. The fibre source and
manufacturing processes meet recognised international environmental standards, and carry
certification.

This book is for Samantha Thurston;
you made me a better person.
You have given me my world.

CONTENTS

PART THREE: THE RISE

PART FOUR: THE LEGEND

JOHNATHAN THURSTON

THE CAREER

NRL

323 Games (29 Bulldogs, 294 Cowboys)

178 Wins (20 Bulldogs, 158 Cowboys)

90 Tries (10 Bulldogs, 80 Cowboys)

923 Goals (third-most all-time)

2222 Points (third-most all-time)

Premierships (Bulldogs 2004, Cowboys 2015)

The Deadlys Indigenous NRL Player of the Year Award
(2006, 2007, 2009, 2011, 2013)

Preston Campbell Medal (2010, 2017)

RLPA Player's Champion Award (2005, 2013, 2014, 2015)

Arthur Beetson Medal (2017)

Provan-Summons Medal (2014, 2015)

Clive Churchill Medal (2015)

Dally M Medal (2005, 2007, 2014, 2015)

STATE OF ORIGIN

37 Games (24 wins, 5 tries)

99 Goals (most all-time)

220 Points (most all-time)

Wally Lewis Medal (2008)

Peter Jackson Memorial Trophy (2012, 2017)

WORLD CLUB CHALLENGE

Graham Murray Medal (2016)

TESTS

38 Games (35 wins, 13 tries)

165 Goals (most for Australia)

382 Points (most for Australia)

Harry Sunderland Medal (2013)

GOLDEN BOOT AWARD FOR BEST PLAYER IN THE WORLD

(2011, 2013, 2015)

HUMANITARIAN AWARDS

Ken Stephen Medal (2012)

Honorary Doctorate of Letters, James Cook University (2015)

Australian Human Rights Commission Medal (2017)

Queensland Australian of the Year (2018)

JOHNATHAN THURSTON
THE AUTOBIOGRAPHY

Edge a little closer friends cos this is what it means
When you rise up from the ashes and life's beauty intervenes
Humility speaks volumes when a champion stands tall
Never let them tell you that you're *'just a bit too small'*
And, in handing out his headgear, so the fable lifts him higher
Cos in every heart that feels his pride, it lights another fire
For his club, his state, his country – for his people, just the same
The one who always tried his best – *'Hey tell me that kid's name!'*
It is written in the dreaming now for all the world to see
And forever to remember ... the remarkable JT

Rupert McCall

A COWBOY AND A CROWN
PROLOGUE

MY LEGS WERE JELLY. GONE. I could barely walk. *Take your time. You need to get your legs back.* The crowd roared. The screams were deafening. *Compose yourself. Block it all out.* Easier said than done.

I can't remember who gave me the ball, but there it was in my hands. Now it was just me and a ball. A kicking tee and the goalposts.

The siren had sounded and it was all on me. I was one kick away from delivering the Cowboys a fairytale title: the NRL premiership I had been brought to North Queensland to win. It was a moment 10 years in the making. I was also one miss away from going on suicide watch.

The gravity of the moment hit me.

Block it out.

I looked into the crowd. I scanned the heaving mass of colour, attempting to find faces amid the flags, banners and pumping fists. Not just faces, but two very familiar ones: those of my partner and my daughter.

OK ... Where are you, Sam? Where are you, Frankie? I need you now.

I needed to see them. Their eyes would calm me. Their smiles would ground me. And their love would take away the enormity of what I faced.

Soon the noise was gone. I was alone in the stadium. Just a kid and his ball. But I still couldn't feel my legs.

I can't do this. I am spent.

I needed to take my time. I needed the blood to return to my limbs. I had never been this buggered. Legs filled with lead, hips bruised and beaten. So I looked back into the crowd, searched for those familiar faces. And slowly my legs came back. I was good to go.

Let's do this.

I looked at the posts, the towering white sticks growing from the hallowed turf of ANZ Stadium. I did the calculations in my head.

Distance? Check. *Angle?* Check. *Hook?* Check. *Wind?* Check.

I placed the ball on the mark and began steeling myself. It was all up to me. This was the biggest moment in my career. The day I had dreamed about since I was four. Siren sounded, game on the line, ball in my hands.

Was I a champion or a chump?

Shut up. Block it out.

I had to get rid of those thoughts. I had to tell myself it was just another kick. I had to block out everything and get on with it. Again I looked for Sam. Scanned the crowd for Frankie.

Suddenly I couldn't hear a thing. The crowd was gone and so was the head noise. Silence. I was just taking a kick for goal. A kid in a park doing that thing he loves.

I got down on my knees and placed the ball. I was a metre away from the sideline, and 21 metres out from the try line. I hadn't taken the ball back as far as I normally would because there was such a strong breeze swirling in the sold-out stadium that night. The wind was going to hold up my hook. Yeah ... that hook.

I usually go back 24 metres when I am that close to the sideline. Taking the ball back that far allows for the amount of hook I put on the ball. It gives the footy time to curl back and, hopefully, go straight over the black dot. But for this kick, the biggest kick of my career, I only went back 21 metres.

So there I was, tee placed, ball aimed towards the target, a study of concentration and steely nerve.

'Na, JT,' said the referee. 'Out there. The try was scored further out. Come on, mate ...'

Shit.

I was rattled. 'Oh,' I said. 'Sweet.'

Fifty centimetres? Are you serious? Jeez.

Stunned but silent, I picked the ball up and placed it on the mark the referee was pointing at. It was almost the greatest mistake of my life. Instead of moving the ball across and then back, which would allow that little extra for my hook, I simply moved it across.

Anyway ...

I went about clearing my head as I placed the tee on the ground. I was looking through the posts to find my new mark when my concentration was suddenly shattered.

'JT,' shouted a voice, a very familiar voice. 'You want 500 bucks, old mate?'

I turned and Allan Langer (Alfie) was smiling. The Broncos legend turned Broncos trainer stood behind me, water bottle in hand, grin slapped across his face.

'Well, miss it and it's yours.'

Now I was laughing, at least inside. Bloody Alfie.

I looked back at the ball and cleared my head. Again. Then I stood up, the breeze at my back and took five steps back.

I checked my mark. My aim was true. I then looked down at the ball. I was going to come over the top of it a little bit more than usual to keep it lower and out of the breeze.

I wiggled my toes as I stared at the ball. My legs had finally returned to me. I imagined the feeling of the ball hitting my foot. I felt good. I was set. I took another little look at my mark behind the posts: I was smack bang on target. I pulled up my socks and went back in to address the ball.

You got this.

Now it was just me, the ball and the posts. I could hear nothing and I felt nothing. I took my final steps to get into my kicking position: five back, two left, and another back.

There were no nerves, no fear and no hesitation. I imagined the kick in my head. In my mind, I moved in and nailed the footy, sent it sailing between the posts.

Now to do it for real. I moved in, taking another step back and another across before beginning my march, and I launched my foot into the ball.

Whack!

I hit it sweet. Exactly where I wanted. Time seemed to stop as I watched the ball. It was heading towards its target, beginning wide as planned and now coming back.

That's it. Come back some more ...

And it did. I thought it was going over. I raised my arm, celebration set. It was going over for all money.

Oh no …

The breeze began holding the ball up.

It's going to miss!

And it did.

I was suddenly cold. Shocked still. My heart seemingly stopped. As did time. The ball had hit the right post. I had missed by a centimetre. Maybe two.

Fuck! How did that miss? Fuuuuck!

I was shattered. I could have ended the game there and then. Won the premiership. It was the moment I had waited a lifetime for. And I failed.

Fuck!

You don't need to be a lip reader to work out what I said. And I was filthy with myself for not taking the ball back half a step when the referee moved my mark. I would have nailed that kick had I just taken it back half a step. But I hadn't made that minor adjustment and demons were now in my head.

That's it. You blew it.

The boys came rushing in. Kyle Feldt (Feldty), Michael Morgan and James Tamou.

'We got this,' one of them yelled. 'Pull your lip up. This is ours.'

Then Lachlan Coote and Gavin Cooper (Coops).

'Let's do this,' Coops shouted.

Soon every single member of the team had given me a slap on the back. 'It's not over,' someone said. 'Job still to be done.'

And just like that I forgot about the kick. I was ready to go. Enter golden point extra time.

Our assistant coach, David Furner, walked over and delivered a message from Paul Green, our coach. 'We're going to kick off if we win the toss,' he said.

Really? Why would we do that?

'What?' I said. 'Kick off?'

In the first five minutes of golden point you will get the ball three times if you receive. Generally you only get it twice if you kick. I wanted the extra set.

'Na, we want the ball,' I said.

He shook his head.

I too was shaking my head as I walked over to the coin toss. My good mate Justin Hodges, the Broncos captain, was already standing next to the referee. I gave him a hug.

'Heads,' I called as the coin was launched into the air.

And sure enough it was a head.

'We'll kick off,' I said through gritted teeth. I didn't think it was the right decision.

Kick off? Two sets with the ball?

But I wasn't going to overcall the coach, not now, not ever.

I threw the ball to Feldty and took up my defensive position on the field: the wing. Ha. Ha. That is the best place to defend.

The whistle resumed what had already been an 80-minute war. Kyle Feldt launched the ball into the air. It was one of his towering kick-offs, a satellite-scraping screamer.

I rocketed downfield, racing towards the target zone. I followed the ball, the Steeden swirling. It was a grenade. Still, I can't believe what happened next ...

I was about 15 metres away from Broncos No. 7 Ben Hunt when he dropped the ball – it bounced off his chest and slipped through his hands. I was preparing to put my shoulder into him when the football hit the ground. Astounding.

Hunt was shattered. He turned his back and shook his head. I ran towards Feldty.

'Oh, yeah,' I yelled. 'This is ours.'

It didn't cross my mind to give Hunt a spray. I saw him, down on his haunches, struggling to contain his tears. He was devastated. I might have said a word or two to another player, a few choice words to get inside his head, but the Broncos players are like brothers to me. I know most of the boys really well. We have played Origin together and have a close bond. I have so much respect for that team.

So I said nothing to Hunt, instead barking orders to my team.

'This is it, boys,' I said. 'This is our chance.'

I pleaded for calm. I told them to prepare for what was to come: a full set of six, right in front of the posts. And even better, the first play was to come off a scrum. Receiving the ball from a scrum restart was ideal for a field-goal attempt. Six defenders were going to be out of the defensive line, and there would be no markers to rush me down.

We quickly set up the play. I asked for two blockers. I was going to have the shot on play one.

I went through it in my head. I knew I wouldn't have a lot of time. The Broncos would know it was coming as soon as I took my mark. I was going to have the man who locked the scrum rushing at me. The pair in the back row too. I would be a marked man.

I went back to the 20 to give myself some space. Still, I would have to catch and snap. I stood with my hands out and waited for the ball. Again I was one kick away from winning a grand final …

And then it was in my hands. Jake Granville (Jakey) had pulled the ball from the scrum and fired it my way.

Oh no ... Broncos everywhere.

I was confronted by a maroon-and-yellow swarm, buzzing bees, stingers set. There was no way I could get to a drop kick. So I stepped off my right foot and I ran.

Not again ...

I was tackled about 15 metres out. I played the ball and Jason Taumalolo went on a charge. He was tackled just metres from the line. We were now too close to the try line to have a shot at goal from first receiver. There would be too much pressure with the defensive line just metres away.

'This is your kick, Cootey,' I said as I pointed towards Lachlan Coote.

Cootey could kick them pretty sweet. He had already won a game by booting a field goal earlier that year. I pointed to the spot where I wanted him and he moved into position. I thought I could give him enough space. Jake hit me from dummy half and I flung it to Coote.

'Noooo,' I heard him yell. Too late, the ball had been let loose.

Hunt, out for redemption, was charging at him. Coote was no chance of having a shot. He took the ball and stepped to his right before charging left. He shovelled the ball to Kane Linnett near the sideline.

Not again.

This was fast becoming a nightmare.

Coote took the ball from Jakey and fired it to Tamou for a settler. He was tackled 12 metres out from the Broncos' try line. Suddenly I had the ball in my hands. I was, again, 20 metres out and right in front. I looked up and had some space. It was now or never.

Whack!

My foot crashed into the synthetic Steeden.

Yuk!

I had come over the top of the footy. I hadn't dropped the ball cleanly and I miskicked it. I had hit belly instead of a point. My heart sank to my stomach as I watched the footy climb into the air, over defenders and into the night.

Maybe ...

It was low and flat, but it was straight.

Oh yeah!

It went over. Cue the celebrations.

I raised my hand into the air. Triumph. I turned and launched myself at Lachlan Coote, for no other reason than that he was the closest. He took me in his arms and lifted me into the air. I was then mobbed by the boys. One by one they jumped on me, all screaming, crying and hugging. Madness. Ecstasy. But for me, more than anything, relief.

I had done it. Finally. I had won a premiership with the Cowboys. Right then and there, the weight of the world was lifted from my shoulders. I was the one who almost lost the game by missing the conversion kick. I again missed a chance off the scrum. Now I had made up for it.

Yes, I had kicked a field goal to win a grand final in golden point extra time. But in that moment I had merely redeemed myself.

The celebrations came. Oh, did they ever! I cried, laughed and screamed. I hugged, kissed and high-fived. It was madness.

Whack!

Coops came into for a hug but head-butted me instead. The force of the blow split me open. There was blood but no pain. Nothing could hurt, not in this moment.

*

A lot of the rest is a blur. I remember doing an interview. It would have been pure gibber. I was an emotional wreck.

Soon I was on stage being presented with the Clive Churchill Medal. It should have been a great moment. It wasn't.

I don't think I deserved that award. I wasn't the best player on that day. I felt nothing but embarrassment as my name was called. I made an error in the first half, which had led to a try. Early in the second half I got a poor last-tackle kick away. It led to a penalty goal.

I wasn't the man of the match, but here I was getting this medal, one of the most prestigious awards in the game. And it really brought me down. I was sweating as I walked offstage. I didn't want the thing. It wasn't mine to own. I looked at the boys. There was Jason Taumalolo: he deserved the medal more than me. He had a huge game. And there was Jake Granville, equally deserving. To be honest I think Anthony Milford from the Broncos should have got it. He had the most influence of any player in the game.

'Well done, mate,' said coach Paul Green as I rejoined the group.

I shook my head. 'I don't deserve this,' I said.

He got angry. 'Shut up,' he said. 'Of course you do. Don't you dare let anything spoil this moment.'

He was right. It was time to celebrate, best on ground or not. We were the premiers. And I had this medal whether or not I deserved it.

I went off to find Sam and Frankie. I wanted to share the grand final win with them.

'Yes,' Sam screamed when she gave me a hug. 'You did it.'

I couldn't talk. I just hugged her and gave her a kiss. I grabbed Frankie and launched her into the air. I took her out on the field and put her on my lap.

What a moment.

And then it all becomes a blur ... again. There were friends, family and high-fives. Beers and bourbons. We partied in the sheds.

Later we walked out onto an empty stadium, the fans long gone home. It was just us: the Cowboys, the NRL premiers. We sat around the trophy and sipped on beer. It was a very special moment. I looked at the posts and reflected on what had happened right here, only a few hours before. Crazy. Misses and hits. From zero to hero. Wow.

I have had so many great moments in my career, but this was the best.

I had been brought to the Cowboys to win a premiership. And now it was job done. It had taken me a lot longer than I would have liked: 10 years of trying. But finally, we were the NRL premiers.

And I had played my part.

But this story doesn't begin in 2015. Not at ANZ Stadium with a Clive Churchill Medal and a premiership trophy. It begins in a Brisbane backyard. With a boy, a ball and a bloody big dream.

JOHNATHAN THURSTON
THE AUTOBIOGRAPHY

THE KID

PART ONE

SLIPPERS, SPACE INVADERS AND SOFT DRINK

CHAPTER 1

IT WAS MOSTLY PINK, SOFT and fluffy on top, rock-hard and ribbed on the bottom. And boy, did it hurt.

'No, Mum,' I pleaded. 'Not the slipper. Please. I'm sorry.'

Too late ...

Mum had already turned her night-time footwear into a weapon. Kicked from her foot and caught in hand, the slipper was a whip: cocked and ready to crack.

'You are getting it, boy,' she howled. 'You can't behave like that.'

Mum's slipper had a cream sole, grooved for grip, or maybe to tattoo? On top it was soft and fluffy, its brutality masked.

We got yelled at when we were bad. We got the slipper when we were worse.

'Come here now,' she said, her voice all no-nonsense and direct. 'You're getting a smack. Come over here and get it now.'

Oh no. Not the slipper.

I stayed put.

'Now,' she said, even louder. 'Make me come and get you and you'll get two.'

She meant what she said. I slowly edged her way.

'Soft?' I asked. 'Don't hit me hard.'

I tried to look cute. It didn't work.

'Ahhhh,' I screamed as the rubber sole turned into a whip and smacked into my bum.

I jumped around, a cat on a hot tin roof. She cocked the slipper again.

'I'm sorry,' I cried. 'Sorry. Sorry. Sorry.'

'Have you learned your lesson?' she said, the slipper still locked and loaded. 'I don't want to have to do this again.'

I nodded. I didn't stop the hysterics until I got to my room. I shut the door and went to the mirror.

Jeez!

My bum was all rising welts, a size six forming on flesh. She got me good.

Yep. Little JT could be a bugger ... surprise, surprise. I was as naughty as I was nice. And mostly I got what I deserved. Mum was the one to dish out the discipline. Oh, Dad had a big hand – *huge* – and it smacked me more than I would have liked, but mostly he was the threat and Mum was the reality. Mum would use Dad as a warning.

'Do you want me to get your father?' she would ask.

Duh.

Of course I didn't. So Dad was more last resort and less regularity.

Cruel?

No. I deserved everything I got. The slipper only came out when I went too far. We don't smack kids these days, but back then it was part and parcel of raising a child. I got nothing I didn't deserve. In fact Mum should have upgraded to a belt!

So don't go calling DOCS, but, by all means, if you need some advice on slippers, give her a buzz.

Now let's get into my childhood: a tale of soft drinks, Space Invaders and, of course, Steeden footballs.

'Hey, Johnny, you want to be our ball boy?' Dad asked.

I looked at him and shook my head. 'Nup,' I said. 'I'm good.'

Why on earth would I want to spend my afternoon chasing footballs when I could be playing in the mud with my mates?

'I'll pay you dollar,' he said. 'All you have to do is kick the football back.'

Now he had my attention.

How many cans of Fanta could I buy for a buck? Maybe 10. *Red frogs?* Like 100.

'OK,' I said. 'But you better pay up. And I'm going to spend it at the canteen after the game. Don't tell me I have to save it for a car or something stupid.'

My professional rugby league career began when I was four. I was employed as a ball boy for the Acacia Ridge Hotel A-grade rugby league team. I couldn't have cared less about football. I did it for soft drinks and sweets. Somewhere in Brisbane, on a suburban ground, this future Kangaroo picked up a football for the very first time because his dad offered him a dollar.

My father, Graeme Thurston, was an A-grade footy player. He played for Acacia Ridge Hotel and also another club called Browns Plains. And apparently, he was pretty good.

'Oh, he was a tough bastard,' one of his mates told me later. 'Real hard. I loved playing with him. When it was on, you wanted him by your side. I'm glad he was in my trench.'

Dad played a bit of hooker and also back row. He wasn't a big bloke, but what he lacked in size he made up for with heart. Apparently he would take anyone on. I can't remember too much of what he was like as a player, I was too busy chasing balls and thinking about how many red frogs I could buy with a buck. Others have filled me in.

'Not a thing like you,' said another of his mates. 'Good, but a completely different player.'

So I pulled up my socks and positioned myself on the sideline. The referee blew his whistle; it was game on.

Whack!

A pair of giants collided. That must have hurt.

Crunch!

Another couple came together on the next play. It was brutal, and I loved it. The men were huge – well, they certainly looked that way to an all-skin-and-bone four-year-old – and they were smashing each other. It was violent, fast and loud.

Was it better than throwing mud at my mates?

Maybe ...

Soon the ball was hurtling towards the touchline. End over end, the football was a heat-seeking missile on a mission to take out the corner post. I would later find out it was called a grubber kick. But whatever, it was time to earn my buck. My little legs pumped as I ran down the field. I moved as fast as I could.

Damn. That's going to end up on the highway.

But then, all of a sudden, it pulled up. The thick, wet grass – only the playing field had been mowed – stopped the ball dead.

Pheeewwww!

I didn't want to chase it over the fence. I picked it up and booted it back onto the field. And I reckon that was my very first rugby league kick.

And I get a dollar for doing this?

I can't say I fell in love with rugby league right away – that didn't happen until I was about six. Until then it was all about spending the dollar Dad would give me, without fail after every match, at the canteen.

One ground had a Space Invaders machine, the old coffee-table type with the wooden base and glass top. Oh, how I loved that friggin' thing.

I would be on Dad as soon as the whistle went, my father exhausted, battered and bruised after his 80-minute war.

'Can you give the dollar to me in 20-cent coins?' I would ask.

He soon learned to keep small change.

I would then go and stack the coins on the top of the machine, and, one by one, they would disappear into its belly.

Yep ... Space Invaders, soft drinks and sweets; that is how I discovered rugby league.

I was born into a big family. And when I say big, I mean *big*. My mum – Debbie Saunders – is one of 13. She has nine brothers and three sisters. So that means I have nine uncles, three aunties and a shitload of cousins.

Ha!

I am not real good at maths, so I am not going to count. But what I can tell you is that family has been a *big* part of my life. My childhood home was a brick three-bedder in Brisbane. Brand new when we moved in, it was a housing commission house on Commodore Street, Sunnybank Hills, in the southern suburbs of Brisbane. And it became a hub for family Thurston and Saunders.

With a *big* backyard, and an even *bigger* front yard, our house was the perfect place for a *big* family to get together. I can't remember a time when the house wasn't packed, jammed and almost bursting the bricks it was made of.

My early life was all barbecues, family and fun.

Did I mention I had a *big* family?

They might as well have moved in; in fact, some of them did. The rest would come round every other day. And that is exactly how my Mum wanted it.

Debra Saunders is the matriarch of my family. She has three sons, a daughter-in-law, nine brothers, three sisters, and a *shitload* of nieces and nephews. My mother made it her mission in life to keep our family together. The second eldest in her family after Uncle Robert, she is the glue that holds my *big* family together.

We have had plenty of drama over the years: fights and fists. But Mum has always sorted it all out. Yeah, she is the boss. No doubt about it. Just ask her. But seriously, the old lady could put her foot down. And when she did we all listened.

Remember the slipper?

Dad, a fitter and turner by trade, used to work long hours. He would leave before I woke up and get home after sunset. He also spent a lot of time on the road. But Mum was always home and we became inseparable. Later on she would go and work for the Queensland Police Force as a liaison officer up in Brisbane. But in the early days she was always there to give me a big fat hug whenever I needed one.

Or a smack with that bloody slipper!

*

Being surrounded by people was my norm; I can't imagine growing up any other way. I have no doubt it made me the person I am today.

I was a second child. Both my mum and dad have children from previous marriages. I have an older brother: Robert, from Mum's first marriage. And I have an older sister: Katrina, from Dad's first marriage.

Dad emigrated from New Zealand – yeah, yeah, I'm half Kiwi – before I was born. His daughter, Katrina, and former wife stayed in New Zealand. I didn't meet my sister until I was eight.

Robert lived between our house in Brisbane and his dad's in Melbourne. He is five years older than me, and, yes, we were always at each other. Mostly it would be over video games. We used to hire a Sega Master System in the holidays.

Remember *Double Dragon*? *Out Run*? *Alex Kidd in Mirade World*? Well, classic arcade games like this turned the lounge room into a war zone.

'Give me the control pad, Johnny,' Rob said. 'It's my go. You just died.'

I looked at him and smiled, before turning back to the screen.

To continue press X.

I pressed X.

'It's my bloody go,' he yelled. 'You can't play again.'

Rob jumped up and moved his skinny little arse in front of the TV. I couldn't see a thing.

'Move,' I screamed. 'Get out of the way. You can play next.'

He wouldn't. So I threw the controller at his head.

'You're dead,' he screamed, his right foot powering forward to begin his charge.

I was off the moment the controller left my hand.

There were sliding doors leading from the lounge room to the backyard, and another set leading to the front yard. Mum always left both sets open because I had run into them once or twice. I went towards the doors leading to the front yard, and with a lightning step to the left I was through and out on to the patio.

Whack!

This time I stepped off my right foot, the evasive action stopping me from crashing into the privacy screen attached to the patio. I was heading full speed towards the tree.

Bang!

Another step, again a left. Now I was running circles around the gigantic trunk, and more importantly around my brother.

'Sissy,' I yelled, the tree safely between him and me. 'You big girl.'

He suddenly stopped before changing direction.

Whoops!

I was now running straight towards him.

'Yeah?' he said, pinning me to the ground, knees buried in my chest. 'Let's see how hard a sissy can punch.'

For the record, it was hard. And that is where the Johnathan Thurston sidestep was born, the big left and the leaping right. My famous footballing footwork was developed out of necessity. Honed by a privacy screen and practised around a hulking tree as a means of avoiding a belting. Before evading defensive lines, I was evading my big brother. I had my own agility course in my backyard.

And it was as good as any I have seen in the NRL. We didn't need cones, or hurdles: we had a clothesline, a gumtree and a privacy screen. The threat of being belted if caught was better than even the most demanding coach. I was always being chased, and sometimes I got caught.

'Mum,' I screamed. 'Rob hit me. He chased me all the way down the street and belted me.'

Mum laughed. 'Well, you should have run faster, son,' she said.

I was a massive sook growing up.

'Toughen up, princess,' Mum would say. 'You want to play with the big boys then you'll have to act like one.'

It was pretty cool when my little brother came along. I was so used to being the youngest that it was great to finally have someone I could boss around. Shane was a tiny little kid, always the smallest in any group. And yeah, I belted him a couple of times. But I also looked after him. One of my jobs was to make sure he got to, and home from, school ...

'Mum,' I screamed. I was hysterical, tears rolling down my cheeks after catching the bus home. 'I've lost Shaney. He was there and then he wasn't. I can't find him anywhere.'

I was terrified. We were coming home from school and he just vanished; on the bus with me one minute, gone the next.

Mum laughed. 'Go and look inside,' she said.

And there he was, eating cereal, bum on the floor, watching cartoons. I ran up and punched him in the arm.

'What did you do that for?' he asked. 'You got off the bus and left me. The doors closed and I was on my own.'

Oh ...

I'd like to say I didn't lose him again, but I did.

Our home was the second house built on what would become a sprawling suburban estate. Surrounded by bush when we moved in, the suburb is now all roads, houses and families. But back then there was open space everywhere, and we put it to good use. Sometimes it was cricket, mostly it was football, and when we had money for petrol it was a Yamaha PeeWee 50. Oh yeah. We rode that midget motorbike until the tank ran dry.

The house was brick; it had three bedrooms, a lounge room and a kitchen. I never had my own room. I always shared, first with Micheal – more about my cousin in the next chapter – and then Shane. Sometimes it was both. We had bunk beds and it was first in, best dressed. Whoever went to bed first would claim whatever bunk they wanted, so I slept on both the top and the bottom. We were a family that shared everything.

I spent a fair bit of time in the living room. My little brother always had the run of the TV, so mostly we were watching *Gumby*, *Postman Pat* and *Fireman Sam*.

I was always last out of bed. By the time I got up Shane would already be eating his *Weet-Bix* while watching TV. We would sit there, mindless morning zombies, until Mum screamed at us to get ready for school.

'What are you two doing?' she would yell. 'We have to leave in two minutes.'

I didn't have a bedroom full of toys. There were no posters covering the walls. And there were no books on the shelves. No, my room was full of balls, bats and racquets. You had to be able to kick it, pass it or hit it – or I didn't want it.

We ended up getting an old TV in there a few years later. And then a Sega. Game on. We only ever used the bedroom for sleeping until we got that games system. And then we never left.

My bedroom was messy, there was shit everywhere. We would throw our clothes on the floor. Dump our bats and balls in the corner. I don't think I cleaned it once. Sorry, Mum.

I also used to break out. Our room had a casement window that opened at the bottom with a roller. You could make enough room to sneak out. And I did plenty of that. Again: sorry, Mum.

You are probably working out that I was no angel. Yep, I was a cheeky bugger. Guess I still am.

FINDING FOOTY

CHAPTER 2

'HEY, JOHNNY,' DAD SAID, BIG smile on his face. 'Reckon you can score a try today?'

I shrugged.

'I'll give you a dollar if you can,' he said.

My eyes lit up.

'In fact, I'll give you a dollar for every try that you score,' he continued. 'So you'll get three dollars if you can get three.'

I smiled. 'How much money you got?' I asked.

He laughed, at least until the end of the game.

I scored nine tries.

'You got a 10-dollar note?' I said, hand out the moment the full-time whistle was blown. There was barely a spec of dirt on my oversized black-and-white jersey.

'I'll owe you a dollar until I score next week.'

Dad gave me the 10. 'Just keep it,' he said. 'This was a one-time deal.'

Dad never offered me another incentive when it came to rugby league.

I played my first game of rugby league for Souths Acacia Ridge Junior Rugby League Football Club (JRLFC) when I was six. And apparently I was pretty good from the get-go.

I started playing football not long after one of my cousins came to live with us. Micheal Janson, my mother's nephew, moved into our house for a while when I was six. I am not sure why but one day he was bunking down with me and it was great. We all called Micheal 'Mickey Motor', and he fast became my best mate. He was right into his football and he ended up getting me into it too. He had already played a season with Souths and he wanted me to join him.

'Come and play with me, Johnny,' he said. 'We can be in the same team.'

Micheal was a year older but the 6s and 7s were combined.

'Yeah, righto,' I said. 'Beats watching you.'

And so it began ...

Soon I was surrounded by footballs; my backyard was full of them. So too the front yard, the neighbour's yard and that bloody ball-swallowing bush down the end of the street.

Yep. It was footy, footy and footy at the Thurston house. Seriously, we played so much we wore the grass out. With an endless supply of both teammates and opponents – think *big* family – both front yard and back were reduced to tufts of green swimming in baked brown dirt.

My uncles never said no when I nagged them for a game.

'Righto,' Uncle Stephen, who lived with us for a few years, would say. 'I'll go and get your other uncles too.'

Soon Uncle Brett would be there, Uncle Phillip and Uncle Dean too. Sometimes we had enough to make it 13-on-13: a full-on international-rules match. And my uncles were all so young. Mostly in their early twenties, they were full of energy and spark. And they had to be to keep up with me.

'We can't play here,' Uncle Stephen said, first looking at the desert that was our backyard and then the grazes and cuts on my legs, given to me by the rock-hard surface. 'Which of the neighbours aren't at home?'

Mostly it was the older lady down the street. She had the thickest, greenest grass I had ever seen – at least until I had finished with it. I actually caught up with her years later when I went back to that street to do some filming with Channel 9. She told me it had taken years for her grass to grow back.

Anyway, after a quick knock-and-run, house empty and replacement field ready to roll, we started the game.

Back and forth, tries a plenty, we were still going when the sun went down.

'Next try wins,' Uncle Stephen barked. 'Winner takes all.'

He picked up the ball and started his run.

OK. Hand it over.

Did I mention that I was a bad loser? Yeah, I was a terrible sport. So my uncles would let me win. Well, most of the time.

I was waiting for Uncle Stephen to drop the ball, already thinking about my victory dance.

And Johnny does it. The crowd goes wild.

But Uncle Stephen was running. Fast.

What's he doing? He can't score. He always lets me win.

He burned down the sideline, a cheeky smile on his face, try line closing fast.

Surely he's going to drop it? Or just throw me an intercept?

He didn't. Uncle Stephen planted the ball and raised his arm towards the sky.

'Yeah, the trophy is mine,' he beamed. 'Last-minute try to win the grand final. I'm a bloody legend. Give me the Clive Churchill Medal now.'

I looked at him, my face blank.

What's happening?

And then I cried. 'Na, next try wins,' I demanded. 'Game's not over. It's next try wins.'

But it wasn't. Uncle Stephen was already putting the imaginary Clive Churchill Medal around his neck. He had opened and was drinking his celebratory beer.

Game over.

So I ran, back through the *always* open sliding door, bolted across the lounge room and into the kitchen. Mum's arms were warm and accepting as always.

'I'm never playing with Uncle Stephen again,' I said, my eyes wet, my face red.

Whether it was cricket, football or the last jellybean in the jar, I had to win. The rough stuff didn't worry me a bit; I could take a beating, but only if I won. I was even worse when it came to cricket; I was never out.

'Na, I didn't knick it,' I would scream, even if it tore off a chunk of willow from the side of my self-scooped imitation Gray-Nicolls One Scoop. 'That's not out.'

I would throw the bat away in disgust when the decision wouldn't be overruled. And then, of course, I would go running to Mum.

'I love you, son,' she would say. 'But stop being a baby. Go on. Get back out there.'

*

So yes ... This mummy's boy had a cry on his first day of school – of course. 'I don't want to go, Mum,' I said. 'I want to stay home with you.'

She gave me a hug and sent me on my way. I was dropped at Acacia Ridge State School for my first day of school in a taxi. I have no idea whether or not it was because we didn't have a car. Maybe it was getting fixed. I am not sure but I clearly remember both Mum and Dad taking me to school in a cab.

I also remember crying.

My first teacher was Mrs Shaw and I liked her a lot. Maybe she reminded me of Mum. Anyway, school ended up being OK.

All my report cards from primary school were good. I was hungry for information and did my work. I was never in trouble and believe it or not, I would describe myself as a pretty good student, at least until I got to high school.

But ...

I was also one of those kids who would have 'easily distracted and needs to choose his friends carefully' written in the comments section of his report.

Want to guess what my favourite subject was?

Yeah, you are right: it was sport. I liked class, but I loved recess and lunch: that is when we played sport, cricket in the summer, footy in the winter.

Later on, in Years 5 and 6, I got to play both cricket and football for the school. We would travel around taking on other schools and that was something I really enjoyed.

Have I told you that I was competitive?

Whack!

I hit it sweet, straight out of the meatiest part of the willow. I was running down the pitch, my eyes following the path of the ball. I was a Test cricketer in the making, an opening batsman, an opening bowler, and no doubt, on this day, on my way to scoring a ton.

Oh no!

I hadn't got as much on it as I thought. It was coming down and heading towards a pair of cupped hands.

Hands that belonged to a girl!

And *she* caught it. Yes! *She* caught it.

I threw my bat down hard, before steaming off the field.

A friggin' girl?

I fancied myself as a bit of a cricketer. I loved it as much as footy. Maybe even more. And then a girl got me out.

I kicked the kit. I huffed and puffed. I don't think I spoke to anyone for the rest of the day. I just fumed. I walked over to Mum. I looked at her, waiting for her to say something to make me feel better.

She giggled.

So I went back and kicked the kit again.

I was into a bit of everything when I was young. It wasn't just footy and cricket. I also played a lot of snooker, table tennis and squash. If it had a ball, I was in. I was pretty handy at snooker in particular. Maybe I should have become a snooker pro. It certainly would have been easier on the shoulders; the liver, not so much.

I excelled in all forms of athletics. From the 100 metres to cross country, I pretty much won them all. I went to state level for both track and field. I think the only discipline I sucked in was shot put, but then again, the shot was heavier than me.

My best friend during primary school was my second cousin Latoya. We started school together on the same day and got on from day dot.

Latoya's grandmother lived near our school. My mum and dad both worked late, so I would go back there and wait for them to pick me up. And yes, I probably played Barbie dolls with her, experience that would come in handy later in life when I became father to three girls.

I had male friends too, well at least one. Dusty Morton was one of my great childhood friends. My dad played footy with his father and we had a lot in common. We used to spend a lot of time together when our old men were playing footy or having a beer.

You probably know JT as a proud Aboriginal: a footballer who wears black, yellow and red boots to publicly acknowledge his heritage, a guy who campaigns for the rights of his Indigenous brothers, someone who won the Human Rights Commission medal for his contribution to Indigenous education.

But I was no Indigenous ambassador back in primary school; I was just a kid. Seriously. I didn't even know what an Aboriginal was until I went to school. And even then, it meant nothing except for the fact that I was one. Well, in part ...

My mum is an Aboriginal, born and bred in Queensland. I started identifying myself as an Aboriginal in primary school. I knew I had New Zealand heritage, but being so close to my uncles and cousins, and also living in Australia, I identified with Mum's side of the family tree. New Zealand was an ocean away. A nation we played in cricket and football. A place where a sister I had never met lived. I was an Australian Aboriginal.

And what did that mean?

Not a whole lot. I didn't know a thing about my family history. I can't even remember having a conversation about it until I was in my late twenties. And that probably wouldn't have happened had it not been for the introduction of the NRL All Stars match, which pitted an Indigenous team against a non-Indigenous one.

I guess I never asked about my cultural background because it was a non-issue. I was never discriminated against and I never encountered any serious form of racism. Plenty of Aboriginal kids went to my school at Acacia Ridge. Maybe that helped. All I know is that I was never disadvantaged because of the colour of my skin.

Lucky I didn't own up to being a Kiwi. Ha. Ha.

I didn't mind school, but I loved football. And my thing was scoring tries. I was small, even for a six-year-old. But I was fast. Real fast. Not many people could get hold of me once I caught the ball. I would take off towards the sideline and run the length of the field. Just ask Dad.

Scoring tries?

Yep, loved it.

Tackling?

Not so much.

I was a tiny fella and I struggled to pull the big boys down. Thankfully, I didn't have to do much 'D' when I was young because I played on the wing. I still try to get out there now, as much as I can. Ha.

But in all seriousness, I had a go. I might have been tiny, but I was tough. Thanks to my dad, my brothers and my uncles, I was used to coping a hit. I was always getting roughed up and never short of a bruise.

My first real memories of playing are from when I moved to Souths Sunnybank JRLFC when I was eight. I went to that club because one of my dad's best mates had a son who played for them. His name was Josif Mladenovic.

We became as thick as thieves. We hung out not only at the footy club, but also at my house and his. Kick after kick, pass after pass, we became inseparable. Yep. Long before JT and Darren Lockyer, JT and Cooper Cronk, and JT and Michael Morgan, it was JT and Josif ...

Josif had an idea.

'Why don't you just stand out there,' he said, pointing to the sideline. 'I can just do a big pass and you can run to the line without anyone touching you. All the tacklers stand in the middle of the field.'

So that is what I did. Josif grabbed the ball at first receiver and threw a perfect spiral pass, hitting me right on the chest. I looked up and there was nobody in front of me. I sprinted my way to the line – not that I needed to with all the defenders still in the middle – and scored the easiest try of my career.

'Yeah, let's do that all the time,' I said to Josif. 'I don't really like being tackled.'

Josif was a bloody good football player. He played in the halves and I played on the wing. And we were just nine when we started thinking structures and plans. Josif was a great passer and talker. I was fast. So every set he would run a couple of forwards before throwing a long ball out to me. And I am talking a 15-metre pass.

I always positioned myself so I was in space. He would get the ball to me, out front and on my chest. From there it was easy. I would just run and score. It wasn't quite Craig Bellamy spec but it worked. And looking back I am pretty amazed that we were running structured sets in Under 8s. We didn't lose a game for three years.

I kicked my first proper goal during my first year with Souths: it had been drop kicks until we moved up into the Under 8s. It was early morning, the grass drenched with dew. The surface was as slippery as an ice-skating rink, as cold as one too. My bare feet were numb; we didn't wear boots until we were 10.

I built a little sandcastle to place the ball on. I had no idea what I was doing but I had seen it done on TV. I stuck the ball on top after eyeing off the little posts made from PVC pipe. I walked back and moved in.

Whack!

I got it. I struck the ball pretty well from the start; I can't remember missing many. I guess I had a fair bit of God-given talent.

My first pair of footy boots came from Kmart: a pair of budget black Trax. I got them when we moved into the 10s and were allowed to wear boots. They must have been complete crap, but I thought they were brilliant. It was like strapping on a Superman cape, but instead of flying they gave me footballing powers: the step, the skip and the speed.

They were black with molded rubber studs. And I loved them; I might have even taken them to bed and cuddled them like a teddy bear. I would score a lot of points in them before wearing them out. My feet didn't grow a lot back then so I had them until they were ruined.

We always watched the footy when it was on. Dad, the brothers, the uncles and me. We would all pile into the lounge room and watch the match of the day on our old-school TV, a square screen buried in a hefty wooden box.

The first season of top-grade footy I can remember is 1989. I watched rugby league before that but I didn't really know what was going on. Mum was a Canberra Raiders fan so I followed them too. Dad went for the Bulldogs and so did my brother; it created some fun. It was always mayhem when the Dogs played the Raiders. We would get right into it.

Supporting the Raiders ended up being a pretty good move – Canberra were an incredible side in the early 1990s, up there with the great South Sydney teams of the 1950s, the Dragons of the 1960s and the Melbourne Storm of today.

There was Mal Meninga (big Mal), Laurie Daley (Loz), Ricky Stuart (Sticky) and Steve Walters. They were a side with talent to burn. And they won a lot more games than they lost.

Mal was always my favourite, all tree-trunk legs and palms of steel. He was so bloody big. I was tiny and was completely in awe of his size. I used to love watching him trample blokes. I used to imagine that it was me running over the top of defenders, left arm in a cast, scoring under the posts.

Fair to say Mal was my first idol. Later it was Allan Langer, Darren Lockyer (Locky) and then Andrew Johns (Joey).

Origin was my favourite type of football. It was a huge occasion in the Thurston house. We would always throw a party and the house would be full of colour and noise. And we hated New South Wales.

So did I dream of becoming a State of Origin star? You betcha. Yep. It started with a dream ...

U10 MATCH RESULTS FOR THE 1993 SEASON

Date   Opposition   Result

Trials
21/2   Springwood   38/8
28/2   St Pauls   55/5
07/3   Mt Gravatt   22/7
14/3   Slacks Ck   37/5

Competition
21/3	Easts	86/5	06/6	Easts	25/14
28/3	Acacia Ridge	30/0	13/6	Acacia Ridge	27/5
02/4	Acacia Ridge	-	20/6	Capalaba	-
18/4	Redlands	-	04/7	Easts	43/3
26/4	Bye	-	11/7	Capalaba	18/0
02/5	Graceville	75/0	18/7	Easts	52/7
09/5	Wynnum	52/0	25/7	Souths	17/0
16/5	Carina	63/0	1/8	Carina	65/0
24/5	Capalaba	43/19	8/8	Capalaba	50/0
30/5	Acacia Ridge	29/14	15/8	Norths	33/13
			22/8	Burpengary	22/7

Total Points For = 882, Total Points Against = 112, Match Average Result = 42/5

U10 PLAYER MATCH STATISTICS FOR THE 1993 SEASON

PLAYER MATCH STATISTICS TOTALS FOR 1993							
Player Surname	Runs	First Tackles	Second Tackles	Passes	Total	Tries	Goals
McADAM	28	68	11	4	111	7	7
HOULAHAN	16	45	8	2	71	0	0
LLOYD	99	152	8	29	288	10	4
THURSTON	143	146	8	30	327	64	19
BOB	15	42	6	2	65	3	0
ROSS	78	113	6	9	206	17	7
MLADENOVIC	81	93	6	10	190	17	11
DEUR	68	38	5	6	117	8	6
REEVE	54	126	26	1	207	3	0
NOLAN	94	110	11	10	225	9	3
FLOYD	69	65	12	0	146	4	9
LANGFIELD	56	68	10	7	141	4	15
McGARVEY	22	35	6	0	63	0	1
JONES	1	14	1	0	16	0	0
HARDING	13	28	2	4	47	0	0
ROSE	44	97	2	15	158	10	3

KICKING AND SCREAMING

CHAPTER 3

'NOT YET, DAD,' I SCREAMED. 'JUST one more kick.'

He stood next to the car shaking his head. 'One,' he shouted back. 'Or you'll be walking home. It's already dark.'

Dad knew there was no such thing as 'one more' when it came to rugby league and me. He would soon be dragging me from Jim Murdoch Oval – the home of Souths Sunnybank JRLFC – by my filthy jersey.

I had stayed back after training to practise my chip and chase. With everyone in my team long gone, the floodlights burning bright and the senior teams running riot, I had claimed a corner of the ground for myself.

I turned away from Dad and went back to work.

OK. This time I'll get it right ...

'Noooo,' I yelled, the bloody ball disobeying me once again. I had imagined the perfect landing, visualised success. I had willed it once it was in the air.

'Ahhhhh,' I yelled, this time loud enough for the Under 19s to stop mid-drill and see what the skinny little kid in the corner was screaming about. I ignored them and raced towards the ball, now at rest and about 15 metres from where I had wanted it to land.

Whack!

I launched the bad bouncing football over the fence, kicking it as hard as I could. This time it went exactly where I had aimed.

Whoops!

Now I had to go and get it. I jumped the fence.

'Why?' I growled, ball back in my hand. 'Why won't you just bounce back?'

For hours I had been attempting to pull off the perfect chip and chase: a short kick that you are meant to regather after it goes over the defensive line. Kicking for yourself, it should bounce back into your arms after you run through the opposition line.

Yeah … should. I couldn't get the damn ball to bounce back to me after I kicked it, no matter how hard I willed it to, no matter what I tried.

'Righto,' I screamed back at Dad, who was now beeping the horn. 'Just one more.'

I turned my attention to the ball, no longer enemy but friend. 'Sorry, I shouldn't have kicked you over the fence,' I said. 'You just need to do the right thing. Please, just bounce back.'

I slowly started my run, positioning the ball while on the move. I dropped it, making sure its path to my foot was straight and true. And then I carefully kicked.

'Damn it,' I yelled.

The ball darted off to the right as soon as it hit the turf.

'Screw you.' I was lucky my mum couldn't hear my language. I chased the ball down and kicked it straight in the guts. 'Have fun on the road. I hope you get hit by a truck.'

I slammed the door when I finally got into the well warmed-up car.

'Keep at it, son,' Dad said. 'You'll get it. Practice makes perfect.'

I sat silent, stewing all the way home. Soon we were in the driveway, a turn of a key killing the car.

'Dad,' I said. 'Can you get me a new ball?'

I was obsessed with football by the time I was 10. I would stay after training, kicking and passing, until the lights went off, or until Dad put me on his shoulder and threw me in the car. I was there every day, chipping, charging and, when things didn't work out, chasing the ball over the fence.

I was always practising, whether in the backyard or at the ground, with my uncles, my brothers, with Josif, or by myself. I would pass, bomb, grubber and chip.

Oh boy, did I chip!

I spent months attempting to master the chip and chase. Hour after hour, day after day, I went out onto that field and willed the ball to come back to me. It refused to behave. The ball was bouncing forward, or to the side, and sometimes even stopping dead. It did everything except bounce back into my hands.

Then, suddenly and from nowhere, came an idea, a light bulb flashing inside my head.

Maybe it's how you're holding the ball.

I had spent all my time worrying about how I was *kicking* the football, not how I was holding it. I looked at the ball and leant it forward in my hands. I had previously been tilting it back. I stuck my foot into it and ran.

Please ... Please ...

The ball bounced and rocketed straight back into my chest. I gave the ball a big kiss before planting it on the ground to score an imaginary try.

Maybe it was a lucky bounce?

It wasn't.

The next ball bounced straight back in my hands. So did the one after that. In fact, they all did, only Dad and his horn stopping the unrelenting procession of short kicks and running catches. And that is how I have chip-kicked ever since. It pretty much always bounces back – not forward, not to the side, and it doesn't stop dead.

Most of the things I do on a football field have been learned through experimentation and persistence. I taught myself all of these things because I was obsessed with being able to do everything. If I saw a player doing something on TV that I couldn't do, well, it was all 'just one more, Dad' and kicking balls on the road until I could to it.

That is just how I was.

And I was like that with most things. If I couldn't do something I would keep on trying until I could.

That Broncos trainer who offered me the $500 to miss the most important goal kick of my career – Allan Langer – also owes me a childhood. Well, sort of. It was because of him, and a couple of others I will soon mention, that I grew up with a football firmly tucked under my arm.

'Alfie' was really big in the early 1990s and he is a guy I spent a lot of time both watching and copying. I would go out to the backyard and attempt to replicate what he did on a football field.

Langer changed the way rugby league players kicked a football. He made the football do things that didn't seem possible. He could get the ball to break to the left or to the right after hitting the ground. He could make it run or stop dead. He could also move the football in the air.

Sometimes he would hold the ball flat, hands on each end, and kick it square in the belly. The ball would wobble along the ground like a grenade. It was a nightmare for fullbacks to clean up.

It was magic and because of Langer, I wanted to be a magician. Alf had all sorts of kicks in his bag of tricks and I watched, paused, rewound and replayed in a bid to learn some of them. So yeah, there were plenty more horn blasts and balls sent over the fence.

I remember spending months trying to get the ball to bend once I had kicked it. At training I would use the goalposts. At home it was the clothesline first, and then the gumtree. I would hit the ball with different parts of my foot to see what reaction I could get out of it. I would also change the way I held it, hoping for a result.

And, just like the chip, I eventually got it right.

I can't blame Alfie entirely for making me live with a football. Others, including Ricky Stuart, Laurie Daley and Mal Meninga, had plenty to do with shaping my game too. The 1990s were a great time to be learning how to play rugby league. During that era the game was being reinvented. Guys like Langer and Stuart were doing things that had never been done before. Stuart's long passing game had never been seen before in rugby league.

Stuart began his career as a rugby union player and he brought his long spiral cut out with him. I used to watch hours and hours of these guys play on tape. They were my first coaches in a way. I threw countless long balls like Ricky and was always trying to be like Alf.

I was pretty much just a running footballer until I was 13. My strength was my speed. Life on the wing was good. I was scoring more tries than I made tackles. But soon I wanted more. I suppose I needed a challenge.

That first challenge came with my passing game. I was pretty good at throwing a ball on my natural side: right to left, but my left-to-right was poor. I could only do what they call a floater, which is a flat pass with no revolutions on the ball. You hold the ball at six o'clock and release it, towards your target, when you get to nine o'clock.

I could also spiral the footy when passing right to left, not a problem. I could hit my mark and throw it a good 15 metres. But going the other way, well I couldn't throw it far at all. I would have to cut the distance with my feet, run the ball to my target instead of using the air. You could get away with doing that if you had to, and most did. It was a lot easier to hide a weakness than to confess to having one, let alone fix it. For me it was a problem because I wanted to be able to do everything.

The solution smacked me in the chest. Literally.

I was playing a game at school when I was hit with the longest, fastest and hardest left-to-right spiral I had ever caught.

'How did you do that?' I asked Russell, the guy who threw the perfect pass.

He shrugged. 'I'm left-handed,' he said. 'That's my good side.'

'Can you show me?' I asked. 'Just do it real slow.'

And he did. I watched on as his left hand took control of the ball. With his palm he took the top belly of the ball, and with his wrist he flicked it towards him. His right hand held the ball underneath, gripping it with his thumb and his index finger: that was the hand that pushed the ball to the target. But it was his left that did most of the work.

'Again,' I said.

And he did: over and over and over and over again until he realised I wouldn't stop asking for more.

I went home, grabbed the footy and tried to replicate what I had seen. I sat on the lounge and ripped at the ball with my left hand, making it spin back towards my chest. I then practised the shove with the right. Then I put it all together.

Soon I was out in the backyard hitting targets: first at 5 metres, then 10 and finally 15.

And I threw them at training too, despite the real risk of spraying a pass into the fence. But I wasn't embarrassed when one slipped – the training paddock is where you train. That is where you are supposed to make your mistakes.

Looking back, I don't know why I was identifying my weaknesses at such a young age. And I certainly don't know how I came up with the drills to turn them into strengths. Maybe it comes back to that competitive streak? Maybe it is a bit of OCD? You decide.

As my skills improved so did my football. I became a bit of a utility as I moved into my teenage years. I went from being a try-scoring winger to playing anywhere in the backline. I still liked scoring tries – certainly more than tackling – but I was soon doing more of the latter than the former.

I was moved into the centres when I was 11. I also played the odd game at No. 6. My game was still very much reliant on speed, but I was slowly learning how to use the ball and my body to set up others in attack, and my shoulders to bring them down in defence.

I didn't lose a game until I was 13. Winning came part and parcel with playing. It was all too easy. And then they moved us up a division.

Oh. Maybe we're not so good.

It was the reality check both the team and I needed – we were cruising until then. It is a cliché, but you learn more about yourself from a defeat than a victory. And we lost plenty in the 13s. Sometimes you need to be beaten to want to improve. You don't have the motivation to get better if you think you are already the best.

Personally, I worked hard on my defence. I was always a small guy and tackling never came naturally. I would rely on my speed to bring them down. I would let them get into a position that suited me, and then use my pace to get to them.

I always went in low; I never went in looking for huge contact. I would use their momentum to get them down. I never attempted to drive and use my weight, and with good reason: I weighed a smidge more than nothing.

I would have been bumped straight to the ground if I had attempted to go high and straight-on. So I didn't. I hit them low, still hard, and let them fall back over my shoulder. Oh yeah, I would have to hold on for dear life and hope it was enough.

And mostly it was.

*

I made my first rep team when I was 12. I was selected for the Queensland primary schools team when I was in Year 7. I had to make the district side first, then the regional side, and ultimately I was picked in the Queensland team. I was pretty excited because the state carnival was an away trip. Until that point I had only ever been out of Brisbane once or twice, and that was down the road to the Gold Coast with the family.

And guess where the carnival was held? Townsville: my future home.

I had never been on a plane before. And I was shitting myself. My brother had been on a plane – he went to Sydney once with Mum – so I quizzed him.

'Will it crash?' I asked. 'Is it safe? Will I get sick? You know those bags they have … they're for spew, yeah?'

I was sweating when I put my seatbelt on.

'Excuse me,' I said to the flight attendant. 'I don't think this belt is tight enough.'

She looked down and it was already strangling my waist.

'It's fine, sweetie,' she said. 'Don't worry. Everything will be OK.'

It did little to reassure me.

My brother Shane had given me a challenge before I got on. He told me that the plane goes so fast when it takes off that it pins you back into your seat. He told me you can't pull your head from the seat. So I made a game out of it and tried to lean forward as the plane began its takeoff. I had to accept defeat on my first attempt, the plane winning.

We arrived in Townsville a couple of hours later. I had no idea that this place would eventually become my home. All

I can remember about Townsville was the Willows Shopping Centre and the heat. It was winter but it was still hot.

We ended up playing a bunch of games, and the week ended with me earning my first ever Queensland jersey. I was picked in the state side and handed a maroon jumper. I beamed with pride when I put it on for the very first time. I imagined it was the real deal: a Queensland State of Origin jersey. I felt invincible.

And that is the moment my lifelong rivalry with New South Wales began.

We played the NSW schools side in a three-match series. I went into my first Queensland camp that week too. We spent the week in Warwick, south-west of Brisbane. It was the middle of winter and it was proper freezing. I had the shits because they made us all go to a local school during the day and do schoolwork. How dare they! I thought it was all going to be football but we only trained in the afternoon.

My parents came to watch when we finally got on the field. So did a bunch of my uncles and family friends. Again I felt like a star. I was wearing a Queensland jersey and a whole mob of family had travelled across the state just to watch me play.

And you will be happy to know, at least if you are a Queenslander, that my domination over New South Wales began from the get-go. We won the series.

Go the Maroons!

TRACKSUITS AND TANTRUMS
CHAPTER 4

FAST-FORWARD TWO YEARS AND I'M being dragged out of the backseat of the family car.

'I'll just stay here,' I said. 'It's too hot. You go and I'll wait in the car.'

The summer sun had scorched away the green and turned my local footy ground brown. The soft spring grass was now like hard compacted straw.

'Come on,' Mum said. 'Get out. Go and have a kick with the boys.'

I looked out the window and the ground was packed. From toddlers to teenagers, boys were running, passing and kicking. Footballs were flying.

'Na, you go,' I said to Mum. 'You take Shaney and I'll stay here.'

Mum shook her head. 'But you have to sign on,' she said. 'If you don't register today you won't be able to play.'

I shrugged my shoulders and shut the door. I didn't care if I never played rugby league again. And it was all over a tracksuit.

*

'Hey, look at Dane,' one of the boys had said at a football carnival the year before. 'What's he wearing?'

I turned and looked towards a kid walking into the clubhouse, bag hanging from his right shoulder. His name was Dane Campbell. He was one of the kids in the team we were about to play.

'Is that Broncos gear?' another kid in my team asked.

It was. Dane was covered from head to toe in the maroon, yellow and white of the Brisbane Broncos. Wearing an oversized jacket made of that parachute-type material. He had oversized full-length pants to match. He was also wearing a Broncos polo and had a Broncos bag.

'Wow,' said one of the boys. 'He must be good.'

Not that good. I'm better than him.

'He must have been signed by the Broncos,' said someone else. 'He's on his way.'

I was 13 when I first saw a kid wearing a Brisbane Broncos tracksuit – and boy, did it piss me off!

Why has he got one? Where's my tracksuit? I'm better than him.

This Dane kid could play, in fact he would go on to play in the NRL for the Knights, but he was no better than me. The only thing he had that I didn't was size. He was a big unit and I was a skinny little thing.

Soon everyone seemed to have a Broncos tracksuit, well, everyone except me. There they all were, walking around in their shiny new gear, chests puffed out and looking a million bucks. And there I was, slumped in a corner wearing a dirty old Rip Curl jumper. The Broncos started handing out scholarships when I was 13. And by the time I was 15 every decent player I knew had a Broncos tracksuit in their wardrobe.

But not me.

Despite making every representative team I could, I had never even spoken to anyone connected with the Broncos. And boy, did it give me the shits. Yeah, I was pissed off. Proper pissed off.

The Broncos were the team I wanted to play for. My love–hate affair with the Broncos began in 1988 when they were born. Until then Queensland didn't have their own team in the NSWRL – the best rugby league competition in Australia – and everyone in Brisbane was forced to support a side from either New South Wales or the ACT.

Everything changed in 1988 when the Brisbane Broncos were formed. Suddenly Queensland had its own side. And it seemed like everyone in Queensland except for me switched to support the Broncos. I loved Mal, Ricky and Loz so I kept on supporting Canberra.

But it was difficult for me because Brisbane were a juggernaut. In 1993, just five years after they were formed, their average home crowd was 43,200. That is the biggest average crowd in the history of rugby league. And it is no wonder when they had a side that included Langer, Steve Renouf, Kevin Walters, Julian O'Neill, Glenn Lazarus, Trevor Gillmeister and a young Wendell Sailor to name a few. They went on to win their second premiership that year, beating St George 14–6. So even though I didn't support them, I wanted to play for them.

And that is why being brushed for a tracksuit hurt me to my core. I would have traded my entire collection of Air

Jordans, my video games, and maybe even my little brother for one!

But the only side that showed any interest in me was the South Queensland Crushers. At some point I was invited to have a look at their set-up. I was impressed, but for whatever reason nothing ever came of it. I couldn't even get a look-in with Brisbane's second team. No one would be interested in me for another five years.

Yep. No one.

I kept on making all the rep teams but no NRL team would even talk to me.

Nothing.

I started getting really frustrated. I didn't know why I was being overlooked. At no point did I question my ability. I knew I was good enough. I considered myself a better player than most of the kids who were being signed, and that is what really pissed me off. I was still small, but that wasn't stopping me from outperforming them on the field.

It was about then that I met a bloke called Cameron Smith (Smithy). I had been playing against Cameron since I was 13. He played for Logan Brothers and was part of a bloody good side. We spoke for the first time at a tryout for an Under 14s Brisbane team.

'G'day,' he said, hand outstretched. 'I'm Cameron.'

I shook his hand. 'Johnny,' I said.

And that was how we met.

'What do you play?' I asked.

'Halfback,' he replied. 'And you?'

'No. 9,' I said.

Yep. That's right. I had been picked as a hooker and Cameron Smith as a half. Ha.

We were soon on a training field, preparing for our trial. We had been put into the same group for a defensive drill. I looked him up and down. We were going to be tackling each other and I thought I had him covered.

Whack!

I was on my back. Hurting.

Fuck! What is this guy made of? Steel?

I felt like I had just been hit by a truck. And it got worse once I was on the ground. Smithy locked my knees together and threatened to rip me in half.

'Man, what are you doing?' I said, still lying in the dirt. 'This is just training.'

He simply offered a smile.

I soon learned that this Cameron Smith guy did everything at 110 per cent. He never cut a corner and went as hard as he could, all the time and every time.

And I also learned that he was deceptively strong. He wasn't much to look at, but after being hit just once I knew he was as tough as any front-row forward. He was all elbows and knees, wiry muscle and granite-hard bone. He was stronger than any bloke our age.

I made a mental note.

Don't ever end up in a group with him again.

I also decided that this was a guy I wanted to play with instead of against. I would get my opportunity ...

But still I couldn't get that Broncos tracksuit. And it was really getting me down.

Things weren't much better at home. One of my neighbours was making my life hell. I was playing a game of backyard cricket with my brother when I whacked one.

Shit!

It went straight over the fence.

My neighbour was in his backyard watering his lawn. 'You lose a ball?' he asked, with a smile.

I nodded.

'You want it back?' he asked.

I nodded again.

'Well, you're welcome to come get it,' he said. 'Come on, jump over. You'll have to find it. My eyes aren't so good. I think it went in the garden.'

I walked over to the fence: rows of greying wood, nailed to beams with rusted nails. I jumped up and hooked my fingers over the tops of the fence palings. My brother pushed at my feet, launching me with a boost.

Whoosh!

A metal bar flew through the air the moment before my brother sent my head towards the sky.

Whack!

The bar crashed into a paling, wood splintering and then smashing, inches from my face. The arsehole had taken a swing at me with a metal bar. He would have hit me in the head had my brother lifted me a moment before.

This bloke was a prick. Seriously. Every time a ball would go over the fence, he would want to rip my head off. He would scream and yell. One time I kicked a plastic football over the fence. Soon his little head was looking at me.

'You want this back, boy?' he said, holding up the football.

I nodded.

He then jammed a knife into the ball. 'Well, fuck you,' he said.

He had no idea that one of my dad's A-grade mates was sitting in the backyard, watching it all.

'No,' Dad's mate screamed. 'You didn't just tell a kid to get fucked and stab his ball.'

Dad's mate jumped the fence and chased him towards the house. He was ready to flog the shit out of him. Lucky for my neighbour, he made it inside in the nick of time. Door safely locked, he called the cops.

We didn't get many balls back once they went over that fence. We ended up banning bombs up that end of the yard while playing footy. And when it came to cricket, it was most definitely six and out.

Soon summer was coming to an end and it was time to play football. Or was it?

Mum looked down at me, her face as sad as it was angry. 'Get out of the car now,' she said. 'You'll bloody cook to death in there. It's a bloody oven.'

I was already starting to sweat, the air a February furnace. I would be medium–well-done in 20 minutes.

'OK but I'm not going to sign up,' I said. 'I don't want to play.'

Dad had his turn. 'Don't be stupid, son,' he said. 'You love footy.'

No. I used to love footy.

'Maybe I'll just have a year off,' I said. 'I'll see how I go. I'll probably come back.'

That was a lie. I had no intention of playing rugby league again. It wasn't that I didn't like football. It was just I didn't think anyone was going to give me an opportunity to make a future out of it. I had dreamed of becoming an NRL player my entire life and now it seemed like an impossible dream. I had put so much into it and had got nowhere. My coach was great, I loved the boys in the team, but I had just had my fill. I wanted to go and get up to mischief with my friends. I didn't want to spend another year watching players I was better than walking around like kings in their Broncos gear.

'OK,' Dad said, 'but why don't you have a chat to a couple of people first. It's a pretty big decision. And I think it's the wrong decision.'

He dragged me up to the clubhouse and sat me down with the club president, Adrian Griffin.

'Mate, you have plenty of talent,' he said. 'You could go all the way. I understand you're frustrated, but I reckon you could regret this in a few months.'

I wasn't listening.

'Why don't we just sign you up?' he said. 'You don't have to play but if you change your mind, you can. If you don't sign now, that's it. You want to be able to play later if you decide you want to. The paperwork has to go in now.'

I had no intention of playing but this would keep Mum and Dad happy. I signed on the dotted line.

Thank goodness!

Of course I ended up changing my mind and I played that year. But I wouldn't have if not for the advice of Mum, Dad and Adrian Griffin. I can honestly say my rugby league career could have ended there and then. I wouldn't be here today, writing this, had I not signed on to play Under 15s.

I might have ended up in jail ...

SKELETONS
CHAPTER 5

THIS IS THE PART OF my story that I didn't want to tell. A chapter I am not proud of and part of my life I wish I could change. I have been keeping these skeletons in my closet for a long time. It is time to let them out.

I considered skipping over this part of my life. It certainly would have been easier to leave it out of this book. But this is part of my story. These things happened. And I feel I owe you the truth.

The mistakes I have made in my life have helped shape me into the person I am today as much as the things I got right. Before I got to the top I was at the bottom. I have spent much of my life trying to be good to make up for the bad.

I hope the following confessions can do some good. If just one kid reads this and is inspired to make a life-changing choice, I will be glad to have told you about the bad that went along with the good.

I also want to say sorry to the people I have hurt. I can't stand the thought that people out there may think that I am a fake. That I am not the person I am publicly portrayed to be because of some of the things I did in the past. I'm sorry. And I can promise you I am not the person I was back then. Now to the tough part …

It began with a bottle of rum and a bunch of mates. We went to the bottle shop with a fistful of coins and paid a guy to go in and buy us a bottle of rum. We mixed it with Coke and drank the entire bottle.

I was 13. That was the first time I got drunk. We downed the booze in a park and went to a party. I was sick the next day, my first hangover. I couldn't remember what we had done or how I got home. I said I would never drink again.

But we were standing outside the very same bottle shop the very next week. Soon we had another of bottle of rum and we were back at the park. Another party. Another hangover. This would become my standard Saturday night for the next two years.

But things got worse. Sometimes there were no parties. Sometimes we wouldn't be let in. Or sometimes they would finish before we were ready to go home. So we would hit the street.

'Over there, Johnny,' one of my mates said. 'That Hilux. It'll be easy to get into.'

He was right. The Hilux was an older car. It didn't have an alarm and the lock was low-tech. I slowly walked my way towards the 4WD parked on a dark street, all quiet, all the residents fast asleep. I pulled out my screwdriver: a flathead with a yellow handle. I paused and looked up and down, left and right. Nothing. No one. All clear. So I jammed the metal end of the tool into the lock and reefed it left.

Pop!

I winced as the metal broke, the noise startling both me and my mates.

'We're good,' said my mate.

No house lights had come on. The street was still dark and empty. I opened the door.

Click!

I winced again, in the dead silence of night the latch cracked like a thunderclap. I had another look around. Nothing. No one. All clear. So I stuck my head into the car and went straight for the glove box. I opened it up and stuck my hand in. I found only papers. No sunglasses. No wallets. Nothing I could sell.

I was backing my way out of the car when something caught my eye. It was a bit of metal, lit up by the streetlight. I stuck my hand down and grabbed it before giving it a shake.

Ching! Ching!

It was a moneybox. I grabbed it and left the car.

'Let's go,' I said. 'Quick.'

We turned and sprinted. Legged it all the way down the street and around the corner. We didn't stop running until we were in another suburb. We opened the box in an alleyway behind a shop.

'What's in it, Johnny?' said one of my mates. 'What did we get?'

I ripped off the lid. 'Holy shit!' I said. 'Take a look at this!'

It was full of money. It took us five minutes to count it all.

'That's over $2500,' I said. 'Fucking score!'

We lived like kings for the next two weeks. New clothes, new shoes and rum: the good stuff for a change.

*

We started with sheds. There were four of us in my group and we would go out together on Saturday nights. We would walk the streets with a footy and look for a house with the lights out. We would kick the footy over the fence and go and knock on the door to ask for it back. If no one answered we would jump the fence. And then we would break into the shed.

We were after lawnmowers and whipper snippers. We got $120 for a working lawnmower and $80 for a good whipper snipper. One of my mates knew an older fella who would come round and buy them from us.

We started with sheds and ended up moving on to cars. I would always carry a screwdriver in my pocket.

We had a few run-ins with the cops. We were chased a few times after being sprung but we outran them every time. They were always stopping us too. We couldn't go a night without having them stop us for a once-over.

I won't name any of the guys I got into strife with but they are still mates of mine today. And believe it or not they all made it out the other side. They all got through school and ended up completing a trade. They are all successful in their own right now and some of the best blokes you could ever meet. We were never bad people. We just did bad things.

My football really suffered during this period. How could it not have? Late nights and drinking ... Needless to say I wasn't focused on football at all. I was also getting into trouble at school, at least when I was there. I didn't show up on most days. I think I might have even been suspended.

*

I am not proud of any of this. To be honest I feel like shit just thinking about it. But I can't hide from it. These were my mistakes and my mistakes alone. I can't blame my mates, I can't blame my family and I can't blame my cultural heritage. I had a fantastic upbringing and the things I did were no reflection on my parents or anybody else. Mum and Dad would have killed me had they known.

I was young and I was stupid. And now that I am older, and a role model to some, I hope others won't make my mistakes. And for anyone heading down the wrong path, remember it is never too late to change your life. Work out what you want to be or do and go for it.

I was 15 when I realised that my behaviour was going to stop me from realising my dream of becoming an NRL player.

So I decided to change my life ...

Salisbury State High School.

FAIRLIE TERRACE,
SALISBURY 4107
Phone 277 1489

Johnathon THURSTON   FORM   9A3

SEMESTER 1 REPORT. 1997.

ENGLISH
RESULT: D
Failed to present one or more of the written requirements.
Needs to be encouraged to read more.
Is capable of better results!
A pleasant, co-operative student.

MATHEMATICS
RESULT: 32%
GRADE AV: 50%
Has some ability to recall the facts and concepts studied.
Participates well in class activities.
Well behaved and courteous at all times.

SCIENCE
RESULT: D
Progress would improve with a more consistent effort.
Needs supervision to work productively.
Often disrupts lessons by talking or disturbing others.
Lab reports not always well completed.
Limited knowledge level and has difficulty solving problems.

CITIZENSHIP ED
RESULT: C+
Lacks interest and fails to give the effort required.
Talkative in class and needs to pay attention.
Needs to display more self control in class.
Is working below ability.

GENERAL SHOP A
RESULT: 49%
GRADE AV: 58%
Practical work is generally satisfactory.
Research and assignment works are below average standard.
Work ethic and attendance are poor.

GRAPHICS
RESULT: 6%
GRADE AV: 35%
Classwork drawing standards are below those required.
None of the required homework was submitted.
Exam results were poor.
A more conscientious effort is required.

HEALTH & P.E.
RESULT: C+
Theory work has shown satisfactory recall of facts,
and has some understanding and application of knowledge.
Demonstrates outstanding skills in most practical units.

DAYS ABSENT: 16   TIMES LATE: 2

_____   _____   _____
FORM TEACHER   PARENT/GUARDIAN   PRINCIPAL

SAVIOURS AND SETBACKS

CHAPTER 6

THE PRINCIPAL LOOKED ME STRAIGHT in eye. 'So you want to turn your life around?' he asked. 'Well, this is the place for you. I can promise you that we'll help you get to where you want to be. But you have to want it.'

I was sitting in an oversized chair, palms sweating, Uncle Dean by my side.

'Of course he wants to,' Uncle Dean replied on my behalf, speaking matter-of-fact to Bob White, the principal of St Mary's College, Toowoomba. Gary Reen, the coach of the football team, was also at the meeting. 'And he's going to.'

Reen turned to me. 'Is that right?' he asked.

I nodded.

'Well, your grades aren't good enough,' he said, 'so you can show me how much you want to be here by going back to Brisbane and improving your marks. If you can get up to a satisfactory standard then we'll have a place for you here.'

I wasn't sure I could improve my grades; I was a struggling student.

'Maybe I should just leave school at the end of the year,' I said to Mum when I got back to Brisbane. 'I could finish up Year 10 and go and get an apprenticeship. I don't need school. Maybe I can become an electrician.'

'Like hell you will,' she blasted. 'You're going to that school whether you like it or not. Now go back to your old school and fix your grades. Do it or else there'll be hell to pay.'

So that is what I did. With Mum's hell-or-high-water demand, I started turning up to all my classes and I paid as much attention as I could. And instead of drinking, smoking and stealing, I studied.

Uncle Dean got me the interview at St Mary's. I was halfway through Year 10 and my life was a mess.

'You'll end up in jail, son, if you keep on this path,' Uncle Dean said. 'You need a change of lifestyle. I think you need to move away from Brisbane and the blokes you're getting into shit with. I think going to Toowoomba will sort you out.'

I nodded. He was right. I knew my life had to be turned around. I was never going to become an NRL player if I was locked away for stealing cars.

So I went back to my school after the interview at St Mary's and put my head down and my bum up. I worked hard and improved my grades. I had a big smile on my face the next time I sat down in that oversized chair, palms sweat-free as they held onto the best report card I ever had.

'OK, we just have to find you someone to stay with,' said White, the principal. 'And a football team to play for. Ever heard of the Toowoomba All Whites? I'll set you up.'

Uncle Dean beamed when I gave him the news. 'That's great, Johnny,' he said. 'This will be the best move you ever make.'

And it was. It would be the move that stopped me from becoming yet another wasted life. And I can't thank Uncle Dean enough. He not only got me the interview but also paid my tuition fees. Uncle Dean knew I needed help and he was willing to give me whatever he could. He knew the only way to save me was to get me out of Brisbane.

Thanks, Uncle Dean.

I moved to Toowoomba a man on a mission. I was finally ready to get serious about football. I was going to leave all my baggage in Brisbane and clean up my life so I could become the best footballer I could be. I was excited by the prospect of going to St Mary's. It wasn't just going to be good for me as a person but also as an athlete, because it was a rugby league school. The Walker brothers (Shane and Chris) had just finished at St Mary's and were making a name for themselves in the NRL. I dreamed of following in their footsteps. I would be playing for a strong school team that was watched closely by scouts from the NRL. I would get an opportunity to impress.

I moved in with the Seddons – a great family who welcomed me into their home as if I was their own. They had a nice suburban house in Toowoomba and I was given everything I needed: a room, a bed, food and an instant family. The Seddons were rugby league people too. Their son Eugene was a good player who had trialled with South Sydney just before I got there. That was the first time I realised that there was a world outside of the Broncos. I had always thought that it was Brisbane or nothing. But when I moved in with the Seddons I realised there were another 15 teams out there and all I needed was one of them to give me a start.

Easy, right? Ha.

Anyway, I now had a light at the end of the tunnel. I still believed I was better than everyone else, but now I had the motivation to prove it. I was ready to make the most of my fresh start.

My first mission was to stay out of trouble. It was easier said than done because I was still a little rascal. The new environment helped. My mates weren't into the same things that got me into trouble in Brisbane. It was a different lifestyle. Sure, the guys I met through school and footy would go to parties and get up to some shit. But it was child's play compared to what I had been doing in Brisbane.

And Mum checked up on me. She was relentless. 'Are you being a good boy, Johnny?' she would ask. 'You better not be getting into trouble. I'll come down and belt you all the way back to Brisbane if you muck up.'

And she meant it. Mum kept tabs on me with phone calls to the school, the Seddons and my new footballing friends. Mum also came to see me on most weekends. She would make the two-hour trip with Uncle Dean. So I had plenty of support.

So was I an angel?

God, no. I still got up to some shit, the worst of which happened on Saturday nights. *Yeah, yeah,* I might have stopped stealing cars and smoking pot, but I still had my wild side. I became good mates with a guy called Leo. He had an older brother, Pat, who used to sneak us into a nightclub.

'Quick,' he would shout. 'In here, boys.'

He had gone into the poker-machine room and opened up a window. We would dive through and dart into the crowd.

Did anyone see us?

And they never did. We always got in. We would get drunk before we got there. We didn't have a lot of money back then so we would fill up on cheap booze before heading into town. I don't think I ever spent a cent in that nightclub.

We had some good times in that place. Wearing my best pants: a pair of bone corduroy duds; my only collared shirt: a button-up with short sleeves; and my school shoes: black, the only pair of dress shoes I had – I thought I was hot shit. I tried to chat up chicks. Unfortunately I didn't have much luck. It must have been the shoes.

I was always a window-jumper but some of the boys borrowed IDs from their older brothers. One of my mates got pulled up.

'Na, bro, this ain't you,' said the beefy security guard.

My mate snatched the ID back and was gone before the big man on the door could even look up. I had never seen anyone run that quick. He should have gone to the Olympics. That sort of thing happened a lot, but we never got caught. We always got away clean. And thank goodness. Mum would have skinned me. Now, let's get back to the footy.

I was in pretty good shape when I moved to Toowoomba. I was still all skin and bone, but both my fitness and skills were fine. Despite the shit I had been through, I managed to stay in good nick. Even when I was letting loose, I was training hard and taking football semi-seriously. But now I was ready to go to the next level. I was 16 when I arrived and I was put straight into an Under 17s team at the Toowoomba All Whites. It was then that I made my full-time switch to the halves.

I hit the ground running and things moved pretty fast. The All Whites were a great club and I was playing with good players. Still, I was a little surprised when I was selected to play for Queensland in the Under 17s State of Origin team. I can't remember much about that match. The only thing that really stands out is the fact they didn't pick Cameron Smith. I was completely gobsmacked by the omission. Smithy was the best hooker in the state by a mile. I couldn't work out why he had been brushed. Anyway, the game was at Lang Park and I must have done OK because I ended up being signed by a manager.

High-profile player agent Sam Ayoub got in touch with my mum after the carnival and told her he was interested in taking me on. He took my parents out to dinner in Brisbane and said he wanted to become my agent.

Why? I still have no idea.

Nobody had ever shown even the slightest interest in me. Player managers were at all my games by the time I was 13. They were jumping on players, pen in one hand and contract in the other. Always on the lookout for the next big thing, they would also go out and visit the players' parents, telling them how good their sons were and where they could take them. But no one came to see me. There were no handshakes after games and no knocks on my mum's door.

Enter Sam.

Sam had some pretty big clients. He managed Queensland legends like Jason Smith and Adrian Lam. I had seen him at games and I knew who he was. And I had no hesitation putting my career in his hands – after all, it wasn't looking like it would be much of a career.

Sammy saw something in me that others didn't. I have asked him what it was and he can't give me an answer. He just says he saw a spark. Well, he must be a bloody good judge if you ask me. Ha.

At the time, Sam was working with Wayne Beavis, Steve Gillis and Al Gainey in a mega-management business called All Sports. Between them they had just about every player in the game.

Sam didn't need to waste his time on a kid who didn't have a deal and didn't ever look like getting one. I will be forever grateful to Sam for taking me on. I have had plenty of managers try to poach me over the years but there is no way I would ever leave Sam. My loyalty is a small repayment for the faith he showed in me.

I was stoked to finally have a manager. It wasn't as good as getting a Broncos tracksuit but it was the next best thing.

Gary Reen was the coach of the All Whites A-grade team. He approached me with a proposition not long after I turned 17.

'You want to come play in my A-grade team?' he asked. 'I think you're good enough to play against men.'

'Yeah, I'll have a crack,' I said, confident and cocky. 'Sounds good.' And it did, at least until I started training with my new team.

What the hell are you doing? They're going to kill you! Have a look at the size of them ...

My new teammates were all battle-hardened giants, behemoths with beards and bulging biceps. I looked around the field and saw warriors. There were players who had just come back from grade, including Mick Kennedy, David Anderson and Shane Wilson. Anderson had only just finished a stint in Sydney with the Parramatta Eels.

Shit. I'm going to get myself killed.

Anderson must have sensed my fear. 'Don't worry, little fella,' he said. 'We'll look after you. Anyone who takes you on will be taking the rest of us on too. We've got your back, son.'

Despite the reassurance, I went straight to the shop the next day.

'Where's the headgear?' I asked.

Being so young, and so small, I wanted to protect myself as much as possible. I wasn't even 70 kilograms yet. So I got myself my very first headgear and I have worn one in every match since. Still, even with the headgear, I was scared stiff. Yep, shitting bricks.

'You'll be coming off the bench,' Reen said. 'We'll ease you into it. Don't worry about anything. Just get on and do your thing. You won't find it too much different from the 19s.'

We were playing a team called Wattles. They were an outfit brimming with talent, including a local named Tony Duggan.

'Your teammates will look after you,' Reen promised. 'You'll be sweet. Remember, they're all old blokes and they're slow. They can't hurt what they can't catch.'

I sat on the bench, waiting to be thrown into the fray. Behind me were rows of cars up against the fence, blokes inside drinking beers and beeping horns. The atmosphere was next-level.

You got this. It'll be sweet.

My confidence ended up shading my fear. I was never lacking when it came to having faith in my own ability, and while I was scared, I was also excited for the test I would soon face.

'You're on,' Reen said, the call coming in the first half.

Chest puffed, head held high, I raced onto the field like I belonged. I demanded the ball straight away and I got it.

I tucked the footy under my wing and ran straight into the defensive line.

Whack!

Three grown men smashed me. I hit the ground hard, but sure enough I got up and played the ball.

Not so bad. I can handle this.

That run gave me the confidence I needed to forget about who I was playing against. It was just another game of football: same game, different people. And after a few games I was able to compete comfortably.

The elevation saw my game come on in leaps and bounds. I felt like a giant when I went back and played against kids my age. They were just boys. After taking on men who were trying to take my head off, I was back squaring off against kids. It seemed all too easy. Seriously, I ran amok when I went back to the 19s or 17s. It was like stepping back three levels. I felt like I couldn't be stopped.

Moving up to play A-grade was one of the best decisions of my career. I had never been the strongest defender, but taking that step really helped me with my tackling. It gave me the confidence to actually hit and stick when I came back to my own grade. After having 30-year-old rough nuts running at me, the biggest 19-year-old no longer seemed so big.

Playing A-grade also exposed me to better coaching. I was learning things like inside and outside shoulder and the basics of rugby league structure. I wasn't in an NRL system but I no longer felt I was being left behind.

I also started growing. While I was still the lightest, I was no longer the shortest. I shot up all of a sudden.

*

Things were finally looking good. I had made the Queensland Under 17s, I was making a name for myself in A-grade and I had a manager fighting for me behind the scenes. And aside from the odd trip through a nightclub window, I was pretty well behaved. I was focused on my footy, I was rarely drinking, and I made good on my vow to stay away from stealing and smoking. Yep. Life was good.

I was soon living with Rob Walmsley and his partner Kate Fahey. Rob was one of my coaches. They were great to me and I was comfortable with the little bit of money I was getting from ABSTUDY, a government fund for Indigenous students. Mum, Dad and Uncle Dean were coming to visit me on weekends, and I was doing OK at school. I went to Toowoomba with hopes of getting an OP (overall position) – the Queensland equivalent of a Higher School Certificate (HSC) – which would have given me a shot at a higher education. But I dropped out after I began Year 11 and took on vocational subjects instead. I found the OP path too difficult while trying to pursue my football dream. To succeed I would have had to study a couple of hours every night and I wanted to spend the time working on my football game instead. It was rugby league or nothing. And it was about then that I suffered a blow that had me thinking I was heading towards the latter.

I sat on the ground, legs crossed, head up, waiting to hear my name. I was covered in dirt, drenched in my own sweat, bloody and bruised. The Queensland Schoolboys Carnival, held in the stinking hot of Cairns, had just finished. I had given it my all.

A Queensland selector walked over, sheet of paper in hand. 'Congratulations on a great carnival, boys,' he said.

'You all did yourselves, your schools and your parents proud. We'll now be selecting the Queensland team to play at the Australian Schoolboys Championships. If your name is read out, please walk over to the table and collect some paperwork. If it's not then keep your head held high. You all did well and I believe many of you will have a future in this game.'

The selector started selecting, names rattled off one by one. There were fist pumps and high-fives as the names were called. The group on the ground thinned fast, smiling boys leaving one by one, going up to get handshakes and permission slips.

I was certain my name would be called. I thought I had been one of the best players in the entire carnival. I waited, waited and waited some more.

'And that's all,' the selector said. 'Better luck to those of you that are coming back next year. To the rest of you, keep at it and all the best for when you leave school.'

What? You missed me? You need to take another look at your list.

I thought it was a mistake. It wasn't. I had been overlooked. Again. First I was stunned and then I was shattered. Devastated. I picked myself off the ground and walked past the parents, the teachers and the NRL scouts. None of them wanted to talk to me. I wandered away from the crowd to an anonymous corner and I cried.

I'm never going to get a look-in, am I? What's wrong with me?

I was so frustrated. I had spent the year playing A-grade and excelled. I had come on in leaps and bounds. And I was sure that I had had a better tournament than most of the guys they had picked. I was completely headfucked.

Why? Why? Why?

Turns out they all thought I was too small. They went for kids with bigger bodies, guys like Dane Campbell and Mick Russo. Yeah, they were bigger than me, but not better. And a lot of the NRL recruitment managers decided if I wasn't good enough for the Queensland team then I certainly wasn't good enough for the NRL. Roosters' recruitment manager Arthur Beetson told people I didn't have a future in rugby league, as did Manly's Noel Cleal. Too small, they said. Too slow. And they weren't alone. Again I failed to get a single offer.

I was suffering from a stigma that I couldn't tackle. Everyone would say, 'Oh yeah, he can attack, but he can't defend, he's too small.'

And honestly it was crap. I never missed tackles. It all came down to my size. They would look at me and see that I was skinny and just presume I couldn't tackle.

So I finished high school without a rugby league club. Despite my two-year turnaround it was the same old story: no one was interested in Johnathan Thurston. I had no NRL deal and no job prospects.

The future looked shit ...

COLD CUTS AND KNOCK-BACKS

CHAPTER 7

BLOOD. GUTS. BITS OF BONE. My apron looked like a crime scene. Freshly washed and white at the start of the day, the garment was now soaking red. I smelt like a freshly cleaned corpse, bleach failing to fully mask the stench of blood. I put my mop into a bucket, hot soap slapping against chunks of flesh, and shook my head.

Is this my life?

Well, for now – the beginning of 2001 – it was. So I picked up my mop and attacked another pile of fat and filth. Time to get back to work. School done and dusted, NRL clubs not interested, my life was now a room full of meat in the back of a supermarket. With nothing but a rugby league résumé and an NRL dream, I took a job as a butcher's assistant when I left school. And I wouldn't even have scored that job if it hadn't been for rugby league.

One of the men I was playing A-grade with, Bobby Cox, was a butcher. When I finished high school he offered me a job.

'Sure,' I said. 'What else am I going to do?'

I took the job. I really appreciated Bobby giving me the opportunity, but it wasn't getting me closer to my dream of playing NRL, so I hated it.

The butchery was located in the back of a Coles supermarket. My title was shit-kicker. Ha. No, my official title was butcher's assistant, but really that is the same thing.

I almost quit after my first day. Wearing heavy overalls covered in blood and muck, I was locked in a freezer for eight hours moving meat – pallet after pallet of beef, chicken and lamb – off the truck and into the shop.

I remember struggling to lift some of the boxes, even though they only weighed 20 kilograms. Yeah, I was always more speed than strength.

Worse was to come. At the end of the day I had to clean the entire shop.

How long will I be here? Is this all I'll ever be?

And I really did wonder. As I sat there cleaning, sweeping and scrubbing until the tiles sparkled white, I wondered where my life was going. I was beginning to doubt I would ever be more than a good A-grade player who moved meat. Especially after receiving a letter from my manager that stank as much as the smell of meat mixed with peroxide.

Dear Johnathan,

Well no doubt you are back into the swing of things as far as the new season is concerned and undoubtedly looking forward to a successful one at that.

I suppose you are a little disappointed at not securing an opportunity to head south for a crack at the big time this year, but don't let that deter you in your future pursuits.

I don't know if you are aware but the QRL
[Queensland Rugby League] ask for a $10,000
development fee from any club outside your state should
you sign with them. This is a result of you having
represented Queensland in the Under 17s last season.
Naturally this is proving somewhat of a stumbling block
in any talks we are having down here.

Mate I just need to know what you are doing this
season so that we can keep an eye on your progress and
determine what opportunities might exist going forward.

Yours truly,

Sam

So clubs already knocking me back for free would have to fork out $10,000 to the QRL to sign me now? Ouch.

So let's get to the knock-backs, the long list of letters that ensured my life was all mops and meat. The previous note was just one in a long line of 'Sorry, we're not interested' letters and phone calls. My first official knock-back came the year before, in a letter from the Wests Tigers to my management agency. They said they would be watching my progress with 'keen interest' but were 'unable to place' me at their feeder club.

They were the first of many. Soon the Storm and the Roosters would knock me back too.

I decided to put my head down and forget about the setbacks. I was hoping 2001 would bring me some luck. But it wasn't looking good. So I went back to mopping meat ...

Soon I was living solely for the weekend. Monday to Friday became a bore. I was packing boxes and sweeping floors for eight hours a day. The only thing I had to look forward to was football and getting on the piss after we played. I loved playing A-grade with the boys. And I loved chasing girls on a Saturday night. Everything else was shit. I was soon struck down by regret.

Why the hell didn't you try at school? What were you thinking? Take a look at yourself now ...

I did and I didn't like what I had become. I was a butcher's assistant who played A-grade on the weekend. The best I could hope for was to get an apprenticeship as a butcher and play football in the park for fun. Life was looking pretty grim. I started kicking myself for not doing better at school. I began regretting my decision not to go for an OP and I still do. I really wish I had given Year 11 and 12 a go. Yeah, I went to school, yeah, I went to class, but I just sat there ignoring it all for the most part. I never gave myself a chance. I should have applied myself to school like I did rugby league. I will never know how well I could have done or what else I could have been. It is the biggest regret of my life.

My rugby league dream was suddenly revived when I made the Queensland Under 19s in 2001. I was selected to play in the curtain-raiser to the State of Origin. Still eligible to play Under 18s and not aligned with an NRL club, I was plucked by the selectors from A-grade to play with and against the best young rugby league players in Australia. I was stunned.

What the hell are they thinking? Is everyone else injured?

I was floating along, living my life. Work, Footy, Grog, Girls. Repeat. And all of a sudden I was selected to play in the prequel to the last ever game at Lang Park before the famous ground was demolished.

The selection changed my life.

I went into that game determined to have a blinder. I knew I was running out of chances and I felt like it was now or never. I was one of the only guys on the field without an NRL contract. I had to prove that I deserved one.

And I did.

I scored two tries and kicked a bunch of goals in one of my best games. I was a man on a mission and did everything I could to prove the knockers wrong. Having Brent Tate playing outside me helped my cause – he was an absolute weapon. And not even the fact that I scored my second try by running a shepherd could dull my performance.

I took my seat in the stands to watch the main game, knowing I had done all I could. I had no idea what it would do for my career but for the moment I was content to sit back and watch my heroes go to war. By the end of the match I had forgotten all about my tries and goals, about NRL scouts and contracts. I was back to being a fan as Queensland marched their way to a convincing win over New South Wales. I was on my feet every time they scored a try, clapping and cheering and hugging my mates as Lang Park went wild. It was in that moment that I decided I had to become an Origin player. It was the greatest thing I had seen in my life. Being in the crowd and witnessing the emotion, well, I wanted to be the one to prompt a celebration like that.

So that is where my real Origin dream was born. I left the ground and went to bed with a bloody big dream. And the next day my phone started ringing ...

THE ROOKIE

PART TWO

SYDNEY CALLING
CHAPTER 8

'JOHNNO,' ROB SHOUTED. 'QUICK, COME here.' He sounded strangely excited. 'Quick,' he yelled again. 'Someone's on the phone.'

The police? Ha.

'Righto, coming,' I said.

I waltzed into the kitchen. Rob had the receiver in his hand and a smile on his face.

Yeah, not the police …

He shoved the receiver into my palm while nodding with the ferocity of a machine gun.

'Hello,' I said.

'Johnathan?' a man asked.

'Yeah,' I replied.

'This is Nathan Brown,' he said. 'Nathan Brown from the Dragons.'

What the? Nathan Brown? The Dragons player?

I was speechless.

'You there?' he asked. 'Hello?'

'Yeah, mate,' I said. 'I'm here. Sorry, took me a moment to work out whether or not this was a gee up.'

'Na, mate, it's no prank,' he said. 'I just wanted to introduce myself and have a chat with you.'

Now I was smiling ear to ear.

'What's he saying?' said Rob. He was standing right by my side. He moved his head towards the back of the receiver in a determined bid to eavesdrop. I cupped the receiver for a moment and told him to go away.

Proud as punch and as intrigued as hell, I pressed my ear hard against the phone. He had my full attention.

Browny got straight to the point. A former hooker hailing from the NSW North Coast, Brown told me he was doing some recruitment and coaching for the Dragons. He had seen me play the previous night and he had really liked what he'd seen.

'A few people said you're too slow and too small,' he said. 'But every time you ran you made a break in the game. Bottom line is I want you to come to Sydney. How would you like to trial to become a Dragon?'

Wow. Finally I had someone willing to give me an opportunity. Brown wasn't offering me an NRL start, but he said I would play some Jersey Flegg (Under 19s) and the rest would be up to me.

'Ummm,' I said. 'Can I have a think about it? Can you give me a couple of days?'

I wanted to say yes and jump straight on a plane. But first I needed to call my manager, Sam.

I phoned Sammy. 'You wouldn't believe who just called me, Sam,' I said.

'Yes, I would,' Sam said. 'Was it Nathan Brown?'

'Yeah it was,' I replied. 'How did you know?'

'How do you think he got your number?' Sam said. 'The Yellow Pages?'

Oh yeah. Right …

'Anyway, they aren't the only ones that are interested, JT,' Sam continued. 'I have another club that might be a better option for you. What do you think of the Bulldogs?'

Well, I loved the Bulldogs. I had been a Raiders fan growing up but my dad and my brother supported the Doggies so I knew a lot about them. I had watched plenty of their games at home and they were an awesome club. They had enjoyed huge success since the 1980s and were regarded as one of the most professional clubs in rugby league.

So yeah, I told Sam I thought the Bulldogs were pretty damn good.

'Well, good, they're going to fly you down to Sydney for a look,' Sam said. 'Pack your bag. And I've already spoken to your mum. She wants me to keep an eye on you if you come to Sydney and she's pretty keen on you going to the Bulldogs because I live nearby. There's nothing wrong with the Dragons but the Bulldogs are around the corner from me.'

A week later I was standing in an office at Belmore Sports Ground being offered my very first deal.

'From what we've seen we're prepared to bring you down to Sydney,' said Mark Hughes, the former Bulldogs player turned recruitment manager for the club. 'We're prepared to give you a shot. We'll put you up in a house and get you a job. The rest is up to you. But we want you to come down now.'

Now? Wow.

That wasn't what I was expecting. It was mid-year and I was all settled in Toowoomba. I was expecting them to offer me something for 2002.

'Ummm,' I mumbled. 'Now? I'm not sure. Can't I come at the end of the year?'

I wanted to play for the Bulldogs but I wasn't ready to make the jump. Not then. It was mid-season and I was committed to my A-grade team back in Toowoomba. I didn't think leaving halfway through the season was a good idea. I didn't want to let my team down and I also thought it would be difficult for me to force my way into any of the Bulldogs teams.

But Hughes, whose nephews Glen, Steven and Corey all played for the Bulldogs, was adamant I join straight away.

'This chance might not be available in six months,' he said. 'But it is now.'

I knew it was the place for me, but I wasn't ready to commit. 'I want to come at the end of the year,' I said. 'I want to finish this season with my team.'

Hughes smiled, knowing he hadn't yet fired off his big gun.

'OK, mate,' he said. 'Well, let's take you to the game tomorrow. You can decide after that. Now let's go and have a look at where you'll live and then we'll go and get a feed.'

I was taken to the 'Belmore house', which is – surprise, surprise – a house in Belmore. Owned by a couple called Pete and Mary, it was where all the young out-of-town Bulldogs lived. Pete and Mary took care of us like we were their own kids. I'll be forever grateful.

I met a few of the residents: future Wallaby Rocky Elsom; Ben Harris, soon to be both a Bulldog and Cowboy; future South Sydney captain Roy Asotasi; and would-be NRL wrecking ball Jason Williams. It all looked pretty good to me. I wasn't concerned about the prospect of living in a share house. I had spent the last couple of years boarding with strangers who ended up becoming my lifelong friends. I had also been billeted out during my various rep camps over the years.

'What do you think?' Hughes asked.

'All looks sweet to me,' I replied. 'Except for that Williams bloke. He looks like one mean dude. You wouldn't want to end up in a room with him.'

Hughes grinned ...

We headed up the F3 to Newcastle the next day to watch the Bulldogs take on the Knights in an NRL clash. And in the bowels of Marathon Stadium, Hughes wheeled in his cannon.

'Hi, mate,' said the giant lying on the massage table. 'I'm Steve Price.'

No shit. As if I don't know who you are ...

'You got time for a chat?' he asked.

'Yeah, sweet,' I said, completely in awe. 'Here? Now?'

He nodded.

Steve Price was not only the captain of the Bulldogs. And he wasn't just a Queensland Maroons legend. Pricey was also a Toowoomba boy, and for me that was as good, maybe better, than the other two.

He had my undivided attention.

Between grunts and groans – the massage was rough at times – Pricey told me I had to move down straight away. He told me that coming down at the end of the year would be the worst possible thing for someone like me.

'You won't last, mate,' he said. 'The pre-season will do your head in.'

Pricey told me how people get homesick during the preseason and that is when most people quit.

'It can be very lonely out there getting flogged,' he said. 'It's much easier if you go straight into playing games. You don't have time to think about how lonely you are.'

It was surreal. Here I was in an NRL dressing room speaking to the captain of the club my father and brother barracked for. Here I was watching the Queensland legend getting a massage.

'Yeah, you're right,' I agreed.

Ha. Who was I to argue?

My mind was made up. I was going to the Bulldogs and I was doing it right away.

So, time to sign a contract? Ha. No. There was no contract. I was offered a training trial. I shook hands with Mark Hughes and agreed to become a Bulldog the same day. I wasn't going to get paid a cent so I wasn't a professional footballer yet, but oh man, I was about to feel like one. Did I tell you how much I wanted my own NRL tracksuit?

The contract offered me accommodation in Belmore, plus assistance in finding a job or, failing that, $100 a week through to the end of the season.

So yeah, it was a tracksuit and 100 bucks a week. I had finally hit it big.

There has been a bit of talk about who found me and who was responsible for getting me into the NRL. Well it was certainly Mark Hughes who recruited me to the Bulldogs. He was instrumental in getting the deal done. And apparently he became interested in me after a recommendation from Bulldogs boss Bob Hagan's son Justin, who had seen me play in Brisbane.

And Nathan Brown made me an offer to come to Sydney before the Bulldogs stepped in. I never really knew why I knocked him back, but I have since learned it was because my mother didn't want me living on my own, and Sam stepped in and arranged the Belmore house deal. Turns out Browny, who would go on to become the Dragons coach a couple of years later, had arranged for me to live with his mum in a place at Cronulla. I never knew he had gone to such lengths to sign me until later on. I have bumped into Browny over the years.

'You should have been a Dragon,' he always says. 'And you know you were the first bloke I ever tried to recruit?'

Turns out Browny watched me in that rep game and he couldn't work out why I was the only one on the field without an NRL deal. He had been forced into an early retirement with a neck injury and had been sent on his first recruitment mission for the club.

'I carried a contract in my back pocket after that,' he said. 'If I had one the day I saw you, I would have signed you on the spot.'

And Tommy Raudonikis – the Magpies legend – was the first to push me to an NRL club. Tommy lived on the Gold Coast and was doing some recruitment work for the Wests Tigers. He had seen me play. And despite what everyone else thought, he saw my true potential. Tommy organised a dinner with Wayne Pearce and did his best to get me a deal with the Wests Tigers.

Anyway, no one was fighting over who found me just yet.

BECOMING A BULLDOG

CHAPTER 9

EVERYTHING I OWNED FITTED INTO an old cricket bag that I had been using since Year 6. Yep. That was the extent of my life: all my possessions squashed into a Slazenger. I pulled the zipper and put it all on a plane. I was standing in the belly of Belmore Sports Ground a few hours later.

'This is for you, mate,' said the gear steward. He was pointing at a pallet.

'Really?' I asked.

I was staring at more gear than I owned: shirts, jumpers, jackets, pants, shorts, singlets, dress shirts, ties and hats. And it was all Nike.

'Na, that must be for the NRL boys,' I said. 'I'm just here for a trial.'

He shook his head. And with that my wardrobe was tripled.

How good is this?

I had spent my life wanting a Broncos tracksuit but could never get one. So I thought about all the times they had brushed me as I slipped on my very first Bulldogs shirt. I thought about all the knock-backs and what it had taken me to get here. I thought about all the people who told me I was too skinny and that I couldn't tackle.

And then I smiled.

Finally I had my tracksuit, all blue and white and brilliant. And for a skinny bloke it felt pretty snug. I exclusively wore Bulldogs gear from that moment on.

I was sent straight out onto the paddock for a training session with the Bulldogs Jersey Flegg side after the gear steward kitted me up.

'G'day, mate,' said the Flegg coach. 'I'm Ricky Stuart. You ready to rip?'

Yeah. My childhood hero was now my coach. Of course I was ready to rip.

'Shit, yeah,' I said. 'Let's go.'

Did I mention that part of the reason I wanted to play for the Bulldogs was because Sticky would coach me? I don't think I did. Well, the bloke I used to mimic in the backyard had retired from playing in 2000 and taken up a role as the Bulldogs' Jersey Flegg coach in 2001. It was his first step in what would become a great and long coaching career. Stuart is now an NRL premiership-winning coach, currently head coach at the Canberra Raiders.

Really? I'm standing on a field with Ricky Stuart.

I was starstruck when I walked out to meet him but that feeling of awe soon passed once I was on the field.

'What the fuck is that?' Sticky screamed at one of the boys. 'You're only going half effort.'

I was thrown straight into a fitness drill called a 'four in five'. We had to complete four laps of the football field in five minutes.

'You look stuffed,' he said when I finished. 'But good job. You did it in 4.10. Looks like you're not as unfit as they told me you would be.'

Yep. Sticky just gave me a compliment. Well, I think it was a compliment.

I had never lifted a weight in my life. Never. And my first gym session at the Bulldogs was one of the most terrifying experiences of my life.

'Full body session, boys,' said veteran Bulldogs trainer Garry Carden. 'Let's rip in.'

I had no idea what he meant. I was put into a group. I watched on as one of the boys bench-pressed 100 kilograms. He pumped out 10, rapid-fire and strain-free.

'What do you lift?' he asked.

I looked at the bar.

No fucking idea.

'Yeah, about that much,' I said, pointing to whatever he had just thrown around.

Thankfully Carden was within earshot. 'Start him at 60 kilograms,' he barked before walking away.

So off came the two 20-kilogram plates. I backed my way onto the bench, a stranger in a strange land. I didn't even know where to put my hands.

Here goes ...

I pushed at the bar and pulled it off the rack.

Jesus! Fuck me!

It felt like I was holding up a small car.

'Let's go,' Carden shouted again. 'Push 'em out.'

So I did. One, two … two and a half.

Fuck!

I couldn't even get out three. One of the boys grabbed the bar and racked it. I was bright red, partly due to exertion, mostly because of embarrassment.

'Just the bar next time,' Carden said.

I looked around expecting to see the boys having a laugh. But they weren't.

Thank goodness!

It was pretty obvious I had some work to do in the gym. All I could do was my best. I had to get stronger. I looked around and some of the boys were lifting 140 kilograms. I was on the wussy weights, but I was determined to improve.

The Bulldogs Jersey Flegg side was jam-packed with talent and I had my work cut out to make the side. Some of the best teenage players in Australia were in that team, including Glenn Hall, Roy Asotasi, Ben Harris, Dean Byrne, Brett Oliver, Andrew Emelio and Matt Utai. And they had all been there since the start of the year and done the hard yards. They had earned their start in the side.

And who was I?

I was a Johnny-come-lately, the new kid on the block. I was the kid from Queensland out to steal someone's spot. Well, that is how it felt. I can't imagine the team's No. 1 playmaker Brett Oliver was glad to meet me. I knew I had to earn the team's respect.

So I went as hard as I could. I nailed myself in the fitness drills. I was a bull at a gate. I was superfit when it came to my cardio and I was determined to show them that I belonged. There was no easing my way in. I had just left my life in Queensland to have a shot at becoming an NRL player. I trained like my life depended on it – because it did.

I moved into the Belmore house.

'This is you in here,' I was told, the host pointing at an immaculately made single bed. 'And that's Jase, your roomy.'

I looked towards the occupied bed.

Shit.

Jason Williams was propped against the wall, all 120 kilograms of him being held up by a thin sheet of gyprock. He was covered from head to toe in tattoos. He smiled, flashing his gold-crowned gangsta-style teeth.

'Hey, I'm Jase,' he said in a soft voice before extending his heavily tattooed hand. 'Nice to meet you, bro.'

I wanted to ask him what prison he just left.

'Ummm,' I said. 'Yeah. You too, mate.'

Turns out that Jase was one of the nicest blokes I could ever meet. He was a gentle giant off the field and a killer on it. He will be a lifelong mate, but at first he was just plain scary.

'You're a skinny little dude,' he said. 'We'll have to fix that, hey.'

He soon had me eating raw eggs and skolling protein shakes.

'Yuk,' I cried. 'Tastes like shit.'

He laughed. 'Na, bro,' he said. 'You'll get used to it. I love this shit now.'

Jase had an incredible diet – he would eat 10 kilograms of food a day. I would often wake up to find him sitting in bed with a pen and a notepad.

'You studying for an exam, big fella?' I asked.

He laughed. 'Na, JT,' he said. 'Just working out my food for the day. You want me to do a list for you too?'

Why not?

So I gave it a crack. Soon the bloke who drank cans of cola for breakfast and ate whatever was given to him was weighing his food in the morning and placing it in plastic containers.

'I can't eat all this,' I said. 'It all weighs more than me.'

But I did. Bite after bite I ate it all. Soon we were at training – in the Bulldogs gym – and I was sent to the rowing machine for a hardcore pyramid-style drill.

Oh no!

I started feeling sick as soon as I began my first stroke.

This isn't good!

I ignored the rumble in my stomach and kept on pumping away.

Bleeeeewraaahhh!

I spewed all over the floor: raw eggs, cereal, toast and protein shake splattering the rower.

Gaz Carden was soon standing over me. I was curled up on the floor.

'There's a bucket and some rags in the closet,' he said. 'You'll clean up every last bit.'

He walked off laughing, a smile plastered across his face. I think it was his mission to make us spew. Trainers are twisted people, and exceeding your limit is a job well done. Gaz was brutal in the gym. He ended up giving me my very own bucket that stayed next to me at all times.

I eventually became great mates with Gaz. I had dinner at his house once a week and he has been a big part of my career. And one day I will buy his wife a new set of dinner plates.

She used to send me home with a meal every time I went over. I never once returned a plate.

As for Williams and his diet ... Well, I went and handed him all my food-filled plastic containers when we broke for lunch.

'You get double today, mate,' I said. 'I'm getting a can of Coke.'

I never got the $100 a week that was written into my agreement. No, I got a job. My second real job after my stint as a butcher's assistant was at Pickles Auctions, a company that bought and sold used cars. Again my title was shit-kicker. Ha. No, I was a car washer. Bulldogs recruitment manager Mark Hughes had the job lined up for me as soon as I arrived. I was to work during the day and train when I finished. I didn't have a car – actually, I don't think I even had a licence – so I used to get up at sunrise and walk to the factory for a 7 am start.

The work wasn't bad: there were no freezers, boxes or blood. You beauty. And the people I worked with were pretty good too. As I said, it was my job to wash cars. Pickles had a pretty big operation. They had a bunch of machines to speed up the process. I would stand at the end of a giant machine wash. I would wait for a car to come out.

'Let's go,' someone would yell.

And with that four of us would go mental with rags, rubbing and scrubbing. We would dry down the cars, shine up the wheels, wipe the windscreens, and give the interior a spruce. The used cars looked brand-new once we were done.

Mostly I was working with little Chinese guys who didn't speak a lot of English. They were actually pretty funny when I could understand what they were saying. And that is what I did for eight hours a day: 7 am to 3 pm, Monday to Friday. There were no concessions back then, because I was a nobody. I wasn't a football star, so there was no slacking off, turning up late or going home early. I was just like everyone else in that factory.

It was pretty tough rubbing down cars after some of the weightlifting sessions we did in the gym. Shit, some days it hurt just to get out of bed, so wiping down cars could be tough. But I was OK with it all. I was getting paid a few hundred bucks a week, which was a lot better than the $100 I would have been forced to live off if I didn't have that job. And I knew I wouldn't be doing it forever. I knew that it was just what I had to do until I made it as a football player. I didn't mind the job. But I hated being homesick …

I broke down just three days after moving to Sydney. Ricky Stuart found me hunched over in the tunnel following a field session. Head down, hiding in the shadows, I was crying.

'You OK, mate?' Sticky said as he put a hand on my shoulder. 'What's up?'

I turned and looked through my tears to see the bloke I idolised as a kid.

'Oh, shit,' I said, embarrassed that he had caught me having a cry. 'Yeah. Yeah. I'm sweet.'

Stuart got down on his knees, joining me in the shadows. 'No, you're not,' he said. 'And it's OK. You're not the first bloke I've found like this. Football players aren't as tough as everyone thinks. Come on, mate. You have to tell me what's wrong.'

I wiped away the tears and let it out. 'I feel so alone,' I said. 'I miss my family. This is too hard. I just feel like I have nobody. I'm not sure I can do this. I don't want to let anyone down but I think it would be best if I went home.'

Stuart put his arm around me. 'Mate, you're homesick,' he said. 'And there's nothing wrong with that. We all get homesick. You wouldn't be human if you didn't miss the people you love. The good news is it's not a disease. I can promise you it will go away.'

I cracked a small smile. 'It will go away?' I said. 'You promise?'

Stuart nodded. 'And you're *not* alone,' he said. 'Take a look around you. You're now part of the Bulldogs family. You have a club full of brothers, fathers and uncles. We're all here for you, mate. I want you to come and talk to me next time you feel alone. I'll be there for you.'

I picked myself up off the floor and extended my hand. 'Thanks, mate,' I said as I shook his hand. 'I'll be sweet. I'm just a bit of a sook sometimes. I'll be OK.'

And I was OK, for a while. I ripped into the training, went to work, and did my best to get to know the guys in the team. But I wasn't being picked in the team. And I found life tough without football. I walked into Sticky's office four weeks into my stint.

And I cried.

'You know how you said I could always come to you?' I asked. 'Well, here I am. I need to go home. I'm not coping.'

He looked up from the stack of papers he was studying.

'Still homesick?' he asked. 'Or is it something else?'

I shrugged.

'I just don't know if I can do this,' I said. 'I guess I'm homesick.'

Stuart nodded. 'Mate, it's OK to be homesick,' he said. 'Is that all it is? Do you have any concerns with the systems we have here or the football program?'

'Well, I wouldn't mind getting on the field,' I said. 'But I understand I have to earn it. I just can't see a light at the end of the tunnel right now. And it's making me miss home.'

Stuart shuffled himself upright, his back leaning hard into his chair.

'You'll get your shot,' he said. 'And you'll get over this homesickness. You're not really thinking about quitting, are you?'

I shrugged. 'I'm not sure,' I said.

And I wasn't. I wanted the opportunity and I was grateful for it, but I wasn't getting a start. I didn't want to quit – well it was in the back of my mind – but I certainly wanted to go home and see my family and friends. I was lonely. All the training, working and not playing had taken their toll. I was very disheartened.

'Look,' he said. 'You have a big future here. You just have to be patient. Why don't you go home for the weekend, see your folks and come back nice and fresh? I'll let you go only if you promise you'll come back.'

I gave him my word, albeit reluctantly.

So I jumped on a plane and headed back to Brisbane. I left all my problems back at Belmore and went about clearing my head. And I had a great weekend with my family and friends. It was so good to see them. I told Mum I didn't want to go back.

'Like hell you're staying here,' she said. 'Johnny, this is everything you've ever wanted. You've worked so hard to get here. You're going to get on that plane and go back and make a name for yourself. You'll forget about all this when you're a rich and famous football player.'

I laughed. 'Me?' I said. 'Rich and famous? Ha. But yeah, I should probably give it a chance.'

The weekend was over before I knew it. Mum ordered me a cab.

'Can I stay?' I said, tears in my eyes as I got in the taxi. 'I can try and get a club up here. Maybe they'll want me now that I've been at the Bulldogs.'

She shook her head, gave me a kiss and slammed the door.

'Good luck, son,' she said. 'You show them what you can do.'

I cried the whole way to the airport. I wanted to tell the taxi driver to take me back once we arrived at the terminal. But I only had enough money to pay what was on the meter.

My life would have been a whole lot different if I'd had a wallet full of cash. I am sure I would have never returned to the Bulldogs.

I was back in Sticky's office two weeks after I returned. There were no tears this time.

'Are your parents free this weekend?' he asked. 'I've got a couple of plane tickets for them to fly down and watch you play.'

That was Sticky's way of telling me I had finally made the team.

'I'm playing?'

He nodded. 'Yes,' he said. 'Well done. I told you you'd get your shot. And that's what you're getting. It's now up to you to make the most if it.'

My parents were free of course. And they were there to watch me have a spew on the sideline before the game.

Bleeeeehhhh!

I emptied the contents of my stomach onto the grass.

'Nerves?' one of the boys asked.

I shook my head. 'Na, I think I ate a bad apple.'

I made my way to the bench. And that is where I waited until I was finally thrown into the game. It was midway through the first half when I ran on. And boy, did it feel good.

Finally. This is what I'm here to do.

I realised how much I loved playing footy and what it meant to me as I ran out onto the field. I looked pretty good in blue and white too.

'Yep,' I called, with outstretched arms. 'I'm here.'

And soon the ball was in my hands and I was stepping my way through a gap. I pinned my head back and went like the wind. The try line was beckoning.

Almost there.

I was about to score a try with my first touch.

Thud!

A desperation tackle from a defender I didn't see stopped me from scoring my first try. I was only inches away from the line. I was so close.

Damn.

Oh well, I might not have scored but making the break gave me the confidence that I belonged on this field with these boys. I knew I was every bit as good as them. And Sticky was pretty impressed with my game. He told me I had exceeded his expectations and that based on that performance I had earned a spot in his side.

About time!

Suddenly all those worries I'd had a couple of weeks before were gone. I was no longer lonely, no longer homesick, and no longer wanting to leave. It is funny what a game of football can do.

I was promoted to the starting side after a couple of more games off the bench. Dean Byrne was promoted to reserve grade so I was thrown into the halves.

And things happened pretty quickly from there.

After another six or so games, I too was called up to play reserve grade. I went from not even getting a start in Jersey Flegg to running out on the field in second grade to play with blokes I had spent my childhood watching on TV.

The Bulldogs reserve-grade team was a ripping side, featuring Steve Reardon, Shane Marteene, Steven Hughes, Reni Maitua and Adam Perry to name a few.

My first match in reserve grade was against Parramatta. I started on the bench.

'Righto, get on there,' said the trainer. 'You're in for Hughesy.'

Steven Hughes had been injured early in the match and I was chucked into the centres.

Centres? Shit. I haven't played there for a while. Oh well …

I ran out and looked up at the Eels player I was marking: it was future international Willie Tonga.

This is going to be interesting …

I think I would have been overawed playing my first proper senior match, especially given that I was playing out of position, had it not been for my A-grade experience with Toowoomba. I had played against men before so I just took it as another game.

I went out and did my thing and had a blast. I put my wing partner – Matt Utai – away a couple of times and scored a try myself. I even took over the goalkicking late in the match. It was more than I could have ever expected. I thought I might get a few minutes off the bench at the end, not 77 minutes, a try and a couple of goals to boot. I finished wanting more.

And that is exactly what I got.

Soon, a game or two later when we played Cronulla, I was lying on the dressing room floor at Shark Park in tears. I had just been taken off the field after copping a huge knock to the head. I looked up and Garry Carden was standing over me.

'Fuck, the only thing he needs is a Gatorade,' Carden said. 'He's crying so much that he is in danger of dehydrating himself. Other than that, he's fine.'

I finished the year playing another three games in reserve grade and became the starting No. 6 in Jersey Flegg. I also became the full-time goalkicker. As I said, it all happened very fast. That homesickness I felt was but a distant memory. Stuart was right: it wasn't a disease.

We went on to win the Jersey Flegg competition, beating the Sharks 12–10 in the grand final. And I played my part by making a gutsy cover tackle to stop a try that would have cost us the match. The jubilation I felt when we won the game far outweighed any of the pain I had previously felt. I was as happy as I could be.

And I have to thank Sticky, not only for being supportive but also for being a great teacher. I really learned a lot from Sticky that year. He was a former half, one of the greatest ever, so I was always picking his brain. I was still predominantly a ball-runner so I wanted to improve all the other areas of my game. Ricky taught me about game management, something that was utterly foreign to me. I don't think I had even heard the term before I got to the Bulldogs.

Sticky also helped me with my general play kicking. It has always been OK, but a kicking game is always something that can be improved. There is no such thing as a perfect kicking game. I needed to work on finding space. I needed to get the ball away from the wingers and the fullback.

My passing game had always been strong but Sticky helped me improve by working on pass selection. Being a great passer isn't just about being able to fire a football. You need to know when to pass the ball and when to hold it.

As I said, all my doubts were gone as soon as I got on the field. I knew this was the place I wanted to be.

Now all I needed was a contract ...

I signed my first ever contract on 12 October 2001. It had taken me a long time to get a deal, so I was pretty stoked when I finally got to put pen to paper. I agreed to a one-year contract with a one-year option in my favour. I was to be paid $20,000 in 2002 and a minimum of $30,000 in 2003 if I activated the option. It wasn't a whole lot of money but back then it felt as if I had won the lottery. Getting paid to play football was a dream come true. What's better than a tracksuit? A tracksuit and some cash, of course.

I also had some clauses written into the contract that would allow me to earn a fair bit more. I was going to receive $300 for every reserve-grade match I played and $3000 a game if I managed to get a match in the NRL. I thought I was a long way off playing NRL but it was nice to know there was a big reward if I managed to jag a game.

Sammy negotiated pretty hard to get me this deal. The Bulldogs were at first offering me a two-year deal for $16,000 and $25,000, so Sammy did well to get it bumped up. Sam never leaves a dollar on the table in a negotiation.

I had also expressed interest in starting an apprenticeship and asked the club if they could help, but they decided my maths wasn't strong enough, and neither did I have the 'passion' to commit to a four-year electrician's apprenticeship.

Oh well. I had plenty of passion for footy, and I could count by one, two and four, which is the only maths I needed on the field. I ended up becoming a porter at the Novotel Sydney Olympic Park. But I didn't figure I would need that job for long considering I was now a professional football player. Ha.

A RAPID RISE AND A FAST FALL

CHAPTER 10

AFTER SPENDING SIX WEEKS BACK home – laying bricks for cash and drinking beers with family and friends for fun – I returned to Belmore. And I was dreading my first ever NRL pre-season.

It can't be as bad as they say. Can it?

I had heard horror stories about pre-season training. It was all sweat, spew and scorching sun, according to anyone I had ever asked. I was also nervous about joining the NRL boys. I had been selected in an extended NRL squad for the pre-season. I was going to get to train alongside some of the biggest names in rugby league and I was as nervous as hell.

So I tiptoed my way down the tunnel hoping for an anonymous entry. I quietly walked into the dressing room and carefully placed my bag on the floor next to a plastic chair. I thought I hadn't been seen.

'Na, mate,' said Brent Sherwin, the Bulldogs NRL halfback. 'Don't put your bag there. You have your own locker now. Come over here. I'll show you.'

I smiled. 'Seriously?' I said. 'Na. Not me. I'm not even a proper reserve-grade player.'

Sherwin laughed. 'Na, you're one of us now,' he said. 'And don't smile. You might not think that's such a good thing when Gaz is finished flogging you.'

At that point I didn't care how tough the pre-season was going be. And nothing could wipe the smile from my face. I had just been accepted into the NRL by way of locker. I was ready for anything.

It was both exciting and daunting to join the NRL squad for the first time. Sure I knew a couple of them from playing reserve grade, but most of the guys were more heroes to me than teammates. I was about to train with Willie Mason (Mase), Steve Price, Mark O'Meley (the Ogre) and Braith Anasta to name a few. These guys were Australian Kangaroos and State of Origin players, the best of the best. I felt like a very small fish about to go for a swim with great whites.

I didn't have a lot of time to think about the company I was keeping. Soon the only thing on my mind was pain. We went out onto the field and began our pre-season with a notoriously brutal fitness drill called the 'beep test'. The 'beep test' measures how fit you are by way of survival. You run a prescribed distance and have to make it to the line before hearing a 'beep'. You wait, catching your breath, until another 'beep' starts a fresh run. At first there's a lot of time between the beeps and it is quite easy to get to the line. But the time between the beeps shortens with each run. Eventually it becomes impossible. You keep on going until you fail to make the line before the 'beep'. You are told what level you made it to when you drop out. I think I was in the 12s.

I went as hard as I could and ended up one of the last players standing – well, standing until I collapsed. I was proper fucked. And then I was told to get up and go for a run …

Each day saw a new type of torture: riding, running, lifting, sprinting, pushing and pulling. The only thing that was constant was that we moved until we dropped. The gym work was especially difficult. I had never even trained full time, let alone faced a Bulldogs pre-season, so I found it tough. I couldn't walk at the end of most days. I was sound asleep by 7 pm.

I was determined to impress and promised myself I wouldn't be broken. While I didn't think I could earn a spot in the NRL that year, I made it my mission to earn the respect of the team. I didn't want to have another cry in the tunnel. The training broke plenty of players, but I got through my first ever pre-season in one piece. I had my moments, but I made it out the other side. And I was the better for it.

I headed into season 2002 the fittest I had ever been. And I was stronger than I had ever been, heavier too. I ended up putting on 3 or 4 kilograms and entered the season weighing 78 kilograms. My body was beginning to change shape. Maybe I was becoming a man? Ha. That extra weight and strength gave me an oversized injection of confidence. I set myself the goal of making my NRL debut that year.

My first mission, of course, was to nail down my spot in reserve grade. When I had achieved that I was going to do all I could to get my NRL crack. I got my first taste of the big time when I was taken to Toowoomba for an NRL trial match.

*

Corey Hughes, the NRL hooker, walked up to me the morning after my very first NRL trial match. He smiled as he threw out his arm.

'Congratulations on your game,' he said. 'You really killed it. Well done.'

I had scored four tries the night before in a dream match, played in front of my family and friends. I had come back home and I had nailed it.

'Thanks, mate,' I said as I stuck out my hand to meet his for a shake.

Hughes pulled his arm away and with the speed of a striking snake gave me a smack in the face.

'Ha,' he said. 'Got ya. You got a big head or what?'

The entire team laughed as one.

Oh no. What was that?

I went bright red, the butt of the joke and firmly the fool. Oh, I felt terrible. He burned me good. I backed away pretty fast. The boys continued to laugh. Yep. That is how I was welcomed to grade, with a slap in the head and an ego-crushing comment. But hey … at least they now knew who I was.

The weekend had gone better than I could ever have hoped. I had made the most of my opportunity by putting my name up in lights. And I did it in Toowoomba, the place where I had turned my life around, on a ground where I had played and triumphed with the All Whites. Jersey covered in dirt, body battered and bruised, I walked to the fence and shook hands with people I knew after the match.

'Hey, deadly,' a little Indigenous fella yelled. I turned, thinking he was talking to me. 'Na, not you,' he said and then pointed at Braith Anasta. 'Him. Yeah, you deadly, Braith. We love you.'

I burst out laughing.

'What?' said Anasta. 'What are you laughing at?'

'That's hilarious,' I said. 'Yeah, you deadly, Braith.'

I continued to laugh. I couldn't stop. And from that day on the boys called me 'Deadly'. No one ever called me JT at the Bulldogs, it was always Deadly. And all the Canterbury boys still call me Deadly to this very day. It wasn't the best nickname but it wasn't the worst. Not when blokes in my team were called Smack (Corey Hughes), Ogre (Mark O'Meley), Nugget (Adam Perry), Shifty (Brent Sherwin) and Pig (Brett Oliver). But for now, they weren't my team. I was sent back to reserve grade following the trial. But soon I would be Deadly again ...

I started the year well. I had locked down the No. 6 jersey in reserve grade and was in good form. Both Kevin Moore (the reserve-grade coach) and Steve Folkes (the NRL coach) were happy with my progress.

I was called into Folkes' office after seven games.

Have I done something wrong? Shit, did I muck up on the piss?

I couldn't remember disgracing myself, but I could never remember anything I did when I was drunk. I nervously knocked on his door.

'Come in,' Folkes said. 'Take a seat.'

I sat and sweated on what was about to come next.

'We're going to have to fly your parents down to Sydney this weekend,' Folkes said. 'Have they ever been to Penrith?'

I shook my head. 'I don't think so,' I said. 'Why would they go to Penrith? Isn't that place a shit-hole?'

Folkes laughed. 'To watch you play in the NRL,' he said. 'You want them to be there to watch you make your debut, right?'

And it hit me. I was being picked to play in the NRL.

Fuck, yeah! Woohoo!

I was so pumped that I couldn't get a word out. All I had ever dreamed of was playing first-grade football and here I was, in front of an NRL coach, being told that my dream was about to come true. It was pure jubilation. A lifelong goal reached.

'Oh, and don't tell anyone other than your parents,' Folkes continued. 'We don't want anyone finding out. You won't be named in the team. We want to keep it a surprise for Penrith. That will also keep the media away from you.'

I nodded, but I wondered how I would go keeping this news quiet. It was the best thing that had ever happened to me. I wanted to tell the world.

'Oh, and you won't be going to work tomorrow,' Folkes said. 'You'll be doing your first full week with the team.'

I turned up to Belmore the next day as nervous as I was excited. I was a kid on his first day off school. I had done the pre-season with the boys but I hadn't had a lot to do with them since then. And I knew I had to slot right in like I belonged. I didn't want to be stuffing things up at training and getting in the way.

'Hey, it's Deadly,' one of the boys shouted. 'You Deadly, JT. Come on. Jump in.'

And with that I felt at home.

'I want you to add some spark,' Folkesy said later. 'Get out there and break the game open.' He told me I was going to come off the bench. His plan was to move Braith into the forwards and put me in at No. 6.

Sweet.

It sounded good to me.

I trained well all week. I knew all the plays because they were the same as the ones we did in reserve grade. The Bulldogs unified their calls across the grades so we could slot right in. The only difference was some of the boys had their own individual calls. For example, Nigel Vagana – our strike centre – had a call for when he wanted to be hit with an out-ball. Luke Patten (General) had a call for an in-ball. I learned them, committed them to my memory bank and was all set to go by the end of the week.

I sprang out of bed on game day and cracked a huge smile. *Finally.*

The wait had been excruciating. I don't think I slept much the night before. I was like a kid on Christmas Eve.

Now what do I do?

It was a night game so I had a whole day to kill. I had never had a game-day routine so I was at a loss. Some guys are religious with their routines. They will do the same thing before every match. Some watch movies, others play golf, some even go out and mow the lawn. I ended up hanging out with Mum and Dad. They had flown in the day before so it was a good opportunity to spend some time with them. They kept my mind off what was ahead.

Soon it was time to go. I put my prized tracksuit on and walked to the Canterbury League Club, where a bus would take us to Penrith Stadium for the clash against the Panthers. I jumped aboard.

'Hey, Deadly,' someone said.

I nodded and smiled before making my way to an empty seat. I planted my bum and settled in for the ride. I don't think

I said a word for the duration of the hour-long trip. I just sat back and took it all in. I watched the boys: some played cards, others listened to music and a few just stared out the window, their minds seemingly vacant.

I don't think I thought about the game once. I was just stoked to be on the bus with the NRL team. I was one of them now: an NRL player proper. It would have been pointless to make a mental plan for the match anyway. I was on the bench so I didn't know when I would be on or where I would be playing. I only had to remember one word: spark.

I felt 100-foot-tall and bulletproof when I walked off that bus. Dressed in my tracksuit – *yeah, my very own tracksuit* – I was all chest out and head held high as I made my way into Penrith Stadium. We approached a posse of Panthers fans, Willie Mason walking in front of me, Andrew Ryan (Bobcat) behind.

How good is this!

Then came the insults.

Bulldogs suck. Woof! Woof! Dirty dogs. You suck!

Again … *How good!*

I had never been booed at before.

Yeah, you made it now, Johnny.

Yep. This was the NRL. Boos and all. I couldn't believe I was part of this team. The boys had just won five matches in a row. There was an air of arrogance about them. It was almost as if they thought they couldn't lose. They didn't give a toss about insults. They took every slur as a compliment.

I walked into the dressing room and sat down. Again I just watched; I wanted to take it all in. Some of the boys got massages and others got strapped. Some cracked jokes and others listened to music, all headphones and 1000-yard stares.

Suddenly the nerves kicked in.

Wow. This is really happening. This is the NRL.

I shook it off and kitted up. I needed to keep myself busy.

Just another game. All good.

I can't even remember who handed me my first jersey. I was that nervous I don't think I even took notice. I just grabbed it and whacked it on. I do remember looking down at it when I put it on.

This is your first NRL jersey. Sweet. Maybe I'll get it framed ...

It was a Saturday night and Penrith Stadium was packed. We were bombarded with more insults when we left the safety of the sheds to warm up on the back-field.

And this is only a warm-up?

Soon we were running out onto the field proper. Pre-match speech done, all revved up and ready to roar, I sprinted out onto the ground to a deafening roar. Whatever they were shouting was inaudible, just a mess of sound. I was jumping out of my skin, all adrenaline and ready to let rip. And then it was back to the bench.

I took a couple of deep breaths and the frigid night air snapped me back to earth.

Stay calm. You can't waste your energy now.

The referee blew his whistle and the game began.

Shit, this is fast.

This was the closest I had ever been to an NRL match and the speed of the game staggered me. So did the collisions.

Whack!

One of the boys put on a heavy hit and a Panther went crashing into the ground. I wasn't a good spectator. I shook as

I watched. I twitched as I waited. And finally I jumped to my feet when I got the call.

'You ready, Deadly?' Bulldogs football manager Garry Hughes asked.

Of course I was.

'You're on.'

And with that I became an NRL player.

I charged onto the field.

Righto, this is it. This is your moment. Make it count.

I took my place in the defensive line and turned my attention to the opposition. Tony Puletua, a Panthers giant, was staring me down. He gave me a nod before getting the ball. Soon he was steaming at me, his legs tree trunks and his body brick.

Here we go!

Puletua would have been at least 30 kilograms heavier than me and he was coming at me like a steam train. I felt no fear, no hesitation as he charged.

Whack!

I hit him with everything I had, which wasn't much. And he was as hard as nails. The impact threatened to bounce me but I held on with everything I had. Hands still on body, I slipped down and grabbed at his legs. And somehow I managed to drag him down. Geez, it felt good.

But I didn't have time to dwell. Before I could think the ball had been played and I was chasing someone else. And that is how it went for the rest of the night. I rushed from play to play, legs pumping, heart racing, never dwelling, always chasing. The speed of the game was staggering.

The biggest difference between the lower grades and the NRL is the speed. Everything in the NRL is just so much faster. There are no stops or breaks. You can't blink. Sometimes you can't even breathe.

'Your ball, Deadly,' said Nigel Vagana, the Kiwi international playing at right centre. 'Go on, have a run.'

A scrum was setting just metres out from our own line.

'Are you fucking kidding?' I said. 'You want me to run it off our own goal-line?'

He nodded.

'They'll pick me up and put me in the stands,' I said. 'No way.'

He stared daggers. 'This is your debut,' he said. 'Go and have a carry. Get it out of the way.'

I shook my head and then got as far away from the scrum as I could. Yep, the future Dally M Medal winner dogged it. There was no way my first hit-up in the NRL was going to end in disaster. I would have been picked up and thrown over the dead-ball line. It would have been all Gorden Tallis on Brett Hodgson, State of Origin style.

I remember avoiding my first run but I don't remember making my first run. The rest of the night is but a blur, a rush of emotion. All I know is I went OK and we won. I sang the team song in the shed after the match and had a beer on the bus. I met Mum and Dad back at the Canterbury League Club – where we had our after-match function – and had a bourbon and Coke.

'You made it, Johnny,' Mum said. 'I'm so proud.'

I could have died there and then.

I kept my spot in grade and a career highlight came in round 21 when I went over for my first NRL try. And believe it or not I scored it in North Queensland against the Cowboys. I ended up getting a double at Dairy Farmers Stadium. No wonder I love that ground.

I might take a minute to tell you a couple of things about this Bulldogs side – because they were a team like no other. They had a culture that will never be replicated, that couldn't be replicated. The Bulldogs were a side that bonded over booze. It was in pubs and nightclubs that they formed friendships that would never be broken. Their unofficial motto was party hard and work harder.

And oh boy, did they do both!

I had never been a big drinker, but I was forced to learn fast. Being a Bulldog was as much about booze and benders as it was rugby league. The Bulldogs were a unique side in that they were together seven days a week. They would train together, play together and drink together. That was their culture.

Most of their games were on Friday nights, and they would go out after the game and drink until Monday. Seriously. That was a normal weekend. They would all go out *together*, crash at the same house *together* and do it all again the next day ... *together*. That was part and parcel of being a Bulldog: we did it all *together*.

It might sound like a bad thing, all the alcohol and nights out, but it made that team the closest outfit I have seen. They were all best mates and would do anything for each other both on and off the field.

Not even distance could keep them apart. The boys pretty much lived in one of two places: the Eastern Suburbs or the Sutherland Shire. So come the weekend they would pick a destination and head out as a group. The blokes from the

Shire would crash at someone's pad in the Eastern Suburbs one week and vice versa the next. One week it would be the Coogee Bay Hotel, the next Northies at Cronulla.

And these boys could drink. Blokes like Willie Mason and Mark O'Meley could drink for two days straight. They could put away a carton and still have the coordination to walk on a tightrope. I had never seen anything like it. I would be legless after drinking four bourbon-and-cola cans. I didn't drink beer back then so I was always on Woodstocks; they were a bit cheaper than the Jim Beam.

Management didn't discourage the drinking and nights out. They were of the opinion that we could do what we wanted as long as we didn't get into trouble and we trained harder than any other team. And that is exactly what we did. There were no excuses on a football field. It was flat out or get out. It didn't matter how much piss they drank on the weekend, they all trained like animals come Monday.

The Bulldogs welcomed me immediately. I was taken into the fold as soon as I got there and included in their weekend plans. That was part of their culture – you were immediately taken in as family. I felt pretty special being with those boys when we walked into a pub as one. Everyone knew who we were. People would stop and point wherever we went. We would stride in together – up to 25 at a time – so it was impossible to fly under the radar. Some of the boys had huge profiles. Mason, Anasta, O'Meley, they were some of the biggest names in the NRL. I felt like a rock star.

I didn't have a profile and for the most part I could go unnoticed. No one bothered me. I used to just sit back and watch the way they handled themselves. And 99 per cent of the time they were as good as gold, although looking back, much as I loved and continue to love those boys, I can see that sometimes our behaviour was not always in the best interests of ourselves and those around us.

It was all new to me: free drinks, girls and everyone wanting to be your mate. I had never experienced fans, attention and scrutiny. Girls would throw themselves at the big names and guys wanted to be their best mate.

I didn't really know what to think of it. I just went along for the ride. I had a girlfriend at the time so mostly I just hid away in the corner. And I got away with doing it because I was a nobody. I was barely recognised back then. I had only played a handful of matches and I wore headgear on the field. They would know my name if they asked but mostly they didn't. I was always the guy on the edge of the madness. It was a load of fun.

And then the NRL dropped a bomb. On 23 August Steve Folkes called me into his office. I had gone back to reserve grade the week before, after having a shocker against the Warriors in New Zealand. I was hoping he was about to give me a reprieve.

'Johnno, I've got some bad news,' he said. 'We're about to be stripped of all our points and will spend the rest of the year playing for nothing more than pride. The NRL has just completed an investigation and it looks like we've breached the salary cap. I don't know a lot more but be prepared for a shit storm.'

Salary cap? Shit storm? What the hell?

I became part of what was labelled one of the biggest scandals in rugby league history when the Bulldogs were stripped of 37 competition points and fined $500,000 for deliberately breaching the salary cap. An NRL investigation revealed the club had exceeded the $3.25 million salary cap by over $1 million for two consecutive years. The stripping of 37 points guaranteed that we would finish with the wooden spoon.

Then NRL CEO David Gallop said the club had broken rugby league's heart. 'There is no question that persons within the Bulldogs have let down their players, their fans and their club desperately,' he said. 'The NRL feels deeply for the players and fans of the Bulldogs who are victims in this. But it feels just as strongly that the players and the fans of other clubs in the finals should not risk their dreams being shattered because a club was allowed to get away with breaking the rules.'

I was stunned. Just two weeks before I had been part of the most remarkable game of my career up to that point. Down 19–0 against the Knights in Newcastle after 40 minutes, we mounted one of the game's biggest ever comebacks to give Hazem El Masri a shot at winning the game. In a thrilling finish, Luke Patten went over in the corner to score a last-minute try and take the score to 21–20. El Masri had a sideline kick on his non-preferred side to make it 16 wins in a row.

And I was shitting bricks when he lined up the kick after I bombed a dead-set try, dropping a ball with the try line open earlier in the match. El Masri could erase my mistake with one clean strike. And he nailed it.

Cue the party.

We were on cloud nine after the match, celebrating like we had won a final. There were beers on the bus and we even stopped at a pub on the freeway to continue the party. We were on top of the world, still undefeated and flying. We had proved to ourselves we could do anything by coming back to win that game. The premiership was ours. We didn't think anyone could stop us. But we were wrong.

I walked out of Folkesy's office feeling completely numb.

Seriously, can they do that? Surely it's bullshit. Na. It can't be right.

I couldn't believe what I had just been told. No rugby league team had ever been rubbed out of the competition for a salary-cap breach. I don't think a team had been wiped out for any sort of breach. My confusion soon turned to anger.

We would have won the comp. We've been robbed a premiership. This is bullshit.

And I stayed angry because no one ever explained why and how this had happened. The only information I got was from reading the papers. So yeah, I was filthy at the world. It was meant to be such a big year for me. I was playing first grade and on track to be part of a premiership team. And now I would spend the rest of the year playing reserve grade because my NRL match payments would have constituted another salary-cap breach. I was screwed.

The shit storm that Folkesy predicted hit like a hurricane. Belmore was turned into a circus, cameramen hanging from trees to get a shot, microphones stuck through fences in the hope of a sound grab. We were getting into Hollywood-style car chases with the press when we left the ground. Reporters camped out at our homes. It was madness.

Media outlets began publishing each player's salary. I just laughed when I saw mine. I was on $20,000 a year. But some of the others didn't find it amusing at all, especially our captain, Steve Price.

Is that all he's on? Wow. That isn't much.

That is what I thought when I saw Pricey's salary published in the paper. It wasn't a lot in comparison to what some of the other guys were getting. And it certainly wasn't a good look considering he was the captain of our club. Internally, the wage reports created some problems. I think it was what eventually prompted Pricey to quit the club.

There weren't any jokes about paper bags or car-park cash payments. For the most part we didn't talk about it. That doesn't mean there was no finger-pointing. We all knew who was copping the cash. It wasn't too hard to work out. But did those we suspected know they had been receiving illegal payments? *Probably not.* The players didn't know whether or not the club had been declaring their wage to the NRL. There was no way to know, at least back then.

I was largely shielded from the drama. I had been dropped back to reserve grade the week before the grenade and I spent my days with Kevin Moore and the second-grade squad. And even when I ended up with the NRL guys, the media were never interested in me. Guys like Braith and Willie were hammered; I was pretty much left alone.

A scandal like this would have broken most clubs – but the Bulldogs weren't most clubs. In the end it was the bond I spoke about earlier – forged with sweat on footy fields, cast in bronze with booze and benders – that saved the club. Instead of being divided, the Bulldogs became even closer. It became 'us against them'. It was the start of the 'siege mentality' that the club has made famous. We were all watching together when the Roosters won the premiership.

'They're not the real premiers,' one of the boys said. 'They didn't beat us.'

We all vowed to come back bigger and better. We wanted revenge.

CONTRACTS, CASH AND A BLOODY BIG BLUE

CHAPTER 11

I WAS SOON NEGOTIATING MY next deal. Having finally cracked the NRL, I was in a position to earn a full-time wage. The Bulldogs kicked off contract talks with a letter saying they saw me as a '10-year-plus player', and that I could become 'a starting five-eighth at the very top level' or 'easily slot into the halfback position'. As you can imagine, I was stoked.

Sam wasn't so stoked about the money though. The Bulldogs were offering a starting playing fee of $70,000 ($90,000 including my hospitality traineeship) in 2003, with a $2000 incentive per NRL game up to 10 games, and $1000 thereafter.

They argued that I was still a back-up to Braith Anasta at five-eighth, and they saw me as a comparable player to Brett Seymour at the Broncos. They were basing my worth on what Seymour had signed for at the Broncos.

It all sounded pretty good to me. I didn't really care about the money. I just wanted to be playing NRL for the Bulldogs. But soon Canterbury had some competition. Sam called and asked to meet me at a café in Belmore.

'I have you a very big offer from another club,' Sammy said. 'Take a look at this.'

He slipped a typed letter across the table. There was a giant bunny in the right-hand corner.

'Souths?' I asked. 'The Rabbitohs? You have to be kidding. They're shit.'

Sam almost spat out his coffee. 'Just take a look at the offer,' he said.

Then it was me spitting out my coffee.

'One hundred and sixty thousand dollars a year,' I blurted. 'For two years. That's like 300 grand.'

Sam smiled. 'It's $320,000, Johnno,' he said. 'And you could also earn more with bonuses. We could probably squeeze them for a bit more too.'

The offer, sent to Sam from Rabbitohs CEO Paul Dunn, was huge. I backtracked. 'Yeah, Souths aren't that shit,' I said. 'I guess they have some potential.'

'It's certainly something to think about,' Sam said. 'You've obviously attracted some attention and some people think you have a pretty bright future ahead of you.'

I shrugged. 'Yeah, let me sleep on it,' I said.

But I didn't need to.

Souths were on struggle street. They had just lost 11 of their last 12 games at the time of the offer and they were getting flogged by 30 every week. Coached by Craig Coleman, their best-known players were guys like Adam Muir, Owen Craigie, Scott Geddes and Wade McKinnon. Kicked out of the competition in 1999 when the ARL was restructured into the NRL, it was their first year back after winning a landmark court case to be reinstated.

I called Sam the next day. 'Na, I am not interested,' I said. 'I don't think it would be a good move. I reckon they're pretty desperate. I'd rather stay at the Bulldogs for whatever I can get.'

Sam agreed. 'The money will come later,' he said. 'You need to be at the club that can help make you the best footballer you can be. At the moment I think that's the Bulldogs.'

So Sam went back to the Bulldogs and played hardball. Armed with the offer from Souths he had some bargaining power. But the salary cap scandal was in full swing by the time they were ready to offer me an official deal and the club did not have a lot of room to move. A lot of the NRL boys were agreeing to take pay cuts so I couldn't be greedy.

'Mate, I just got off the phone with Steve Mortimer [Bulldogs CEO],' Sam said. 'They've come in at $73,600 for 2003 and $120,000 for 2004. I reckon that's all we'll get out of them.'

'Take it,' I said. 'I just want to stay with the boys.' I could sense something special was about to happen and I wanted to be a part of it.

I thought 2002 couldn't get any worse – and then I was picked to play for New South Wales. Yep. This proud Queenslander was told he would be wearing a filthy blue jersey and playing against his beloved Maroons in an Under 19s State of Origin match. Ha. Seriously, I didn't care. Not back then.

I was selected to play in the New South Wales Under 19s team because I now lived in Sydney and played for a club based in New South Wales. I had played for the Maroons the year before when I was based in Queensland. It was a strange system and a lot has been said about the State of Origin eligibility rules over the years. Sonny Bill Williams, a proud Kiwi, also played for NSW a year after me. You didn't get to choose who you played for back then – you were told. And I had no problem with turning out for the Blues.

Yeah, it was a bit strange putting on that jersey and lining up against a bunch of my friends – but I was just happy to be testing myself against the best players in the game.

I went up against a lot of my mates, Cameron Smith included. But I also had a few future Queensland State of Origin teammates playing with me for the Blues. We went on to win the match with soon-to-be Maroons Willie Tonga scoring three tries and Ashley Graham two.

Smithy gave us a bit of lip because we were playing for New South Wales, but we had the last laugh.

We ended up carving them up. *Go the Blues!* Ha. Ha.

It was a time of transition for Queensland when it came to State of Origin. They were forced to have a good hard look at their entire football program in 2000 after they were given a 3–0 hiding against a rampaging New South Wales. Beaten 56–16 in Game III, they had 104 points scored against them in the series. The hidings caused a shake-up from the grass-roots level.

In response to the top-level decline and the 3–0 defeat, Queensland set up the rugby league program at the Queensland Academy of Sport (QAS). They began identifying the best young Queensland players and putting them into camps. I went into my first QAS camp in 2002. I roomed with Matt Sing and Shannon Hegarty. The QAS brought its young Queensland rugby league players together and began introducing them to the Queensland State of Origin system. Wayne Bennett set up the program by securing government funding. Since 2001, 51

One of the greatest moments of my life –
the 2015 NRL Grand Final in the bag and
my little Frankie in my arms.
(CAMERON SPENCER/GETTY IMAGES)

Top: That's me on the left, just a few months old and happy to be in the world from the look of it. I'm hanging out with my second cousin Latoya, who went on to be my best friend at primary school.

Bottom Left: This is me as a toddler. Look at those chubby cheeks! And look at the ears … the cheeks disappeared pretty fast, but the ears, not so much.

Bottom Right: Proud big brother. Shane came along when I was three years old. At last I had someone to boss around … (ALL PHOTOS THURSTON FAMILY COLLECTION)

Top: My first footy team, the Souths Acacia Ridge Junior Rugby League Football Club Under 7s. I'm on the left in the front row.

Bottom: Barefoot footy at Souths Sunnybank. I didn't own a pair of football boots until I was 10 years old.

(ALL PHOTOS THURSTON FAMILY COLLECTION)

Top: Winner of the Under 12s State Carnival, playing for Met West at the Brothers Leagues Club in Townsville – my first trip away from home, to what would one day be my home.

Bottom: First time in Maroon! In 1995 I was a State representative on the footy field. Here I am with the

Top: On the field with the Queensland schools side. You can see me in the front row. And guess what? We won the series. Queensland domination started early!

Bottom Left: This is me, my dad and Shane on a family holiday to the Gold Coast.

Bottom Right: Same holiday – Dad, me acting the clown (another thing I started early), Shane and my Kiwi half-sister, Katrina. (ALL PHOTOS THURSTON FAMILY COLLECTION)

Left: When I was 16 I was lucky enough to go to school at St Mary's College, Toowoomba. This got me away from Brisbane, where I'd been acting up a bit … more than a bit. (St Mary's College)

Right: First XIII at St Mary's College, Toowoomba in 2000. I'm in the front row centre, and you can see Jaiman Lowe, who I would later play with at the Cowboys, behind me to the right. (St Mary's College)

Bottom Left: St Mary's College was a great sporting school. Here I am at practice with the school rugby league team. (Errol Anderson/*Toowoomba Chronicle*)

Bottom Right: All dressed up in a penguin suit for my Year 12 formal. I've worn a few of those suits since then, but this was a first. I was probably wondering where my T-shirt was … (Thurston Family collection)

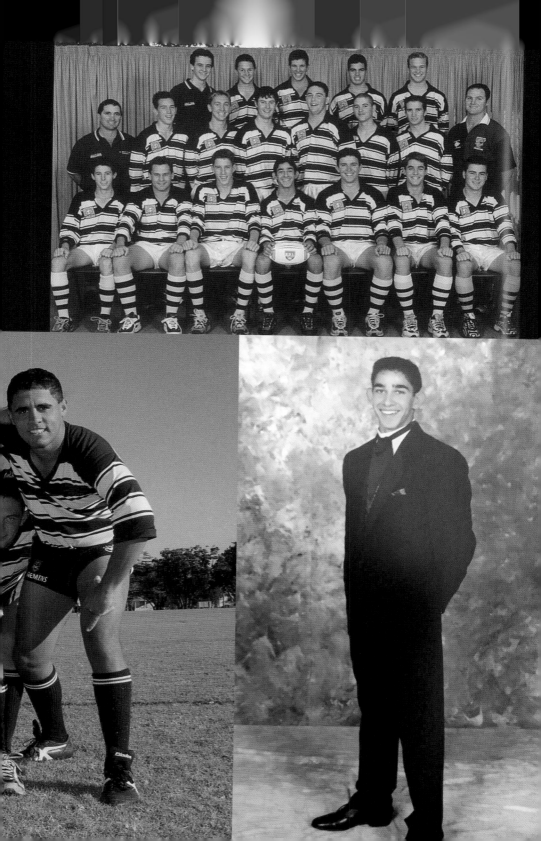

In 2001, aged 19, I signed with the Canterbury Bulldogs. It was a big step up from my job as a butcher's assistant. (BRETT COSTELLO/*GOLD COAST BULLETIN*)

In 2001 I finally got a club tracksuit (and a whole bunch of other gear), and boy was I happy. You can see it on my face here, at practice with the Canterbury Bulldogs at Belmore. That's Nigel Vagana whose back you can see – a great bloke, I learned a lot from him. (NEWSPIX)

Jersey Flegg Grand Final, Stadium Australia, Sydney, 30 September 2001. Together with Matt Utai I'm tackling Luke MacDougall of the Sharks. (JONATHAN WOOD/ALLSPORT)

And we won! Canterbury Bulldogs defeated Cronulla Sharks 12–10. Nothing in my world to date has felt as good as this moment. (Mark Evans/NEWSPIX)

Weekend

The Sydney Morning Herald

August 24-25, 2002 no. 51,468 First published 1831   smh.com.au $2 (including GST)

BULLDOGS

The network that built an empire
News Review

Roy Masters
League's culture of lying Sport

Diana's elusive peace
News Review

Sell your home for extra
Domain

■ Club out of finals ■ Board steps aside ■ ICAC moves in

The day league's heart broke

Anne Davies, Kate McClymont and Brad Walter

The Canterbury Bulldogs were effectively thrown out of this year's competition last night when the NRL stripped them of 37 competition points and fined them $500,000 for "exceptional" and "deliberate" breaches of the salary cap.

An emotional NRL chief executive, David Gallop, called it a "bitter day for rugby league" and said "The game has had its heart broken in an unexpected and tragic way."

He laid the blame for the competition leader's demise squarely on its management, saying "There is no question that persons within the Bulldogs have let down their players, their fans and their club desperately.

"The NRL feels deeply for the players and fans of the Bulldogs who are victims in this but it feels just as strongly that the players and the fans of other clubs in the finals should not risk their dreams being shattered because a club was allowed to get away with breaking the rules."

As angry fans gathered outside the leagues club last night, the football club board stood aside en masse and an interim four-man board of former players – Steve Mortimer, George Peponis, Peter Winchester and Brad Clyde – was appointed.

The decision by the NRL board came just six days after the *Herald* revealed the club had exceeded the salary cap by $1.5 million over the past two seasons and that some payments had been made by the Oasis development – a joint project between the Bulldogs and Liverpool Council.

Also yesterday, the Independent Commission Against Corruption announced it would investigate the council's involvement with the Bull-

Too much to bear . . . a distraught Bulldogs fan, Stephen Ellis, 58, breaks down and sobs outside Canterbury Leagues Club after his team was kicked out of the finals. Photo: Andrew Meares

Top: The year 2002 saw my first outing as an NRL player – in a side that ended up playing for no more than pride, stripped of all our points in a salary cap scandal. It was huge news, as you can see from this *Sydney Morning Herald* front page from 24 August 2002. (FAIRFAX)

Bottom: As if 2002 couldn't get any worse, I was picked to play for New South Wales in an Under 19s State of Origin match. (THURSTON FAMILY COLLECTION)

Top: Playing the Newcastle Knights in round 5 of the 2003 NRL season at Energy Australia Stadium, Newcastle, on 11 April. I'd just been tackled by Andrew Johns; I wanted to ask him to sign those socks. (NICK LAHAM/ GETTY IMAGES)

Middle: Back on the NRL team at last, at Ericsson Stadium, Auckland, on 5 September 2004. I've been snagged by Iafeta Paleaaesina of the Warriors. We went on to win 54–10. (DEAN TREML/GETTY IMAGES)

Bottom: Willie Mason and me tackling Chad Randall during the round 5 match against the Manly Warringah Sea Eagles at Telstra Stadium, Sydney, 11 April 2004. Minutes later, I broke my tibia and fibula, the first major injury of my career. (NICK LAHAM/GETTY IMAGES)

Who would've thought it? Aged 21, with Bulldogs captain Steve Price injured, I got a start in the 2004 NRL Grand Final against the Sydney Roosters at Olympic Park, Sydney, 3 October 2004.
(Brett Costello/Newspix)

With Bulldogs coach Steve Folkes, after the win. I'm so thankful that Folkesy decided to start me off the bench that day.
(Brett Costello/Newspix)

After we took the game, 13–16, I handed my premiership ring to Steve Price. It just seemed like the right thing to do. Pricey was an inspirational leader and an invaluable mentor to me during my time at the Bulldogs. (DAVID KAPERNICK/NEWSPIX)

In the Queensland Origin team at last, Game I of the ARL State of Origin series, Suncorp Stadium, Brisbane, 25 May 2005. We took this game but lost the series … this would soon change. (JONATHAN WOOD/GETTY IMAGES)

Playing against my old team, the Bulldogs. Here I'm crossing the line to score a try ahead of Luke Patten, at Carrara Stadium, Gold Coast, on 27 May 2005. (Jonathan Wood/Getty Images)

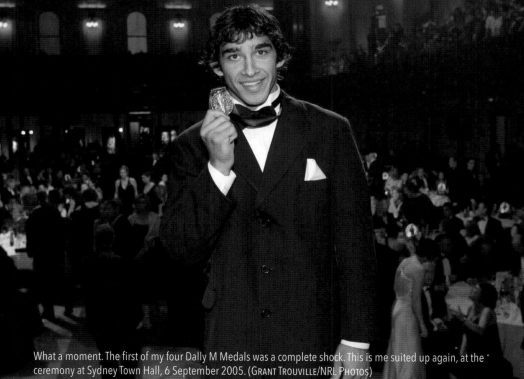

What a moment. The first of my four Dally M Medals was a complete shock. This is me suited up again, at the ceremony at Sydney Town Hall, 6 September 2005. (Grant Trouville/NRL Photos)

Top: Bryce Gibbs of the Wests Tigers tackles me during the NRL Grand Final at Telstra Stadium, Sydney, 2 October 2005. My second Grand Final in two years – but this one didn't work out so well. (Cameron Spencer/ Getty Images)

Bottom: Remember what I said about how good it feels to win a Grand Final? This is what losing looks like – Matt Bowen and me after our 30–16 defeat. All you can do is take the pain and throw it into next year's effort. (Mark Nolan/Getty Images)

players have graduated from the QAS to play State of Origin for Queensland. I have no doubt the program paved the way for Queensland to become the powerhouse it is today. Since 2006, Queensland have only been beaten in two series.

Anyway, in 2002 I was a Blue and I played with Greg Bird, Anthony Watmough and Ryan Hoffman. Soon I would be playing against them ...

Season 2003 began with a woman levelling a serious allegation against me. In February, following a trial match played in Coffs Harbour, I was accused of sexually assaulting a woman in our team hotel. The woman made a complaint to police, claiming she had consensual sex with a player before having non-consensual sex with a second player. I was the second player.

Police investigated the incident and I was cleared of any wrongdoing. I maintain that everything that happened in that hotel room happened with consent.

I was fined $1500 by the Bulldogs for bringing a girl back to my hotel room, which was against club rules. The incident was not made public. I thought I had heard the end of it. I was wrong. More on that later.

I returned my focus to football after I was cleared of wrongdoing and made it my mission to establish myself in the top grade with the Bulldogs. After making my debut, and getting a taste of the NRL, it was my plan to establish myself in first grade. I was hoping to earn a starting spot and play in every match that year. But 2003 was not the breakthrough year I was hoping for.

Things didn't work out how I planned. With Braith Anasta and Brent Sherwin performing at No. 6 and No. 7, I had to bide my time. I was resigned to a utility role in 2003, coming off the bench in six of my nine NRL matches.

I tried to make the most of my opportunities, which were limited, and I scored four tries. I worked hard behind the scenes to develop my game. I also ripped into the weights in a bid to put on some size.

The Bulldogs made it all the way to the preliminary final. I thought they would win the competition but they were tossed out by the Roosters in a 28–18 defeat. I was determined to have a huge off-season and break into the squad for season 2004.

THE DARKEST HOUR

CHAPTER 12

'HEY, THERE'S THAT SHEILA FROM the other night,' said a teammate, pointing at a young woman on the dance floor.

It was 1.30 in the morning, Sunday, 22 February 2004. I was standing next to three of my Bulldogs teammates in the Plantation Hotel in Coffs Harbour, sipping a can of bourbon and cola. We had demolished the Raiders 30–12 in a pre-season trial match that day, and I was excited about the prospect of the season start. Bulldogs coach Steve Folkes had given us a leave pass. Folkesy was an old school coach. He was happy for us to have a drink as long as we turned up at the pool at 7 am for recovery.

I looked towards where my teammate was pointing, through the crowd – heaving and rowdy – and saw a young woman wearing black.

I had never seen her before.

'Who?' I said. 'From when?'

The boys filled me in. Apparently a few of my teammates had met her at the pub on Wednesday night, when we were given a leave pass and told we could hit the town. Some of the boys went to the movies, others stayed at the team hotel and a group went to the pub. I went to the pub but left early, hoping to get a good night's sleep with our game against the Raiders just a couple of nights away.

'She came back with the boys on Wednesday night,' the teammate continued. 'She slept with six of them.'

I nodded and sipped on my drink.

I wish I could tell you that I was shocked by the group sex – but I wasn't. Consensual group sex, a girl sleeping with more than one NRL player at the same time, was not unusual. Looking back now, I can see how distasteful and disrespectful it was. Now, 14 years later, as a dad of three daughters, I don't condone that type of thing. But back then I was just a 20-year-old doing my best to fit in.

I can't tell you my story and omit the most controversial chapter of my career. I can't leave out an event that then threatened to end my career before it even got started.

I'd rather forget these events but I owe you the truth.

Again, this is my story. I can only tell you what I did and what I saw. With this I will become the first member of the 2004 Bulldogs squad to publicly speak about the incident that became known as the 'Bulldogs Rape Scandal'.

And there are no winners here: it is all pain, hurt and ugly.

Back to the Plantation Hotel, where my teammate had just pointed out a woman in the crowd. 'She wants to meet up with some of the boys again,' he said. 'But I don't think they want to see her again.'

I continued drinking, not giving the young woman in black another thought. I was on a high after our trial win. I spent the rest of the night playing the pokies and drinking with my teammates, as well as a few of the Canberra boys, who were also at the pub.

At about 5 am, I jumped into a taxi with a couple of teammates. That 7 am start at the pool was on our minds.

Then one of my teammates was shouting. 'Fuck off,' he yelled. 'Get out of here. You're not coming with us.'

I turned to see the young woman in black. She was trying to get into our taxi. One of the boys pushed her out and gave her a gob-full.

She wasn't impressed. 'You are just a nobody,' she screamed. 'A fuckhead.' She was still shouting as the taxi pulled away.

I figured that was the last we'd see of her. But about an hour later, when I was in my room at the Novotel trying to sleep, my roommate said, 'Shit, that girl is coming. Have a look.'

I looked out the window. She was walking towards our rooms.

Knock. Knock.

She banged on the door of the room next to us, where some of my teammates were staying.

Knock. Knock.

At first the boys tried to ignore her.

Knock. Knock.

'Let me in,' she screamed.

They didn't respond but she kept at it. Eventually one of the boys opened the door and gave her a spray. I don't know exactly what was said but the message was for her to go away and leave them alone.

We could still see her through the glass. One of the boys in my room opened the window.

'Get lost,' he yelled. 'Just go home. We don't want you here. Fuck off.'

The woman started to scream and swear, but eventually she left and I went to sleep.

My alarm went off at 6.45 am. I jumped out of bed, still half drunk. 'Let's go,' I said to my roommate. 'We can't be late.'

Our recovery session was to be held at an Olympic-sized pool located in a training facility that was part of the hotel. I grabbed my towel and goggles before braving the daylight.

'Hey, there's that bird from last night,' a teammate said as we made our way to the pool. 'What the hell is she still doing here?'

I looked over and saw the young woman in black sitting on the side of the road, not far from the hotel office. She appeared to be wet and looked like she was crying.

I shrugged. 'Who cares?' I said.

And I didn't, not until Monday when all hell broke loose.

We were ushered straight into a room when we arrived at Belmore for training on Monday morning. Apparently a story had broken on radio that morning, but most of us were oblivious.

'Boys, we have a very serious matter to address,' said Garry Hughes (Gaz), the Bulldogs Football Manager in 2004. 'I was approached by two detectives in Coffs Harbour yesterday. They informed me that a girl has made some very serious allegations. She alleged that she was sexually assaulted by between three and six players in the early hours of yesterday morning.'

Sexual assault. Police.

I was stunned.

Gaz told us that the woman had been found by hotel staff on the grounds of the hotel and was taken away in an ambulance. Two Coffs Harbour detectives had come to the hotel during our recovery session and spoken to Hughes.

'I spoke privately to a number of players after recovery yesterday,' Gaz said. 'And four players gave statements to police at Coffs Harbour before we came home. I thought that would have settled the matter but there are to be further investigations by both police and the club.'

The press got hold of the story and the allegations went public on Monday morning.

'I need to know exactly what happened,' Gaz said. 'I need the truth and I expect anyone that was involved to put up their hand. This is very serious matter and you need to come and see me if you were involved in any way with this girl.'

I later found out the six players went to Gaz's office after the meeting. They told Hughes that they took the woman back to the Novotel and had consensual sex with her on the Wednesday night. They also told Gaz that they had rejected her on the Sunday morning, first at the Plantation Hotel and then at the Novotel.

Another player admitted having consensual sex with girl on the Sunday morning. He brought her back to the Novotel at the end of the night and had sex with her in the pool area.

When Hughes took statements from the players, he told us he would back us to the hilt. He was filthy on us for breaking team rules – we weren't allowed to bring people back to our team hotel – but he was adamant we had not broken the law.

*

I was not involved in any capacity with the woman who made the accusations. I was not involved with her on the Wednesday night and I did not see what happened in the pool area on the Sunday morning.

However, I was shocked and scared to be interviewed by police for the second time in a year. The press absolutely hammered us and it felt like the public thought we were all guilty even though a charge had not been laid. Every player in the squad was under suspicion. And we couldn't even defend ourselves. We were told that we were not allowed to speak to anyone except a lawyer. We all wanted to clear our names, but we couldn't even tell the police. On 3 March the players were interviewed at the Sydney Police Centre, but our lawyers advised us to say only, 'I am not prepared to answer at this time under legal advice.'

And we copped a hammering for turning up to the Sydney Police Centre in casual clothes, some of the boys in shorts, others wearing thongs. The press said that what we wore showed that we were not taking the allegations seriously.

We were being accused of *rape* – of course we were taking the allegations seriously. That is why we all volunteered to give DNA. The truth is we were at training when we were told we had to go and give our statements. We had just finished a session and were told to go straight to Surry Hills. We went in the clothes we had on.

The season began, and I was soon being called a rapist by fans at football games. I scored two tries in our season opener against Parramatta – and we won 48–14 – but it was hard to celebrate when we were all under such a cloud. A lot of people in the public thought we were guilty of what we had been accused. No names were ever released so fans were speculating as to who had been with the woman on internet forums and the like. I was told my name had been included a few times, I think probably because of the 2003 allegation that I had been cleared of. I had a girlfriend at the time and she struggled when people she knew suggested I was involved. The accusations were really tough on the players with wives and families.

Then Gaz was gone. On 18 March he was sacked for failing to ensure the club's code of conduct was observed by the players and allowing players to breach the dress code. I was shattered for Gaz because he was such a big part of the club and did not do anything wrong. Gaz was the glue that held us together and we wanted to come out and support him – but again we were gagged. Next it was Steve Mortimer, the Bulldogs CEO, who resigned on 22 March.

Could 2004 get any worse for me? Yep.

I went into the 2004 season with great hopes. I'd worked hard over the pre-season and after our near-miss at a grand final berth the previous year, I was full of confidence. I started negotiating to stay at the Bulldogs at the beginning of the year. A great deal has been made of the contract talks that led me to quit the club, so I will put it all on the table.

The Bulldogs offered a three-year contract, saying I would be their number-one five-eighth for the 2004 season, and become one of their 'marquee' players in the future. Here's the money they put on the table:

2004: $160,000 sign-on fee.

$20,000 if I played in a State of Origin match.

$30,000 if I played in all three State of Origin matches.

$10,000 if I played for Australia.

Whatever bonuses I earned would be included in the next year's sign-on fee.

2005: $160,000 plus 2004 rep bonuses.

2006: $160,000 plus rep bonuses from 2005.

I didn't sign the deal they were proposing before the season began; both Sam and I agreed I should play and prove my true worth. But then it all went pear-shaped.

Snap!

First came the noise. Next came the pain. 'Ahhhhh,' I screamed. 'Fuuuuck.' I crashed to the turf in utter agony.

'I heard it crack,' the referee yelled after blowing his whistle to stop play. 'I heard it crack. Get off him.'

The most horrifying noise I had ever heard sounded like a gunshot. The referee heard my bone breaking from 15 metres away. And everyone, even those in the bleachers, heard me scream.

'Ahhhhhhh,' I yelled. 'Ahhhhhhh.'

It was 11 April and we were playing against the Sea Eagles at Telstra Stadium in Sydney. I knew thousands of people were watching me, both at the ground and at home. Every camera in the stadium was pointing my way. But I didn't care. I screamed and screamed.

'Help,' I said. 'My leg.'

I wasn't aware of anything that was going on around me. The agony was all-consuming.

'Ahhhhh,' I yelled again.

After what felt like an eternity help arrived.

'What is it?' asked the doctor, flanked by the club trainer and physio. 'What's wrong?'

'My leg,' I replied. 'It's fucked. I'm done. Get me off.'

The doctor looked towards the sideline. 'Stretcher,' he shouted, as he waved his hand across his throat – the universal sporting sign for he is rooted. 'He's no good.'

That was an understatement. I did my best to put on a brave face. I gritted my teeth and held back the pain, the effort turning my screams into uncontrollable sobs. I was soon on an examination table, the doctor and the physiotherapist prodding, poking and pushing.

'Na, it's not my knee,' I screamed. 'It's my leg.'

The doctor grabbed my leg and gave it a pull.

'Ahhhh,' I yelled, the pain from the pull feeling like a grenade had just exploded in my leg. 'What the hell was that?'

I looked down and saw bone sticking through skin.

'Yeah, you're right,' the doctor said. 'It's not your knee, it's your leg.'

My tibia and fibula were both in his right hand.

The first major injury of my career came five games into the 2004 season – we won 28–26, by the way, though I wasn't thinking about that too much at the time. I was stretchered out of the stadium in a world of hurt after breaking both my fibula and tibia. Until then I had suffered nothing but sprains, cuts, and heavy hits to the head. And it was all pretty innocuous – well, the cause not the result.

As I had done a thousand times before, I jumped out of dummy half after spotting a gap. It closed. Three Manly forwards crunched me and my leg got caught in a tangle of arms and bodies. I fell awkwardly, twisting and turning before being thumped into the dirt.

'How long am I going to be out for, doc?' I asked, painkillers now dulling the hurt.

'Months,' he replied. 'Maybe more. We'll have to get some scans to see what else has been damaged. But with the breaks alone, well ... it'll be a while.'

Months? Maybe more? No! This will ruin me.

I didn't handle the injury well. I struggled. I didn't know what I was in for because nothing serious had happened to me during my short career. I was also off-contract at the end of the year so that was a serious reason for concern. I was only 20 years old. And my team was caught up in a huge scandal. This injury couldn't have come at a worse time. And it all played on my mind.

'You're looking at spending at least 12 weeks on the sideline,' the doctor said when the scans came back. 'You haven't suffered any soft tissue damage but the breaks themselves will take at least three months to heal. We can't insert plates or screw it back together, so we're looking at a natural healing process. You'll have to let your body fix itself.'

I was immediately thinking worst-case scenarios.

My season is over. How am I going to get another contract now? And why now? You just got into the team and were starting to make a name for yourself ...

By this time I had moved out of the Belmore house and into a two-bedroom apartment near Chullora with my girlfriend. And thank goodness I wasn't on my own.

I was soon in a bad place, all thunderbolts and lightning. For the first time since moving to Sydney I was without football. And all those voices in my head, the ones that had me crying in tunnels and offices, soon returned. I was hurt and homesick.

Why me? Why now? Will I ever play again?

*

Just two weeks after my injury, on 28 April, the rape case was thrown out. The Director of Public Prosecutions ruled there was insufficient evidence to launch a prosecution. No charges were ever laid and we were all cleared of any wrong-doing. Some police involved in the investigation have since come forward and said there should never have been an investigation at all.

Several witnesses backed up the account of the player who slept with the woman on Sunday morning, including a hotel grounds man and a couple who were playing golf. Both parties gave statements to police saying they saw the player and the woman in the pool area having consensual sex.

I am adamant no one broke the law. I think the woman who made the allegations did so out of anger after the boys reduced her to tears. I genuinely feel sorry for her. I was angry for a long time but now, looking back, I can understand that she went through a lot too.

We could have handled the situation better. We didn't treat her with respect. She should never have been treated that way.

I don't think management at the Bulldogs handled the situation well. They never came out and backed the players and they also denied us the opportunity to give our version of events that night. The way Garry Hughes was treated was also a sore point with players. He should never have been sacked.

*

Despite the team being cleared, I got so low with my injury that Mum and Dad were forced to come to Sydney.

'I want to go home,' I said. 'I can't deal with this.'

Again the club let me go home, again I had to promise to return and again I didn't know if I would. I had told the club I was just going back to Queensland to clear my head. But I wasn't so sure I would ever come back. The media soon got a sniff and I became a headline:

Homesick Thurston to walk out on the Bulldogs
and quit the game.

Mum ran in with a newspaper in her hand. 'You are going back, aren't you?' she said. 'You have to go back. You're tougher than this, son. You can't throw it all away because you got hurt.'

And she was right. I jumped on a plane and went back to Belmore. Things got better as soon as I was able to train. I once again had purpose and a goal to work towards. Head down bum up, I ripped into my rehabilitation. And that is what I should have done from the get-go.

Looking back, I could have handled things a lot better. I hit the piss pretty hard straight after the injury. I masked my misery with bourbon instead of treating it. That was my way of dealing with it.

Steve Price actually got up me. 'You can't be going out and running amok,' he said. 'You have to be focused on getting back onto the field. Pull your head in. You'll never get back on the field if you carry on like this. The things you do off the field are just as important as the things you do on the field.'

I ignored him and went into the downward spiral that had me thinking about quitting the game. The booze was my way of dealing with the setback but it just made everything worse. I didn't know the importance of rehab and prehab until much later on. It is something I regret. I could have got back on the field a lot sooner if I had acted like a professional.

Despite all that was going on, the controversy and the chaos, the Bulldogs kept on winning. The boys would put aside their personal hell for 80 minutes each week to perform like true professionals. I think they used what was going on externally to motivate themselves on the field.

BREAKTHROUGHS AND BREAK-UPS

CHAPTER 13

I WAS SELECTED TO PLAY reserve grade once I had recovered. The NRL team was flying and I was told I would have to force my way back into the team. That wasn't the only incentive I had to play well. I was also off-contract at the end of the year and fighting for my future. Injury had robbed me of the opportunity to show the club what I was worth.

The Bulldogs went quiet and I started to fret. I reckon I drove Sammy mad.

'Don't stress, JT,' Sam said. 'You'll get a deal. The Bulldogs will pay you what you're worth or you'll go somewhere else.'

'But I don't want to go anywhere else,' I said. 'I want to stay here. Let's just get it done.'

But Sam stuck to his guns. 'No, mate, I've told them you're worth more than what they are offering,' he said. 'I'm going to ask for permission to go to the open market and test your worth.'

'OK, but I want to stay here,' I said. 'Whatever the other clubs offer I'll stay for less.'

And that is exactly what Sam told the Bulldogs. The Bulldogs offered $170,000 for season 2005 and $200,000 for season 2006, and gave Sam just eight days to go and get a written offer from a rival club. They said I couldn't negotiate with rivals after those eight days until the anti-tampering deadline had past. Sam couldn't get a written offer that fast.

I didn't even want to go to the open market. Sam had already had a two-year verbal offer from the Canberra Raiders totalling $450,000. I told him to knock it back because I wanted to stay at the Bulldogs. I told Sam I would stay if they improved their offer by just $10,000.

The Bulldogs rejected the offer. They then said all offers would be withdrawn if I didn't sign by Monday 28 June. I was headfucked.

'So should I just sign what they're offering?' I asked Sam. 'Do they even want me?'

'No, you're not signing anything,' Sam said. 'We'll go to the open market when the anti-tampering deadline ceases on 1 July and get some offers. We'll see what they think when they see what you're really worth.'

I reluctantly left it in Sam's hands. My first official offer arrived on 1 July.

'Are you serious?' I said to Sam when he told me about the proposed deal. 'Two-hundred and ten thousand dollars a year? That can't be right.'

'No, it's not, JT,' he said. 'The Cowboys are also offering $3000 a win and $2000 a loss. And that's just the first year. They're offering a $220,000 sign-on fee in 2006 and match payments, plus $230,000 in 2007 with match payments again.'

All in all, the Cowboys were offering me at least $738,000 over three years.

'Bloody hell, that's huge,' I said. 'And Townsville is a pretty good place, right? Ha. But no, I want to stay here. Can you go back to the Bulldogs and tell them I'll stay for 20 per cent less.'

But the Bulldogs weren't interested. They stood firm at $170,000 for one year. I ended up going to talk to Steve Folkes. I wanted to know where he stood. I told him about the offer I had received from the Cowboys.

'That's a great offer,' he said. 'I won't be standing in your way.'

I am not sure what he really meant by that but I came out thinking he wasn't too fussed about whether I stayed or went. He certainly didn't try and convince me to stay. It was chalk and cheese from the meeting I had next.

I went out to dinner with Cowboys coach Graham Murray and CEO Peter Parr not long after. They were in Sydney for a game and we went to a restaurant in Coogee. To cut a long story short, they told me I had a big future with them. They told me how much they wanted me and explained where the club was heading and where I would fit in.

While the Bulldogs couldn't even tell me I was wanted, the Cowboys all but promised me a starting spot. They said I would be playing No. 6. They also told me I would be playing with Matty Bowen – and that bloke was a hero of mine. It all sounded pretty good.

'So what do you think?' Parr asked me at the end of the dinner.

'It's a good offer,' Sam said, stopping me from making a decision. 'We'll go and have a think about it and get back to you.'

Sam took me in to the Bulldogs a couple of days later to meet Malcolm Noad. He told Noad of the Cowboys' offer and asked him if he wanted to make a counter offer in a bid to keep me at Belmore.

'We can't get to that,' Noad said. 'He would be silly not to take the deal the Cowboys are offering.'

I left feeling numb. 'What does that mean?' I asked Sam.

'It means they've made the decision for you,' Sam said. 'You are signing with the Cowboys.'

I cried, knowing I was no longer going to be a Bulldog.

I cried again when I told the boys. I thought of Mark Hughes, Corey Hughes, Steve Price, Jason Williams, Mark O'Meley, Willie Mason and all the men that had gone out of their way to make me part of the Bulldogs family – and I bawled.

'Boys,' I said when I had finally stopped blubbering. 'I'm off to the Cowboys next year. I can't tell you how hard it was to make the decision to leave but I'll love you all for life. Thank you. And if I get the chance to play alongside you this year I will prove how much you all mean.'

They patted me on the back, shook my hand and wished me all the best. I didn't sleep for a week. I had no idea whether I had just made the best move of my career or the biggest mistake of my life. Anyway, I got back into footy and forced my way back into the NRL.

'You got a passport, JT?' Folkesy asked before the Bulldogs' round 26 clash.

I nodded.

'Good,' he said. 'Because I'm taking you to New Zealand this weekend to play the Warriors.'

Oh yeah!

It felt like I had just been told I would be making my debut again. I hadn't played in the NRL since my injury and I didn't think I would until I joined the Cowboys the following year. So I was over the moon. The Bulldogs were flying and heading towards the finals with a bullet. Suddenly I had a chance to be a part of something special.

We ended up flogging the Warriors 54–10 on 5 September, and I played well.

'Sorry, JT,' Folkes said once we arrived back in Sydney. 'You did everything I asked in New Zealand but I'm going for a different sort of side for the finals. I want a bit of size off the bench.'

I went back and played a reserve grade sudden-death final the next week. We lost.

That's it. I am done as a Bulldog. Bye-bye Belmore.

I went out with the reserve-grade boys and let loose. I treated it like a farewell: all shots and terrible moves on the dance floor. I woke up with a massive hangover.

That's it. All done and dusted. Time to move on. You're no longer a Bulldog.

Or so I thought.

I even found myself cheering for the Cowboys the next day when North Queensland took on the Bulldogs in a preliminary semi-final. The Cowboys had finished seventh and were facing sudden death if they lost. The Bulldogs finished second and would get a second chance, so I ended up cheering for my new team.

You can't cheer for the Cowboys. You're still a Bulldog.

Oh yeah. Whoops. The Cowboys won 30–22. And then, with one call, I was a Bulldog again.

'Yeah, JT,' Folksey said. 'You're playing this weekend. You good to go?'

The loss to the Cowboys had forced Folkes into a rethink.

'Yeah,' I said. 'Of course.'

And with that I was off to the Sydney Football Stadium to face the Storm. One week I am done and dusted and supporting my new team, the next playing Melbourne in a sudden-death final.

I should have been nervous – but I wasn't. This was a win–win as far as I was concerned. My future was set – deal with the Cowboys done – and now, all of a sudden, I had been given a chance to win a premiership. So I cracked jokes at training, I smiled on the bus on the way to the game, and I high-fived all the boys before I took to the field.

I was even happier after the match. We ended up beating the Storm by 43–18. I set up a couple of tries and scored one too. The boys were slapping me on the back after the game.

'Welcome back, Deadly,' they said. 'How good is this? We're going all the way.'

I was on top of the world. Just six months before I had feared my career was over and now I had a shot at winning an NRL title. Wow.

'Bring on the Panthers,' one of the boys shouted of our opponents for the following week. 'Let's smash 'em.'

Oh yeah. Bring it on. I couldn't wait.

And then Folkesy called me into his office. I thought I was about to be promoted from the bench into the starting side. I was dropped.

I was shattered. I don't think I said a word. I just turned and walked away.

That's it. I've played my last game for the Bulldogs.

I didn't see it coming – not for a second. I had played so well against the Storm. *How could he drop me?*

I was shattered. Again I thought I was finished with the Bulldogs, properly this time.

'Anything can happen,' said Pricey, always there for me when I needed him. 'Keep your chin up and train hard. What if Shifty [Brent Sherwin] rolls his ankle?'

Yeah, right.

Anyway, I trained even though I had the shits. It was so hard to be there knowing I wasn't going to be part of whatever they did. Anyway, they beat the Panthers 30–14. I found it a bit easier to be part of the celebrations the next night.

We all went down to Northies at Cronulla to watch the Cowboys play the Roosters in the grand final qualifier. The whole team was there, all shots skolled and on top-of-the-world. The boys were going hard. They had given themselves the day off and they were going to enjoy it before ripping in the next day. I was going to go in as hung over as possible.

'Go, you fucking Roosters,' one of the boys yelled as the game started. 'Cock-a-doodle-fucking-doodle-do.'

While I wanted the Cowboys to win, the boys were all backing the Roosters. The Roosters won the competition in 2002 when we were denied because of the salary cap, and now it was time for revenge.

'We'll show 'em who the real premiers are,' another one of the lads yelled.

The Roosters won and the team went nuts. They celebrated like they had already won the premiership. A few of the boys celebrated a little too hard, and, of course, I joined in. It didn't matter if I wrote myself off with my year over so I went for broke.

I ended up in the back of a taxi with Ben Harris and James Phelps, the *Daily Telegraph* reporter who helped me write this book. We somehow got hold of a bottle of bourbon and were passing it around the cab, drinking it straight. We ended up lobbing at General's [Luke Patten's] apartment at Miranda. He went ballistic.

'We've got a grand final this week, you idiots,' he said. 'Go home.'

I think he booted Benny fair and square in the arse. I don't know what happened after that but I woke up feeling pretty crook. I pulled myself together and headed to Belmore.

'Where's Benny?' one of the boys asked. 'He's a no-show. And he's not answering his phone.'

I had a little giggle. 'No idea,' I said.

Wow. And I thought I was crook!

Poor Ben didn't end up coming to training until Thursday. He missed the team photo and all. I probably need to apologise to him for leading him astray and giving him the bourbon. Ha. Sorry, mate.

Next moment I was summoned to Folkesy's office.

Ah, shit. Does he know about me and Benny? Fuck. What else did I do? Oh … I wasn't drinking with a reporter, was I? Fuck!

I thought I was going to cop it. I walked in looking at the floor, shitting bricks. He told me to have a seat. I waited for him to slap a copy of the *Daily Telegraph* on the desk.

'You ready to play?' he asked. 'You're going to play in an NRL grand final. I'm going to start you off the bench for Pricey.'

What? Serious?

I almost fell over.

Steve Price was injured in the game against the Panthers and I knew he was in serious doubt. But I didn't think that mattered for me because Dennis Scott (Scooter) and Jamie Feeney were both in the extended squad. They were both forwards like Pricey so I assumed it would be one of them.

'You bet,' I said. 'I can't wait.'

He told me I was not going to be named because they were keeping it under wraps. They were going to play some mind games with the Roosters and say Pricey was a chance, even though he was never going to play.

I walked out of there happier than I had ever been. Then I had a reality check.

Shit. My preparation hasn't been great. I better rip in.

I was on the back foot after a week off followed by a massive night on the piss. And then I thought of Ben Harris and I knew I would be right. I was already one training session up on him.

I was walking up the tunnel, towards the field, beaming.

'Ah, fuck,' Dennis Scott said. He was walking into the tunnel and towards Folkesy's office. 'You got picked, didn't you? It's you and not me. Ah, get fucked.'

Scooter thought he was going to get his grand final start – until he saw me. He was filthy.

'Sorry, mate, I was just shattered,' he said to me a couple of hours later. 'I'm still upset but at the same time I'm happy for you. Make the most of it.'

And I decided that I would. He made me realise what an opportunity I had just been given. I was going to do it for him. I was going to do it for the boys. And most importantly, I was going to do it for Pricey.

It was a hell of a week. Every morning we had fans at training. They would be lined up outside, beeping horns, waving flags and shouting our names. Belmore was literally a sea of blue and white. The local butcher even had Bulldogs-coloured sausages.

But while it was crazy on the streets, it was business as usual once we locked the gates. The boys were confident and professional. They trained hard and well. I never doubted that we would win. We were so confident that we were arrogant.

Folkesy gave me my instructions a few days out from the game.

'You'll go in for Braith if things are going well,' he said. 'We'll push him into the forwards and you get on at No. 6 and add some spark.'

He told me to break the game apart. 'If things aren't going so well you might not get on in the first half,' he said. 'But be prepared for anything.'

I trained well. Even though I hadn't been in the NRL team much that year, I knew what was going on. And the boys pulled me straight in and told me I was part of the team.

And what a hell of a team it was. I loved playing with Willie Tonga and Luke Patten out in the backline. They were great players. I was never short of an option when I got the ball in my hands. And I learned a lot from Brent Sherwin. His kicking game was precision. He could land the ball on a dime.

And then there was the forward pack. They were brutal, none more so than Mark O'Meley. I loved playing with the

Ogre. He was an animal. And he really looked after me on the field. So did Mase. I don't think I have seen better when it comes to giving a bit of lip. They went after any player that came for me.

'Yeah, run at us, you fucking soft cock,' they would scream.

We played Parramatta one game and Nathan Hindmarsh wouldn't stop running at me. He ran at me three times in one set of six.

Enter Ogre and Willie. They ripped into him, both with their mouths and shoulders. They ended up belting him every time he got the ball. He didn't run at me again.

And what can I say about Sonny Bill Williams (SBW)? Well, he was just a freak. He was just a kid back then but he was dominant. Geez, he could put a shot on. SBW was also good value away from the field. He was always the designated driver and I would sit in the back with his brother Johnny, sipping on Woodstock cans.

So with guys like this in the team I knew we would win. Don't get me wrong. The Roosters were a great team too. They had Brad Fittler (Freddy), Mick Crocker, Anthony Minichiello (Mini), and Brett Finch (Finchy). They had Craig Fitzgibbon (Fitzy) and Adrian Morley too. It was a good team but they never stood a chance. We were out for revenge. For us this was unfinished business. Nothing was going to stop us. This was our destiny.

It was game day before I knew it. The week was a blur of family, friends and functions. Soon I was sitting on the team bus heading out to the biggest game of my life. We departed Belmore, thousands of fans sending us off to the game in a blue-and-white blitz. We were greeted by just as many when we arrived at Telstra Stadium.

We warmed up inside the stadium, which was surreal because every sound we made was amplified in the quiet. Catching a ball sounded like a thunder crack, the noise hitting concrete before bouncing around the cavernous space. I could hear my heartbeat when all was still. The older boys all had that killer look in their eye: O'Meley, Mase, Braith, Andrew Ryan (Bobcat), they were all on. They flooded the room with confidence and calm.

Before I knew it we were running out onto the field to fireworks, flags and fans. The scene was staggering. I lined up for the national anthem, the eyes of the nation watching.

Is this a dream? Is this real?

Here I was, just 21, and playing in an NRL grand final. Wow. To be honest I struggled to take it all in. With a tear in my eye, I scanned the crowd for my family.

I took my place on the bench and became a mere spectator. And I didn't like it one bit. I wanted to be out there.

'Noooo,' I shouted in the 13th minute and my head went down. Chris Walker had gone over to score the first try of the match. The Roosters were up 6–0 when Craig Fitzgibbon nailed the conversion.

The despair was short-lived.

I jumped out of my seat and fist-pumped the air when Matt Utai crashed over 10 minutes later to bring the score back to 6–4. And I clapped when Hazem El Masri made up for missing the conversion by booting a penalty goal to make it 6–6.

We were down by just one point when I came onto the field in the 46th minute after Matt Utai scored and Hazem converted to make it 13–12. I took on Adrian Morley with my first touch, a show and go. Unfortunately he didn't fall for it. He smashed me. I had a hard time staying composed. Everything felt so rushed and frantic. Everyone seemed panicked. But we soon hit the front when Hazem bounced his way over to score a famous grand final try in the 53rd minute.

'They're going to come back at us,' Bobcat screamed. 'But we can't be beaten now. Not if we give it all we have. This is ours if you all put in 100 per cent. This is it. This is the moment we've been waiting for. Let's do it.'

The next 27 minutes felt like an eternity. The Roosters wouldn't go away; wave after wave of red, white and blue came crashing into our defensive line. It was relentless. We held them out. Repelled each and every charge. And then in the dying moments we cracked. I looked up and Mick Crocker made a bust. I thought we were done. And then Bobcat came from nowhere and brought him down with an ankle tap.

Finally the hooter went and the war was over. We had done it, winning 16–13. I ran at the closest bloke wearing a blue-and-white jersey and jumped on him.

'We're the premiers,' I screamed. 'We did it.'

From there it was a blur of blue and white, bodies everywhere. We jumped up and down, slapped each other on the back and screamed at the moon. The presentation followed and I was given a premiership ring. I went to put it on but couldn't. I looked over towards Pricey.

This is his, not mine.

I walked over and handed it to him. 'This is yours mate,' I said. 'You are the captain of this club and I wouldn't be standing here without you.'

He cried as he took the ring and thanked me by giving me a hug. Folkesy ended up giving me his ring in the sheds but I was able to give it back when the club commissioned the jeweller to make an 18th ring. And I wore it with pride.

I was stunned in 2018 when I heard that Steve Folkes had died. I couldn't believe that Folksey, as fit and healthy as he was, passed away at just 59 from a heart attack. My heart went out to all of his family. I will always remember Folksey and I am grateful for the part he played in my career.

Back to 2004, and after the grand final I had a quiet moment to myself.

Wow. You're only 21 and you've won a premiership. Can it get any better than this?

Well, it did ...

The season ended with a proposition that would make me think about who I was and where I had come from.

'Mate, do you want to play for the Kiwis?' Daryl Halligan asked. 'They want you for this year's Tri-Nations series. You are a Kiwi, right?'

I had to stop and think.

'Well, yeah,' I said. 'Sort of. Technically yes.'

Halligan, a Kiwi legend who was a kicking coach at the Bulldogs, fronted me not long after the grand final. New Zealand coach Daniel Anderson had sent him to make me an offer.

'Well, do you want to be an international?' he said. 'You can be if you declare your allegiance to New Zealand.'

You would think I would have told him where to go right there and then. 'No, I'm an Australian,' I should have said. 'I'm a Queenslander. I bleed Maroon.'

But I didn't. 'Let me think about it,' I said. 'I'll get back to you.'

So what did this future Queensland stalwart and proud Kangaroo have to think about? Well, a lot. I had only played 20-odd NRL games up to that point and even thinking that I might one day be good enough to play for either Queensland or Australia would have been nothing more than a daydream. Seriously. I couldn't even lock down an NRL spot on the bench. And here I was being given an opportunity to play international football against the best players in the world and make a name for myself on an all-eyes-on-me stage.

And there was also a financial incentive. I didn't look into it too much but I knew there would be match payments and bonuses in my contract. So yeah, I didn't say no. I wanted to speak to my dad: the bloke who gave me the Kiwi blood. He sat me down and told it to me straight.

'Much as I'd love to see you play for the Kiwis I don't think you should,' Dad said. 'It would be a huge honour for me and my family, but that's not who you are. You were born in Australia, raised in Brisbane and you grew up supporting the Maroons and the Kangaroos. While you have my Kiwi blood in you, there's no doubt you're an Aussie. And I think that you will one day be good enough to play for both Queensland and Australia. I couldn't live with myself if I stopped you from going on to do that. Knock them back, son. You need to follow your heart.'

Phew!

The decision was taken out of my hands. I seriously don't know what I would have done if Dad had told me it was his lifelong dream to see me wear the black and white of New Zealand.

I called up Daryl Halligan and for the first time in my life I declared what I was.

'I'm an Australian, mate,' I said. 'I might have some Kiwi blood but I'm 100 per cent Aussie. While it's tempting for what it could do for my footy, I just can't pretend I'm something I'm not. Sorry.'

So with that I forgot about playing rugby league again that year and turned my thoughts to becoming a Cowboy.

COWBOY COUNTRY

CHAPTER 14

I THOUGHT I HAD MADE the biggest mistake of my life when I touched down in Townsville.

'Are you serious?' I said to Sam as the aeroplane door opened. 'We're going to melt.'

I had just been smacked in the face by a wall of heat, all humid and hideous. The flick of a latch had turned the cool air-conditioned cabin into a furnace.

My manager laughed. 'You're still on the plane, you big girl,' Ayoub said. 'Wait until we hit the tarmac.'

I looked out the door and could hardly see the ground through the metre-high heat haze.

'Na, I think I'll stay here,' I said. 'This plane will eventually go back to Sydney, right?'

'We can still sign the deal with Canberra if you like,' Sam suggested.

And with that I slung my bag over my shoulder and left the plane.

I turned to Sam when we had walked across the tarmac. 'So what was the Raiders deal again?' I said as I wiped at the sweat on my flooded face.

He laughed and pushed me into the terminal. 'You'll get used to it,' he said. 'And everything up here is air-conditioned.'

'What, even the football fields?' I asked.

Soon we were walking the streets of Townsville. For a moment I thought it was raining.

'Look, I'm dripping,' I said to Sam. 'I'm leaking all over the footpath.'

He laughed, before noticing he was making a puddle too. 'Yeah, you're right,' he said. 'This is hot.'

We were both soaked.

'You won't be complaining about the Townsville weather in winter,' he said. 'But I'll let you complain now.'

We took our shirts off and wrung them, a water bottle full of sweat slapping onto the street.

I sent Josh Hannay, one of the few North Queensland players I knew, a text telling him that I had arrived.

'I'm out on the drink,' he replied. *'At a bar on the strand. Come.'*

I went down wearing thongs, shorts and a singlet, everything else I owned packed away or drenched through. I remembered the words of a couple of former teammates as I walked into the bar, which was air-conditioned, thank God.

'Take it easy on the piss when you get up there,' Bulldogs' back-rower Adam Brideson said before I left.

'Yeah, you're hopeless on the piss, Johnno,' interrupted Todd Polglase, a former Canterbury fullback. 'The worst thing you can do when you go to a new club is go out and make a fool of yourself.'

Brideson agreed. 'You need to earn their respect before you let loose,' he said. 'So drink slow and slip in a water every now and then.'

I vowed to take their advice – but somewhere between drink three and eight I forgot their every word.

'You ready to hit the nightclubs now, mate?' asked Hannay.

Of course I was.

'Yeah, sweet,' I said. 'I'll get a cab to my joint and get changed. Where is it? I'll meet you there?'

The boys started laughing.

'Get changed?' Hannay asked. 'Why?'

I looked down at my shorts and thongs. 'I can't get in anywhere like this,' I said. 'I'll go home and grab jeans and a collar.'

More laughter.

After being ushered straight to the front of the line, entry fee waived, I was knocking back a free drink.

'How good is this?' I asked.

And it was, at least until the next morning. I woke up with the worst hangover I had ever had. And I had this strange dream about dancing half-naked on a bar ...

Whoops!

I put the pillow over my head and went back to sleep. I woke up to my phone ringing later that day. It was Jaiman Lowe, who I had gone to St Mary's with.

'Hey, Tiny Dancer,' he said.

I rocked up to begin my first pre-season with the Cowboys. I walked into the gym.

'Geez, it's hot in here,' I said. 'Is the AC broken?'

One of the boys shook his head. 'Yeah, it's been broken ever since Billy Johnstone got here,' he said of the infamously tough trainer who was the head conditioner at the Cowboys. 'He broke them all on his first day.'

Turns out Johnstone didn't break them. He just threw them all out. Apparently it used to be like an igloo in the gym: all state-of-the-art climate control and precision comfort. He didn't want his players to be soft so he made it hot as hell.

Johnstone also had the televisions and any other things that made the gym comfortable removed. And that included the fans. He turned it into a sauna. Seriously, it was disgusting. Imagine 30 blokes working out in a 40-degree room in 80 per cent humidity. Yeah, everything ends up wet. Oh well. I wasn't going to let a bit of sweat stop me. I was going to rip in and become the best footballer I could be.

No one at the Cowboys put any pressure on me after I signed my deal – but I put plenty on myself. While they said there was a starting spot for me, I knew I had to work extremely hard to lock it down.

And being the new kid in town I felt I had to prove myself from the get-go. I was on huge money – at least I thought I was at the time – and I felt I had to deliver. And looking back it was big money, considering I had only played 20-odd first-grade games. Either way I was determined to make sure I gave the Cowboys a return on their investment.

My strength had always been my fitness, so I wanted to nail the pre-season and make an immediate impression. I started a couple of weeks earlier than most of the squad and I got stuck straight in. I set myself a goal of proving myself to be one of the fittest at the club.

Have I complained about the heat yet?

Well, it was hot. The heat made everything 50 per cent tougher.

And have I told you Billy Johnstone was an animal?

Well, he was ruthless. Every NRL player has heard stories about Billy Johnstone – but nothing can prepare you for his fitness regime. A premiership-winning player with the Bulldogs in 1985, Billy is old-school with a capital 'O' and 'S'. Aside from being part of one of the great Canterbury teams – we are talking Mortimer, Lamb, Gillespie and Tunks – Billy was also a former professional boxer. A local footy legend in the Brisbane competition before moving to Sydney to play with the Bulldogs and then the Dragons, Billy had 27 professional fights.

There is no one like Billy Johnstone. He tried to break me. I knew that was his mission the moment I met him. Only the strong survive with Billy. He weeds out anyone who is mentally weak. And while I have been accused of being a weed, no one was ever going to call me mentally weak.

It did, however, take a while for me to get used to his style of training. We didn't do a lot of running before Christmas. It was all bike, rower and climber. My strength was running, so that was negated. My strength was also my skill with the ball and we didn't touch a football until after Christmas. So that was negated too.

We did a lot of weights and I was challenged. And it wasn't because the weights we lifted were heavy, it was because of the way we did them. It was more a cardio workout than a strength-builder. Ever seen a bloke spewing while lifting weights? Well, I hadn't either until I got to the Cowboys.

Billy's weight sessions weren't player-specific, which they are today. It was one size fits all. Looking back, it was both good and bad. Yes, it taught me how to be tough, God yes it did. But it also didn't help me develop my body. I was only 80 kilograms back then and I needed some size. I needed to be doing big weights at low reps. Instead I was doing the same thing as a guy like Carl Webb: our front-row forward, who weighed 110 kilograms. Our sessions were all 'supersets' and they are designed to lean you down.

But I wouldn't be the trainer – or player – that I am today if it wasn't for hard-arse Billy. And he could be hard. I was on the rower one day when a guy next to me spewed.

'You weak prick,' he screamed. 'Look at that filth. That's what comes out of people as weak as you.'

The poor guy was rooted. He got up and didn't know where he was. He went stumbling around and walked in front of Billy.

'Go and hose it off,' he said. 'Take it out and bring it back looking brand new.'

He grabbed a rower and wheeled it out. He hosed it off and brought it back.

'And you're not just unfit but you're simple too,' Billy said.

The guy looked at Billy, completely bemused.

'You cleaned the wrong rower, you clown,' he said.

He pointed at the one still covered in spew.

'See the bad decisions you make when you're fatigued, boys,' he said.

Pre-season over – *finally* – we got out onto the field. And, football in hand, I started making magic with a little bloke called Matt Bowen, who we called Mango. While he might have been slack when it came to anything involving fitness, Mango was a freak as soon as a football appeared. Yeah, he hated conditioning, but come game-specific training time he was next-level. Mango moved across the ground so easily. He was graceful. And boy he was quick. No one got near him in a 40-metre sprint. His acceleration off the mark was staggering.

I first witnessed Mango's speed back when I was in Year 11 during a high school footy match. Mango was in Year 12 and he had already been making a name for himself. We went to a carnival at Bundaberg and everyone was talking about him.

'You seen this Bowen play?' everyone would ask. 'He's the next big thing.'

I wasn't convinced until I took him on – and lost. We eventually came up against Mango's side and soon into the match he made a break. He wasn't completely through and he was right up against the sideline. I had a bit of a start on him and only had to move a couple of metres to shut him down. And that is when he put his foot down and took off.

Damn! He's quick.

He left me clutching at air.

Geez. Wouldn't mind playing with that bloke one day.

And in 2005 I got my chance.

We formed a bond as soon as I arrived. We had a footballing sixth sense in that we just knew what the other one was going to do. I knew where he would be and he knew where I would put the footy. It was a dream combination from day one. And he was funny little bugger. Mango is a real quirky sort of bloke, shy and reserved for the most part, but he also has a wicked sense of humour and gets out of his box when you get to know him.

But it was on the field where he was at his best. And I knew from the moment I started throwing footballs to him that I was going to have a good year. I just had to give him a little space and he would do the rest.

I began the year training at No. 6 and was selected as the starting five-eighth for our first trial match. I was playing second receiver, and the majority of the plays were being run off me. I picked the plays up quickly and became comfortable being the main ball distributer for the team. A lot of that was thanks to our coach Graham Murray (Muzz).

Muzz was a tactician who never left a stone unturned. He was a real student of rugby league, and put a great deal of thought into every play on the football field. He had a great football brain, as did Neil Henry, who was the assistant coach when I became a Cowboy. Together they made a great coaching team.

Muzz was also a good communicator. We were always kept well informed of his plans. We had a couple of meetings each week and constant chats on the football field. Muzz was also big on video. He would put tapes on and show us what we got right and where we went wrong. He did a lot of research on rival teams and came up with specific game plans to attack the weaknesses of our rivals.

This level of preparation was new to me. Sure we did a bit at the Bulldogs, but at Belmore it was always about us and not them. Both Muzz and Neil were also big on individual preparation. I got a spray off Neil early on.

'What, you think standing around cracking jokes instead of stretching will make you a better football player?' he shouted. 'Well tell me, how many NRL games did you play last year?'

I looked at him like the goof I was. 'Six,' I said.

'Exactly,' he shouted. 'And it would have been a whole lot more if you took your training seriously. You need to act like a professional in all areas of your game.'

I laughed it off but it hit hard at the same time. I never stretched and never took my prehab or rehab seriously. And I knew I would have been back on the field a lot faster the year before if I was a little bit more professional. I think that is when I started treating every area of my training seriously. Yeah, I ran hard and did all the big things at training to the best of my ability, but I slackened off during things I didn't think were as important, like stretching. And it was wrong.

My NRL debut for the Cowboys came in round 1 when we played the Brisbane Broncos at Suncorp. Yep, the big Queensland derby: the Cowboys versus the Broncos in Brisbane. I didn't quite understand the rivalry back then. To me it was just another game. But soon I would learn about all the history between the two teams and what beating Brisbane meant to our fans and our club.

North Queensland were very much the Broncos' little brother. And we had grown up in the shadow of the powerful Brisbane outfit. They had it all: cash, glamour and stars. We had pain, suffering and a long history of losing. But as a club we always stood up against the Broncos. No matter how high the odds were stacked against us, we gave them a game. It was this history of standing up to Brisbane, mostly against the odds, that helped define the fighting culture of our club.

I was given a brief outline of this history the day before the match when Kevin Campion presented me with my very first Cowboys jersey. We had a lunch and in a proud moment, the tough-as-nails North Queensland legend told me what it meant to be a Cowboy. And then he made me one by giving me the jersey.

But the rivalry was just a story until I ran out onto the field. I was confronted by deafening noise as I left the tunnel. The ground was packed with screaming fans. I had never seen a crowd as big for a regular NRL match.

And they weren't just Broncos fans.

I looked around and saw Cowboys fans everywhere. There was as much blue, white and yellow as there was maroon and yellow. Thousands of fans had made the 1400-kilometre trip down to Brisbane to watch us play, many of them piling into the car for a 15-hour drive. And that is when the rivalry became real.

My debut wasn't real memorable. We lost 29–16 and were never in the match. Believe it or not, the highlight of the night for me was getting belted.

Whack!

I was looking back on my inside for a runner when I was hit hard, all shoulder and bone.

Who was that?

I went crashing into the ground, falling like a heap. I was cursing myself for taking the wrong option. And then I saw who tackled me.

Shit. That was Darren Lockyer. Wow.

I was completely starstruck.

You just got tackled by Locky. By Darren Lockyer. How good is that?

Yep. Lockyer was a hero to me. Still is. And I didn't mind the fact that he had just hammered me.

*

I didn't have to wait long to face my former team, with my first clash against the Bulldogs coming in round 2. I was a little nervous about facing my mates – but also keen to get it out of the way. I was expecting them to give me a bit of grief out on the field, but I can't remember anyone saying a word. I don't remember too much about the game – but I do remember getting the win. We ended up beating the Bulldogs 24–12 in front of a near capacity crowd at Dairy Farmers Stadium.

And in round 3, I became an NRL halfback for the very first time in my career. An injury before the Warriors game forced a reshuffle and I was given the No. 7 jersey. I was a little bit unsure of making the move because I had spent the entire off-season as a No. 6 in a distribution role, and I didn't know how I would go with the added responsibility of getting the boys around the park. I was still very much on a learning curve. And now I was learning all the calls and getting the boys to their plays. It was new for me and certainly a big challenge. I looked at it as a way of earning their respect.

We went on to win five of our next six games and suddenly I was being touted as a contender to partner Darren Lockyer in the Queensland State of Origin team. I had no idea, but Queensland were looking for a No. 7 to partner Locky in that year's State of Origin series. And my move into the halves to cover for an injury had put me in contention. So in a matter of months I had gone from a player who struggled to land a bench spot at the Bulldogs to a State of Origin smoky.

I didn't believe it at first. I had a laugh when I picked up a newspaper that claimed I would replace Tigers playmaker Scott Prince as the Queensland No. 7.

Ha. No way. Where do they come up with this shit?

I thought it was fantasy.

I started getting cornered by reporters after games.

'Are you up to it? Are you the man to lead Queensland? Can you be the next great Queensland playmaker?'

I would just roll off the stock-standard answers.

'Oh yeah, I think I'm ready but it's out of my hands. I'm just here to do my best for the Cowboys.'

Deep down inside I dared to believe.

Maybe I really am a chance?

I kept on thinking back to the night I saw Darren Lockyer lead Queensland to victory over New South Wales after I played in the under 19s State of Origin match. I had been dreaming of playing alongside him ever since that magical moment.

Am I really a chance of getting to play alongside the guy who sparked this footy dream of mine?

Turns out I was.

'G'day, mate, this is Gene Miles,' the Queensland selector said, the call coming early on a Sunday morning. 'We're picking you to play Origin, mate.'

I looked around my apartment, expecting to see one of my mates on a mobile phone. I had brought a bunch of my friends up that weekend and I was sure one of them was playing a prank.

'Na, who is this really?' I said. 'It isn't Gene.'

I walked through the apartment as I was talking. All my mates were sound asleep.

'No, it is Gene,' he said. 'Pack your bags, you're going into Origin camp.'

I hung up the phone and jumped up and down on the spot.

'I fucking made the Maroons,' I screamed, the cry startling the boys from their sleep. 'I'm playing Origin.'

The place erupted and the party resumed. We got stuck into the booze and celebrated.

'I better sober up, boys,' I said to the group at about 2 o'clock the next morning. 'I've got to be on a plane in a few hours.'

Billy Johnstone was waiting for me at the airport at 7 am.

'You had a few?' he said. 'You smell like Jim Beam.'

'Shit, yeah,' I said. 'This is my dream, mate. I'm going to be playing State of Origin.'

Another six Cowboys made the team and we all travelled down to Brisbane to join the rest of the squad. I was shaking with excitement the entire flight. I had only ever met Darren Lockyer once, and that was when he smashed me on the football field.

QUEENSLANDER

CHAPTER 15

I WALKED OUT ONTO THE sun-drenched field and first looked at myself.

Is this for real? Look at what you're wearing!

My torso, still all skin and bone, made the size small Queensland Maroons singlet look huge.

'That's the smallest one we have,' said the bloke who handed me my kit an hour or so before.

I didn't care. I grabbed it and slapped it on.

Maroons! You're wearing a Queensland Maroons singlet. Are you serious?

And then there were the shorts. Yep. They were maroon too. All XXXX and QRL.

Wow. This is for real. I'm a Maroon.

I looked towards the field: players passing balls, stepping between cones and stretching.

No way!

I had to shake my head to make sure I wasn't seeing things.

Yep. That's Petero Civoniceva. That's Brad Thorn. And that's Darren Lockyer.

Again I looked at myself and for a moment I was stunned. *I'm wearing the same gear as them.*

I felt like a fraud. Like a kid who had gone to Rebel and bought the training kit. I was wearing the gear of the gods. And then I heard my name.

'JT,' coach Michael Hagan said, 'come on. Let's start.'

And with that I was a Maroon. Well, kind off. I was pretty much a passenger for that entire first session. I was there, standing in at first receiver, shuffling balls, pointing and chasing the play – but I felt I was just watching.

Really? Did Locky just hit Shaun Berrigan with a 30-metre pass?

I was in awe of the skill that was on display. Seriously. Mind blown. Everything was smooth, crisp and fast. Every pass hit the mark. Backs exploded, their runs perfectly timed; there were options aplenty for anyone who had the ball. The forwards charged: left, right and straight – every play of the ball faster than the last.

Yep, it was smooth, slick and sublime.

Lockyer was firing bullets. Smithy was hitting nothing but chest. And Petero was knocking defenders flat. It was a level of skill and intensity I never thought possible. I was Charlie walking into the Chocolate Factory; it was a fantasy made real.

And then Darren Lockyer stopped the session.

'JT,' he said, 'come over here.' He ushered the rest of the team away and I was standing there alone with my hero. 'What are you doing, mate?' he asked. 'Wake up. For me to be able to do my job I need you to do your job. And right now, you're not doing it. You're just catching and passing. I need you to lead the team.'

I nodded. He was right. I was scared stiff of doing anything other than shuffling the ball down the line. I didn't want to overcall Darren Lockyer. I didn't want to jump out and have a run and leave him standing behind, hands on hips.

'You're in the team because I believe in you,' he continued, 'and because I know you can do your job. I need you to take control of the team and get them around the park. That's why the selectors picked you and why I wanted you. I can't play my game unless you take care of yours.'

He must have got a pretty good read on me straight up. He knew how nervous I was and knew that he had to address the situation right there and then. And he was right. I was shitting bricks. I was being very tentative in everything I did.

Right. You heard the man. Let's play some footy.

I was a different person as soon as we had that conversation. I admired him and looked up to him. I wasn't going to ignore him. I wanted to impress him, so if I could do that by being assertive and taking control, well that is what I was going to do.

'Right,' I yelled. 'Two to the left, one to the right, and then my ball.'

I'm glad he pulled me up. It would have been a very different week if he hadn't.

And to know that Locky, a god at the time, was part of my selection in the team made me feel invincible. I walked away full of confidence and self-belief.

I don't remember much else from the camp. I know Pat Rafter, the Australian tennis legend, was there. I know I roomed with Paul Bowman (Bear), but that is about it. I don't think I dropped any plates or made a fool of myself. I was very quiet throughout the entire camp. I don't think I said a word to guys like Petero and Brad Thorn. I just smiled whenever we crossed paths.

Having plenty of my Cowboys teammates around helped. I pretty much stuck to them. I would have been lost without Bowman, Mango, Ty Williams, Matt Sing and Carl Webb, the five other Cowboys who were selected in that team.

Coach Michael Hagan was very relaxed. He never put me under pressure. He just told me to go out and have fun. He told me to use my running game – that is what I had been selected for.

'You're a naturally gifted runner,' he said. 'And it should in fact be easier to break the line in Origin than harder. Why? Because you're not on your own. The best players in the world are running off your shoulder, so use them to create doubt in the defensive line. Your runners will force them to make the wrong decision if you play it right. They'll create opportunities for you.'

Other than to back myself and run, he told me that I had to get the boys around the park. 'And give it to Lockyer whenever he wants it,' he said.

Duh!

The bus ride from the hotel to the match was full-on. I thought I would be prepared after the grand final the year before, but this was next-level. Chris Close (Choppy), the manager, got up before we jumped on and gave the Queensland spiel. He told us what it was all about and got us in the mood.

The atmosphere literally had weight. The game was in Brisbane and the entire city had stopped. It was like the only thing on in the world was Origin, and I was part of the main event.

We had some time off the day before the match and I went shopping in Brisbane with a few of the lads – it was a mistake. For the first time in my life I was a celebrity. I couldn't walk 10 metres without someone pointing, nodding or yelling my name. I was quite embarrassed, to be honest. I didn't really like the attention.

The streets of Brisbane were nothing compared to the ground they call the cauldron: Suncorp Stadium. Wow. The noise was out of this world. The ground was at capacity, fans hanging from the rafters. And they were all there for us. I couldn't see a speck of blue in the stands. It was all Maroon.

The first 40 flew. Literally. My first memory of the game is walking off the field at half-time when we were leading 19–0.

What the hell is everyone on about? This is nothing. This is easy. It's just like any other NRL game. What's the big deal with State of Origin?

Seriously, after my first 40 minutes with Queensland I didn't think State of Origin was what it was cracked up to be. It seemed pretty easy to me.

But 25 minutes later I was a mess. Tackling, running, passing and screaming. I was going play to play, sometimes forgetting to take a breath.

What the hell just happened?

After going to the sheds leading 19–0 and thinking this State of Origin thing was a cinch, I was run off my feet. I had to look at the scoreboard to make sure it was real. Yep, we were losing by a point. It was 20–19.

Are you kidding me? This Origin is something else.

New South Wales had come from nowhere to steal the lead. They had scored four consecutive tries to leave us stunned. NSW coach Ricky Stuart was bouncing around on the sideline like he had won the lottery. We were standing behind the posts, hands on head. I had a played a part in letting them score one of their tries. Midway through their comeback charge, Matt Cooper kicked the ball back inside and I had a shot at cleaning it up. I went to lay my boot into it but was wrong-footed by the bounce. I missed. Craig Fitzgibbon pounced on the ball to score a NSW try. I was desperate to make up for the mistake.

And I would get my chance.

Down by one point and with the siren about to sound, I found myself holding the ball and staring down the barrel of a make-or-break kick. Locky had been going to take a match-saving shot at a field goal the play before but got tackled. So here I was, the very next play, with a chance to level the match.

Or a chance to blow it ...

I didn't have a lot of time to think about it. Ball in hand, all I could see was a blitz of blue coming my way. So I dropped the ball and took a snap.

Yuk!

The field-goal attempt didn't feel good off my foot and Andrew Ryan got a hand to the ball before it cleared the NSW defensive line.

Maybe?

Despite the touch, the ball continued to climb.

Got it!

It scraped over the posts and the referee blew his whistle. I clapped five times before moving back into position. It was my first ever big-match clutch play, but I didn't have time to celebrate. With the game all tied up at 20–20, we were going to golden point. Soon we were defending and under the pump. The Blues were attacking my edge and I watched on as Brett Kimmorley threw an all-or-nothing long ball out towards Matt Cooper. The ball went sailing past my face and seemed certain to put the NSW centre into a hole.

Enter Mango.

In one of those freakish football moments, Mango exploded out of our defensive line and attacked the ball. Hands out, feet pumping, he was either going to win us the game by taking an intercept or lose it by opening a hole for Cooper.

He won us the game.

Bear and Smithy crash tackled Mango to the ground after he went over to score the match-winning try. I soon joined in on the celebration: it was every bit as good as any I had ever had.

Later I had time to reflect on the field goal. I felt like a superhero when the significance of the kick sank in. I believe much of the confidence I have when taking those big plays today can be traced back to that moment. I might not have had the guts to win the 2015 grand final with a field goal had that Origin attempt missed.

The rest of the series was all about a guy called Andrew Johns – a legend of the game and one of my idols. He came back from injury for Game II and put on a clinic. Geez. He took us to school.

In one of the greatest individual performances in Origin history, Joey kicked 40-20s, laid on tries, and nailed all his conversions to lead New South Wales to a 32–22 win. All I remember is chasing him around the field.

He was just as good in Game III when New South Wales flogged us 32–10. Maybe better.

I was initially pumped when Johns was selected to make his comeback match for New South Wales heading into Game II.

Man, you're about to come up against the greatest halfback of all time.

I had watched Joey play all my life and he was one of my favourite players. It was both he and Locky that I tried to base my game on. Joey, like Lockyer, had been at the top of his game for more than a decade. He could win a match in the blink of an eye.

So I was stoked. I was going to be his opposite number. And I was going to give him a run for his money. Or so I thought …

Joey gave me a fair hiding in those two games. The closest I got to him was when I was chasing him from behind after he split the line. He gave me a lesson I would never forget.

Joey laid on tries, made breaks and kicked goals, but he did a hell of a lot more than that. It was what he was able to do for his teammates that really impressed me. Joey just had a presence that couldn't be ignored. When he came out in Game II, New South Wales was a completely different side. Chalk and cheese. He transformed them from a team that had 19 points laid on them in the first 40 of Game I into a team that didn't entertain the thought of a loss. He made them so confident they became arrogant.

Joey was a master, and even though he gave me a footballing lesson, it was a privilege to be on the field with him when he delivered a master class. He is rightfully regarded as one of the game's greatest ever players.

It was not a nice way to end the series after the Game I triumph, but I left the Origin arena with a new-found confidence. I went back to the NRL and felt like I was a brand-new player. I wanted to dominate instead of just compete. I felt so much more confident competing at the NRL level after being exposed to the greats of the game. It was a similar feeling to when I went back to the 19s after playing A-grade. The Origin arena made me a far better player – and I desperately wanted to play for Queensland again.

But I knew I would have to fight for another chance. Even though Queensland was famous for picking and sticking, after the series I didn't feel as though I had earned my place in that side. I hadn't earned the right to be there.

So I went about earning that right ...

THE RISE

PART THREE

A MEDAL AND A FLICKED-UP GRAND FINAL

CHAPTER 16

I WORE A RENTED SUIT and a nervous smile to the Dally M Awards ceremony later that year. Origin over, NRL finals set to start, I turned up to rugby league's night of nights expecting an ordinary evening. Turns out it was extraordinary.

A camera and microphone were shoved into my face as soon as I arrived. 'We are here with Johnathan Thurston,' former NRL player turned reporter for the night Matt Adamson said. 'You have had a tremendous year and are in the running for the Dally M. How do you feel?'

Tremendous year? In the running? Shit ...

'A bit nervous,' I said.

That was an understatement. Suddenly I was sweating and shaking.

The Dally M is considered the greatest individual award in rugby league. Following each and every NRL game, an expert judge awards the best player, at least in his or her opinion, three points. The next best gets two, and the third best, one.

I was in second place on the Dally M leader board when voting went behind closed doors after round 16. But I wasn't nervous when I arrived at the Sydney Town Hall for the ceremony because I didn't think I would win.

I thought I was playing well but most of the points I was given during the first 16 rounds could be attributed to the fact that I had played halfback and five-eighth in a team that was going very well. My good football was a result of that.

There were 10 rounds of voting to be revealed at the sit-down dinner ceremony. I thought Andrew Johns was about to win his fourth Dally M. He had missed the first half of the year with injury but returned to the NRL after giving his State of Origin lesson to me. And he had been at his devastating best. Scott Prince, Ben Kennedy and Stacey Jones had also had great seasons.

So yeah, I rocked up to Sydney expecting an easy night. I rented a suit – I didn't own one back then – and took my partner, expecting to watch on as Andrew Johns was given another crown.

And then came the points.

We were all sitting at fancy tables – round and draped with spotless white cotton, a fresh fork, knife and spoon for every course, and bottles of wine worth more than my suit. I was sitting in between my partner and my coach, Graham Murray.

'Let's take a look at the leader board after 16 rounds,' said MC Warren Smith, a leading commentator for Fox Sports, after the welcoming speeches.

The top 10 players were revealed; I was coming second with 19 votes – one point behind leader Ben Kennedy.

'Let's take a look at what happened in round 17 before we see which of the top 10 players polled votes,' Smith continued.

A highlights package featuring snippets from all the round 17 games was played on a big screen. I didn't feature in any of the footage.

'Only one player in the top 10 polled,' Smith said. 'Scott Prince: One vote.'

Then it was on to round 18. 'Andrew Johns,' Smith said. 'One vote. Johns moves into the top 10.

'Stacey Jones,' Smith continued. 'Two votes. Scott Prince: Two votes. And Ben Kennedy: two votes.'

I stopped sweating.

Yep. Easy night.

But then I started polling votes: one in round 19 and two in round 20. And I stole the lead from Ben Kennedy in round 21, when I was awarded three votes for a man-of-the-match performance in a 26–24 win over Manly.

I was sweating again.

Joey was coming. He was trailing by just six points after also scoring three points in round 21. Joey, who had just landed in the UK to begin a short stint with the Warrington Wolves in the English Super League, was suddenly being beamed live into the room on the big screen via a video cross. Smith asked him about his chances and pointed out his stunning late-season form. Joey downplayed his winning chance – I didn't. He had been lethal in the back end of the season. He was at his very best. I thought he would swamp me.

The gap closed to four points when the votes for round 22 were revealed and suddenly it was my turn to talk – lights, a camera and a microphone once again pushed toward my face.

'After 22 rounds were you expecting to lead the way?' asked rugby league legend Laurie Daley, who was working for Fox Sports.

'No, it's a bit of a surprise,' I said. 'I'm hoping to hang in there but there are pretty good players behind me. You just don't know. I'll wait and see.'

The lights, camera and microphone moved on.

Phew!

I was a nervous wreck. My legs were shaking under the table. I struggled to get through the interview.

'He's a cat on a hot tin roof,' Smith said, he and everyone else in the room picking up on my nerves.

And I only got worse …

I was neck and neck with Andrew Johns – who would become a rugby league immortal – heading into the final two rounds, me with 26 votes and Joey with 25.

'Only two players can now win the award,' Smith said after Ben Kennedy and Scott Prince fell out of contention. 'Let's see if either of them polled votes.'

The room was silent as he paused.

'Andrew Johns,' Smith resumed. 'Three points.'

The room erupted in gasps, cheers and applause as the Newcastle legend stole the lead.

'Johnathan Thurston,' Smith said, his booming voice silencing the crowd. 'Three points. Ladies and gentlemen, this is going to go down to the wire. Let's get to round 26 and find out if it will be Johnathan Thurston or Andrew Johns who takes home rugby league's greatest individual prize.'

My white button-up shirt, also rented, was now soaked through.

'Andrew Johns,' Smith said. 'Three points.'

My heart sank to my stomach as the crowd erupted once again. We had scraped past the Storm in the final round –

30–24 at Dairy Farmers – and I didn't think I had played that well.

So close. Almost. If only.

I plastered a smile on my face as I looked towards Joey on the big screen. And then Smith spoke.

'And with three votes against the Storm and winner of the 2005 Dally M ...' Smith said, 'Johnathan Thurston.'

What? How? What?

It took me a moment to process what I had heard.

You won! YOU WON!

I jumped to my feet, my legs no longer shaking, and kissed my partner. I shook our CEO Peter Parr's hand and then embraced Muzz. I sighed, attempting to find steel, before making my way to the stage.

Shit! SHIT!

All I could think was 'Don't fuck this up'. It was the most nerve-racking moment of my career. Seriously. It was more daunting than lining up that sideline conversion at the 2015 grand final. Somehow I made it up onto the stage. The Prime Minister of Australia, John Howard, draped the medal around my neck.

I looked up.

It's Johnny Howard. It's the bloody PM!

And indeed it was: all spectacles and eyebrows.

I looked down.

It's a Dally M. A fucking Dally M.

And indeed it was: all shiny and gold. All mine. I took a deep breath, knowing the microphone was about to make its way back to my face.

'Johnathan Thurston,' Smith said. 'The first North Queensland Cowboy to win the Dally M. What a moment and what a finish. Can you believe this finish for the 2005 Dally M Medal?'

He looked towards me. 'Step up here to the front of the stage because it is where you belong,' Smith said. 'I can't believe that finish. You just kept on leap-frogging each other. Wow, you are shaking. That was quite something.'

'Yes, ah ...' I said, my voice cracked, my words not quite making it out. 'I'm shocked. Johnsy? He missed out so many games and was still there. But like I said ...' My words failed me.

'You have a rest,' Smith said, saving me. 'What will this mean to Debbie and Graeme, your mum and dad watching on at home tonight?'

'My parents ...' I replied before taking a pause. 'I love them so much. They would be as proud as punch. I'll say a quick hello to them. I love yas.'

'And what about your junior club, the All Whites?' Smith asked. 'Up in Toowoomba they'll all be pretty excited.'

I took a moment to consider the question. 'I moved to Toowoomba when I was 17,' I replied. 'I played all my junior footy at Souths Sunnybank in Brissie. I am sure both clubs will be proud.'

I was hoping that would be it. I was dying – lights, cameras and everyone looking at me. But the questions continued.

'How much of a big call was it to go to the Cowboys from the Bulldogs this year?' Smith asked. 'Did you have doubts that you wouldn't make it up in North Queensland?'

'It did cross my mind,' I replied. 'The Bulldogs gave me my opportunity and were very good to me. But the Cowboys gave me the opportunity to play five-eighth week in and week out, and I would like to thank them and the boys for taking me on board.'

Done. Surely that's it?

It wasn't.

'It was at the Cowboys that you found the form to suddenly play State of Origin beside Darren Lockyer,' Smith said. 'That must have been some sort of moment?'

'Yeah, it was the biggest three weeks of my life,' I replied. 'I was just happy to get a start.'

'The finals begin this week,' Smith said. 'You play the Wests Tigers at Telstra Stadium. Can you beat them?'

'I hope so,' I said.

And with that the questions stopped. I took a deep breath and walked offstage, head held high, ear-to-ear smile plastered across my face, and a Dally M Medal hanging from my neck.

I woke up the next morning and people were calling me the best player in the game. In one night I had gone from just a player of the future to an NRL star. The day before, I was doing my best – and now I was the best. Or at least that's what they said. It was a lot to comprehend.

But I had to put it all out of my head. We were about to play the Wests Tigers in an NRL semi-final. I spent the morning sitting in my room, waiting for the team to arrive from Townsville.

I was the only Cowboys player who had travelled to Sydney for the Dally Ms, which was held on a Tuesday night. The rest of the team were due to arrive in Sydney on Wednesday, ahead of our Telstra Stadium clash against the Tigers.

I was really nervous about seeing them. I wasn't sure how they'd react to all the fuss being made about me. I didn't know how they'd feel about me getting all the accolades for something they had a huge role in helping me achieve. I felt as though they deserved the Dally M as much as me.

'Well done, mate,' said Cowboys prop Paul Rauhihi when the team finally arrived. 'We're all so proud of you. You deserve that, boy.'

The rest of the boys followed. It was hugs and high-fives.

'This is yours too,' I said to the team. 'It's as much the team's as it is mine.'

I became public property after winning the Dally M medal. For the first time in my life, I was constantly being noticed on the street. Before the award – and the 2005 finals series – I would occasionally be stopped at the supermarket.

'Hey, you're JT,' they would say. 'Can we please get a photo?'

After the award – and the finals – I was always stopped.

'JT,' they would scream. 'We're getting a photo.'

Suddenly people wanted to buy me drinks. They wanted my autograph. They pushed their way through crowds to shake my hand. I couldn't even fill the car up at a petrol station without being, at the very least, acknowledged.

Boohoo, big deal, you might say?

And yeah, it didn't worry me. I was young and just took it in my stride. I wasn't about to lock myself in a room. I just kept on enjoying myself and went about my life as usual. It would soon bite me in the arse, but we will get to that a little later.

The only thing on my mind after having that moment with my teammates was the Wests Tigers. I wanted to lead us to a win. I wanted to show everyone I deserved the medal.

And then we got flogged.

*

We had finished the regular season with three wins. Following an up-and-down period after Origin, we had gone on a run to seal fifth place on the premiership table and earn a title shot. Our first finals assignment was the Tigers – a team that had fast become our biggest rival behind the Broncos.

I am not sure what it was, but the Tigers had become the team I loved to hate. Maybe it was because they were on a mission to get us after the Cowboys knocked them out of the finals in 2004?

Anyway, they were a very good side. They played a bump-and-surrender style in attack – meaning they wouldn't fight in tackles so they could hit the ground quick. That allowed them to play the ball quickly and run at a retreating defensive line. They played this style better than any other team I've seen.

We beat the Tigers 44–20 in our first clash of 2005 but they got us by 28–16 in Round 23.

It had only been four weeks since we lost that match, so we went into the qualifying final match as underdogs. With a Dally M, teammates like Mango and Matty Sing, and the whole of North Queensland behind us, I didn't think we could lose.

I was wrong.

In a Telstra Stadium horror show, we were flogged 50–6. The Tigers ran in eight tries to hand us our heaviest loss of the year. Brett Hodgson kicked nine from nine to rub salt into our wounds. We were awful. They were perfect.

The humiliation of that loss could have ended our year. But after earning a life '– a second chance given to us when Cronulla and Manly lost – we vowed to hit back.

We put the defeat out of our heads and went into the second week of the finals full of steam. We were heading into a sudden-death clash against the Storm, and by the time the game kicked off our confidence had returned.

The match was played at the Sydney Football Stadium and I remember it clearly because the ground was empty. It had the atmosphere of a trial match. Playing a match between Melbourne and North Queensland in Sydney wasn't a good idea. It ended up being a tight match. A grind. But we scraped through. Ty Williams scored a double as we edged away to beat Melbourne 24–16. And I played my part by leading the team around the field.

It was a completely different experience from playing in the finals the previous year, when I was a Bulldog. This was my team and I was much better player. I felt like I belonged in this team. I wasn't just along for the ride. I was contributing a lot more.

It was also a different team. We had a good forward pack, Aaron Payne (Payney) was good out of No. 9, and as soon as we had a quick play of the ball, we would flood the middle. We also had a team that could exploit the edges.

Luke O'Donnell was explosive on his edge. There was a bit more structure than we'd had at the Bulldogs and that suited me. The playing group at the Bulldogs drove what we did on the field. At the Cowboys, it was the coaching staff.

And now, after beating the Melbourne Storm 24–16 in the semi-final, we had a shot at becoming the first ever North Queensland team to make it to an NRL grand final. With the team we had, and after a tough win over the Storm, I thought we were a chance.

No one else did.

'Shhhhh,' one of the boys hissed as we made our way out to Sydney Olympic Park on a bus for a training session. 'Listen to this.'

Someone else shouted. 'Hey, driver,' he yelled. 'Turn it up. Turn the radio up, man.'

The bus driver obliged.

'The Cowboys don't stand a chance,' said the voice blaring out of the radio. 'They shouldn't even bother turning up. It's going to be a flogging. The Eels are too good.'

One of the boys yelled, his voice booming over that of the broadcaster.

'Who's that?' he said.

'It's Fatty,' someone shouted.

Queensland legend Paul Vautin (Fatty) had just publicly written us off. Speaking on a Sydney AM radio station, he had declared us as having no hope of beating the Parramatta Eels in the grand final qualifier.

Ouch!

'Fuck him,' yelled one of the lads. 'We'll show him.'

But Fatty had a point. On form, the Eels should have been too good. Parramatta were the red-hot favourites to win the premiership that year. They had finished the regular season as minor premiers, and had belted the Sea Eagles 46–22 in the first week of the finals to make the grand final qualifier.

We, on the other hand – well, we had copped a beating at the hands of the Tigers, before showing glimpses of the team we could be, against Melbourne.

'Buckley's,' Fatty said. 'It won't even be a contest.'

And that was the moment that inspired us to rewrite history by becoming North Queensland's first grand final team.

Sometimes even the smallest of things – a comment, a story or a rumour – can motivate a team or an individual to perform at their best. It's a strange thing. As a professional athlete you shouldn't need any added motivation. It should be a given. Especially when you are playing for a spot in the NRL grand final. But somehow there is no better motivation than getting pissed off.

We blitzed the training session that followed that line-in-the-sand moment on the bus and we went into the Eels match feeling like we were on the edge of something special.

And maybe we were.

We pumped the Eels. Belted them. We came out full of fire, belief and passion, and beat them 29–0. We absolutely gave it to them. The Eels had a chance early. Tim Smith, their No. 7 fresh from winning the Dally M Rookie of the Year award, had an opportunity to put his centre over in the corner. We were on the ropes. But he kicked it for Eric Grothe Jr – who was on the wing – and he sent it dead. From there it was just one-way traffic – and it was all us.

It was a great game. We totally dominated. I set up a try and kicked a field goal; with my left foot, I might add. I left the ground shaking hands with my teammates and patting them on the back. I told them we could win the competition.

And I meant it.

It already felt like we had won the grand final when we returned to Townsville. We arrived home to screaming fans – men and women waving flags and holding banners. The airport was packed. They yelled and cheered. And it went on for the whole week. It was mayhem.

This was the first time I felt the full force of the Cowboys fans: what this football team meant to them and how important it was for this team – and for me – to deliver them the title that they craved.

'What's going to happen if we win the comp?' I asked one of the boys.

He shrugged. 'I wouldn't mind finding out,' he said.

I had played in a grand final the year before. Won a premiership with the Bulldogs. But this was completely different. I was so overcome by the emotion of the fans who greeted us back in Townsville that I went out and bought my first video camera. I wanted to record what was going on so I could look back on it one day. Maybe use it for motivation down the track. And I took that camera everywhere – recording the town and the joy that everyone who lived in it felt.

Soon the Tigers, once again, had my full attention.

Bloody Tigers. It had to be the Tigers.

Wests had, of course, won their way through to the decider. They had beaten Brisbane 34–6 to continue their stunning finals form.

Another chapter in our rivalry would be written.

I was actually happy the Tigers had got through. I was beginning to hate them and I wanted the chance to beat them in the big one. I thought the rivalry would bring out the best in us. We wouldn't be lacking in motivation or desire.

We went into the grand final as underdogs, no surprise after our 50–6 first final flogging. But that didn't worry us. We liked being underdogs – it had certainly worked for us against the Eels.

Things didn't start well. I took the ball to the line early on and almost got through. Caught but arms still free, I offloaded and, following some quick hands, Ty Williams scored in the corner.

Try! What a start.

But it wasn't. Referee Tim Mander was about to award the four-pointer in what would have been a perfect start. And then he took the whistle away from his mouth when touch judge Matt Cecchin approached.

'Check for a possible obstruction by the Cowboys,' Cecchin said. 'I have a no try.'

I lost my shit. 'What obstruction?' I shouted at Cecchin. 'How could you see an obstruction? You were on the other side of the field. You couldn't see a thing.'

He called it anyway.

'How the fuck can you call that?' I blasted. 'You were nowhere near it. This is bullshit.'

The final decision was soon up on the big screen.

NO TRY!

I kicked the ground before composing myself.

'No,' I told myself. 'We have this. Let's go again.'

And we did. Matt Bowen scored the first try of the night, touching down in the eighth minute – striking back soon after being denied – to go to a 6–0 lead following the conversion, I touched the ball twice in the movement.

Yes! We've got this.

But the Tigers soon scored to level the match at 6–6. In a moment Paul Bowman (Bear) would like to forget, he threw a pass in our own goal to avoid being trapped. Bryce Gibbs pounced on the loose ball to put the Tigers back in the match.

And then came a moment of magic no one will ever forget – though I wish I could. I am of course talking about the famous flick-pass try. The Benji Marshall magic. The freak try that has gone down in rugby league folklore.

I have the dubious honour of having started the history-making play. Ball in hand, last tackle, I drilled it into the corner with a well-weighted kick.

Perfect.

We had them right where we wanted them, ball buried on the corner, the Tigers facing a set of trying to work the ball off their own line. I took off to chase. I wanted to get down there and make the tackle. Pin the Tigers down. But I was tripped.

'*Fuck!*' I shouted as I picked myself up and resumed my run.

Brett Hodgson had just fielded the ball, picked it up on his on line and was heading in. I was sprinting towards the play, trying to rejoin the defensive kick chase after pulling myself from the ground.

Hodgson turned the ball inside to Marshall, the No. 6 wrapping around in support. Benji began his run on his own 10-metre line. I saw he had some space in front of him so I rushed to close the gap.

And that is when he stepped and accelerated.

I threw myself at Benji in a desperate attempt to stop his run, but he had my inside shoulder. All I managed was a touch, a passing glance with a fingertip as he rushed by. Matt Sing lunged from behind, the winger grabbing more than me but only enough to check Marshall's run momentarily. We were both lying on the turf when Benji took on David Faiumu, getting on his outside and leaving him in his wake.

I was up and chasing as Benji charged down the sideline, desperately trying to get back into play. I watched on as he charged towards Mango, goose-stepping before trying to take our fullback on the outside.

And that is where I thought the play would end. He wasn't going to get on the outside of Mango. No one did. Mango was too quick. Too good. And Benji didn't, Mango rounding him up and forcing him to the touchline. That should have been the end of it.

But then came the magic, all freak and fluke … a flick. In a famous play that I have been forced to watch over and over, Marshall put the ball into his right hand and threw a flick pass back inside to flying Pat Richards. The rest is history.

I was blowing up behind the posts after the winger touched down to score the famous try and put the Tigers back in the game.

'I was tripped,' I shouted. 'I was taken out after the kick. I couldn't get to the play. Travis Norton was taken out too. Have a look.'

But it was too late; the try had been given. I have no doubt the try would never have been scored had I not been tripped. I would have been in the space Marshall took had I not been illegally taken out.

But I guess that would have also denied rugby league a famous moment, a special play from a special player. And it was special. Brilliant. That flick pass was genius. Marshall was running at full pelt, Mango all over him, and in a high-pressure moment, he not only attempted a near impossible play, but pulled it off. So, well done, Benji.

And a shout-out to Pat Richards – that palm he put in Rod Jensen's face was pretty good too.

We never got back in front after that try – but it was far from one-way traffic. I felt we were always in the game, with the result not sealed until the eightieth minute, when Todd Payten scored to make it 30–16.

The final score was not a true indication of the match. It was a game that we could have won. Should have won.

And I was shattered. Truth be told, I still am.

I sobbed on the field like a baby. I was utterly devastated. I had never felt pain or hurt like it. There is a famous expression in sport: 'There is always next year', but right then it felt like there wasn't going to be a tomorrow. And maybe there wouldn't have been had I known I would be forced to wait 10 years for a second chance ...

THE KID AND THE KING

CHAPTER 17

I THOUGHT DURING THE OFF-SEASON I had come to terms with winning the Dally M medal.

'But are you prepared for what's coming?' Graham Murray asked when I finally returned to begin the pre-season for 2006.

I nodded, albeit hesitantly.

'You know you won't be able to surprise anyone this year?' he asked again. 'Do something good? Well, that'll be expected. Do something wrong? Well, there'll be no excuses.'

I nodded again, unconvinced.

'And they'll be coming for you,' Muzz continued. 'They'll think they have you worked out. They'll watch videos and study your play. They'll know your step. They'll know your pass. They'll know your kick. They'll know how fast you are, know your short balls and long balls, your chips and punts.'

This time I shrugged.

'And they'll be out to hurt you,' Muzz said. 'They'll hit you late when you have the ball and run at you when you don't.'

Muzz paused before looking me in the eye. 'So are you prepared for what's coming?' he asked.

'I will be,' I said.

It was there and then that I made a promise to myself: *You are not going to be a one-year wonder.*

My legacy wasn't going to be: 'Remember that bloke? You know that guy who used to play in the headgear? That Cowboy who won the Dally M?'

I wasn't going to be remembered and forgotten in the same sentence. So I gritted my teeth and bolted out onto the field – virgin green grass, lines freshly painted brilliant white – and I sprinted towards the start line for our first session of the year.

'Four in three?' I asked the trainer, expecting the tradition of his welcoming drill to continue.

'Yep,' he said.

'Let's go, boys,' I shouted. 'Come on. Let's rip in.'

I began my pre-season a bull at a gate. All effort, burn and nothing left in the tank, I trained like I had never trained before. I went to bed each night exhausted. I woke up sore. When times got tough, I used the grand final loss as motivation.

'Get up,' I would tell myself when I struggled to rise. 'Do you want to feel like that again? Go harder. You need to put in more.'

And each day I did. By the time the season started I was fitter, stronger and tougher.

I was also confident. Playing State of Origin had given me the self-belief I needed to become the player I knew I could be. The NRL held no fears – I had competed at the highest level of the game. I had also won the Dally M, a validation as much as an honour.

*

I ran out onto Suncorp Stadium for our round 1 clash against the Broncos asking myself a question: *Are you prepared for what's coming?*

I ran off after 80 minutes of rugby league with the answer: *Yes.*

In a dream start to the season, I scored three tries and kicked six goals in a 36–4 flogging of big brother Brisbane. On their turf, in front of their crowd – all 46,227 of them – I bagged a personal haul of 24 points to help bury the Broncos and bust the second-year syndrome.

And that was just the beginning of a blitz. We travelled back home to beat the Sea Eagles by four points in front of almost 24,000. It was the biggest home crowd I had played in front of since moving to North Queensland. Next up was the Storm – our finals opponents from the year before. I scored two tries and kicked eight from eight as we belted them 40–8. We then proved that kicking 2005 minor premiers the Eels out of the finals was no fluke, by beating them by eight points in our fourth straight win of the year.

And then came the one we had been waiting for.

It had been 187 days since the most heartbreaking day of my life. I ran out onto Dairy Farmers Stadium to face the Tigers for the first time since the grand final loss. Six months since a trip, a flick and a palm to Rod Jensen's face shattered North Queensland's premiership dream. Half a year since I'd sobbed on the turf of Telstra Stadium, inconsolable, struggling to breathe.

But there were no tears as I took the field, 20,262 Cowboys fans cheering, just fire and flame. I had one word in mind as I took to the middle: *Revenge.*

And that is what we got when we destroyed the premiers 32–12 in the grand final rematch. Dulling the pain of our greatest defeat, Jensen – the bloke Pat Richards palmed in the face before that miracle try – bagged a double as we landed the 20-point win. I also scored a try and kicked six from seven to take my season tally to 90 points after just five games.

Next up were the Knights. In other words, Andrew Johns. And I was champing at the bit to play against the legend called Joey in our first clash since I shaded him for the Dally M.

And then I picked up the paper.

> *THE KID V THE KING:*
> *JT to steal Joey's crown.*

My face went bright red.

WTF? Serious?

Later I turned on the TV. The sports broadcaster was at it too. 'Johnathan Thurston is the next Andrew Johns. The playmaking prodigy set to steal the Newcastle great's mantle of best player in the game. And he could do it as soon as this weekend.'

I hit the kitchen table.

No! Really? Why?

'So how does it feel being called the next Andrew Johns?' a reporter asked me the next day.

I bit my lip. 'It is a privilege and an honour,' I replied.

And it was. But here is the response I would have given if I'd spoken the truth.

'It feels terrible,' I would have said. 'Joey is a legend of rugby league. One of my heroes. I grew up idolising him and trying to replicate his game. And I feel like I'm completely disrespecting him for something I haven't said or done.

'You're disrespecting him by comparing him to me – a 22-year-old kid who has done very little in the game. Joey has won three Dally M medals for best player in the NRL, two Golden Boot awards for best player in the world, and a Clive Churchill medal for best player in a grand final.

'He's played 23 matches for New South Wales and 23 matches for Australia. He's also played almost 250 NRL games and scored more than 2000 points. I'm 22 and just starting my NRL career. I've played three Origin matches and I'm still dreaming of representing Australia. Yep. I have a Dally M. But does that give anyone the right to compare me to Andrew Johns?'

But I didn't say that. I just shrugged, smiled and laughed. And I felt like shit.

I was a nervous wreck heading into the match. What should have been a great chance for me to see where I was at by playing against the best in the business had become a public coup: *Kill the King.*

It was a big enough game without all that shit. While we were undefeated so far that season, the Knights were arguably the form team of the competition. They had won four from five, including a 70–32 win over the Raiders, and were sitting just two points behind us on the table. They were coming into the top-of-the-table clash fresh from flogging hotshots the Dragons 54–6, to rack up a staggering 217 points in just five matches.

I suppose I shouldn't have been surprised by all the hype about me and Joey. The comparisons had started even before I had won the Dally M – still, I hated them. As I have said, Joey was one of my idols. He was one of the greatest rugby league players to have lived and I was just a kid. I didn't want to be compared to Joey. He was a freak and I was still a week away from turning 23.

Looking back, I suppose a lot of the anguish came from the fact that I wanted to be better than Joey. I didn't know if I could be – but I had to believe I could be. Please don't think I was arrogant, but some part of me believed that one day I could be remembered in the same breath as him, and I guess my anger at being compared to him back then was because I was nowhere near him at that point.

So why was I such a mess heading into the match? Maybe it was because I might have a shocker and people would say I was no Andrew Johns. Then again maybe it was because I might succeed and people would say I was better than Andrew Johns. Or maybe, well probably, it was because I was fucked either way!

The best thing about rugby league is all that shit in your head disappears when the referee blows the whistle.

'You right, boys?' the man in the middle says, looking left then right.

'Yep,' we say, and then he points to the spot and blows.

From that moment, it is all attitude and adrenaline. It's training and talent. It's also skill, strength and stamina. Kicking tee sent flying, ball in the air, the only thing you're thinking about is getting down the other end of the field as fast as you can, in the hope that it's you who makes that first tackle.

So for the next 80 minutes it wasn't about me and the immortal. Not about the kid and the King. It was just footy.

And in a down-to-the-wire match, we continued our undefeated season start by beating Newcastle 18–16. While all the talk was about me and Andrew Johns heading into the match, it was Mango who won us the game. The man who sent me over the line to score the try that kept us in the game with a two-pass was Mango, who chipped and chased on the last to put us in front. He then won the match by stripping the ball from Clint Newton after running him down to prevent what seemed a certain try.

Phew!

I was so glad to get that one out of the way. I ran to Mango and gave him a hug.

'Fuck, yeah,' I said. 'You're the man.'

And with that, the celebration was over. There was no more adrenaline or attitude. The strength and stamina had been spent, skill and talent left on field. Soon there was just me and Andrew Johns.

'Good game, mate,' Joey said as he slapped me on the shoulder. 'Thought we had you there at the end. Well done.'

I wanted to apologise as I reached out to shake his hand. Wanted to say sorry for the comparisons.

I stopped myself. 'Thanks, mate,' I settled for. 'Yeah, Mango ...'

I couldn't get any more out. He nodded as I sighed. It was then I took a deep breath and walked off the field. I went down the tunnel, into the sheds and straight into what I thought was a cupboard.

And that's where I broke down.

'What's up, mate?' said the doctor, finding me hunched over crying in the doctor's room. 'You hurt?'

I replied by sobbing some more.

'Ah,' he said. 'I'll let you be.' And he did.

I wasn't hurt. I was just relieved. I had got through one of the hardest weeks of my career and I was just letting it all out. I was hoping that would be the end of the JT and Joey thing. Done and dusted. Over and out.

It was only the start.

I was a little bit disappointed that I hadn't made the Tri-Nations tour of the UK at the end of season 2005. I had played State of Origin, won the Dally M and featured in my second grand final, so it hurt not be picked in a squad of 23.

But I had no great hopes of being picked for the Anzac Test, which was to be played on 5 May at Lang Park, given that it was just a squad of 18. Andrew Johns was going to be the halfback and Darren Lockyer the five-eighth.

And then the phone rang.

'You fit and healthy?' said Australia coach Ricky Stuart.

'Mmm, yeah,' I said. 'Why?'

'Because you're going to be playing for the Kangaroos,' he replied. 'I'm picking you on the bench.'

I was completely shocked. Utterly elated. But equally stunned.

The bench? Me? Really?

I wasn't a utility. By this stage I was a specialist half. I couldn't play in the middle and truck it up as a forward. I couldn't catch bombs at fullback or the wing. And I couldn't run crash lines on the edges. I couldn't make 40 tackles if I had to go on as a hooker.

But I wasn't about to say no.

'Yeah, sweet,' I said, fingers crossed. 'I'll play anywhere you put me.'

I arrived in camp to be surrounded by legends. Locky was there, of course. Petero Civoniceva, too. And then there was Andrew Johns. I had never properly met him so I was pretty nervous.

We got straight into training and I was thrown in both No. 7 and No. 6. I went into the halves to fill in for both Locky and Joey during the training drills. And I was blown away. The skill level on display was out of this world. I thought the Queensland sessions were as good as it got. I was wrong.

Watching the speed, accuracy and skill of these players was inspiring. Seeing the ball go from Danny Buderus (Bedsy), to Joey, to Locky was a sight I will never forget. Yep, it blew me away. Everything at that session was just on the money. Next level.

I remember taking a mental note: *This is how it's done. This is how I have to do it. This is how good you need to be.*

It only reinforced my view that I was a long way off being anywhere near as complete as Andrew Johns.

The match was played in front of almost 45,000 people at Lang Park. I sat on the bench for most of the first half, finally getting the call when fullback Karmichael Hunt was taken from the field after being knocked out. Ricky shifted Locky to No. 1 and put me on at No. 6 to partner Joey in the halves.

Wow. Joey. I am about to play alongside Joey. Fucking Joey!

I had to pinch myself. I had fulfilled my dream of playing with Locky but I never thought I would get the chance to play with Joey. My rival was now my teammate. It had been almost a year since Joey destroyed me during State of Origin. Now I was going to get to do the destroying with him.

And it was bloody awesome. I only called the ball a few times, but he hit me on the chest with a bullet on every occasion. I was a bit timid but he made it easy. He was awesome.

We ended up winning 50–12 – but it wasn't as easy as the score might suggest. It was a physical game and I got bashed. No matter what the score is, when you play the Kiwis, you know you have been in a game. They are intense and don't stop hitting. They run hard and tackle hard.

I didn't have too much to do with Joey aside from what we did on the field. I was still in awe of him. I can't even remember if we had a conversation. I was just a pup. I made sure I was last in the dinner queues and last in the massage list in a bid to be polite and keep out of the way of the senior players. Joey was still a basically a stranger to me when I left.

Joey retired suddenly in 2007 when he was struck down by a career-ending neck injury. It was a strange feeling to know I would never play against him again. It was a sad day for rugby league. The whole JT and Joey thing kicked off again too.

I got a text from Nathan Hindmarsh (Hindy) a few days after Joey announced his retirement.

'Did you really say that?' he wrote. 'Wow.'

I didn't know what he was on about. He told me to pick up a copy of the *Daily Telegraph*. So I did.

I'M THE NEXT JOEY SAYS JT.

What? I didn't say that. Fuck!

I was furious. The paper had run a story about me, saying I would love to be as good as Andrew Johns one day. I had no problem with what was written in the article.

But the headline? It was shit. Written in huge bold type, it made out that I was claiming to be as good as Joey.

Here we go again.

I was filthy and feared it would all kick off again. And it did, at least for a little while. I forgot who wrote that story until recently. I was recounting the episode to James Phelps – the co-author of this book.

'Ummm,' Phelpsy muttered. 'Do you know who wrote that story?'

I shrugged.

'Mmmm,' he continued. 'Well ... It was me! I reckon I steered clear of you for a couple of years after that. Shit, you were an angry man!'

I looked at him and laughed. 'Well, you're lucky I forgot,' I said, 'or someone else might be writing this book!'

But as I said, the story was fine ... It was the headline. And I know the reporters don't write the headlines, even if we blame them most of the time!

I ended up having the privilege of playing against Joey on five occasions in the NRL. I won that battle 3–2. He got me 2–0 when it came to Origin. Of course, my best memory of Joey is playing alongside him in that Test match. That is when I really saw his genius.

As far as the rivalry between the two of us went – the whole who is better thing – I always believed I could take him on and win, but I never believed I was better than him. I still don't.

So where do I rate Joey? Well at the end of 2007 I would have put him right alongside Darren Lockyer as the best I had even seen. Another bloke will soon earn the right to sit alongside them, so I will get back to this question.

*

The rest of the NRL season was very forgettable as far as I am concerned. We would only win another five matches that year. Yes: five. After starting the year with six straight wins we went on to lose 13 matches to finish in ninth place and miss the finals by two points.

So much for revenge ...

THE BAD-BOY BACHELOR ... AND SECRET SAMANTHA

CHAPTER 18

I WAS CHATTING TO A girl at a bar in Townsville. She was a pretty good sort and I made it clear I was interested. He came from nowhere, all fists and swinging arms.

'That's my girlfriend, you prick,' he shouted.

And with that he gave me a flogging. He pushed me over the couch and fed me a series of uppercuts. He made a mess of my face, splitting me above the brow. He got chucked out. The security guards brought me ice for my fast-bruising eye.

And I thought being a single NRL player was easy.

In 2005, I became a single man for the first time since I was 17 – and I went about making up for lost time. Life is pretty good for a single NRL player. Let's just say I had no problem when it came to the girls.

Picking up was easy. If you spotted a girl you liked it was as simple as buying her a drink. If she came back to find you later that night, you were in.

Even with the odd belting – and I am sorry, mate, I seriously didn't know she had a boyfriend – being single was fun. I had some of the best times of my life during my single years.

Balancing bachelor life with football took some juggling. I was out and about, in pubs and clubs, until all hours, and that was never going to help me on the field. There were several times when I turned up to training well and truly over the alcohol limit. There were also times when I rocked up blind drunk. It certainly affected the way I trained, but it never affected my performances on the field. I suppose because of that, I kept on doing it. No one ever told me to stop.

I look back and I am gobsmacked that I was able to function as a footballer given how much and how often I was drinking. I don't recover for days now, even after a modest night out. To think I could drink through the night, sometimes the next day, and play a game of NRL that week – it seems like another life. I guess that's what happens to us when we get old. Back then I would be out all weekend and flog myself back into shape in a day.

I had a unit on Sturt Street during this time, which was only 500 metres away from Townsville's party district. I took advantage of it. Sometimes on a Tuesday night, I would walk down to see if anything was happening. I would go and see one of the managers at the bar and have a quiet drink. That quiet drink would end up becoming a bender on most nights.

I got quite a reputation. In Townsville, it's no secret what I was like back then. I am not particularly proud of it, but I don't think I need to apologise either. I was a young single bloke going out and having fun.

I had a couple of fights and committed some misdemeanours during my wilder days. One night, after a bender, I was walking along the street with a couple of girls when a bloke started being a smartarse. He started giving me lip after I brushed him a bit. One of the girls I was walking with jumped in between us and he pushed her over. So I pushed back.

Soon fists were flying and I ended up getting one in. I hit him flush in the mouth and knocked out a couple of his teeth. I also split my hand open.

The fight ended – I'll claim the win – and reality hit.

Shit. My hand. How am I going to explain this? And who saw it? Is this going to end up in the newspaper?

I figured the club would find out about it one way or another so I decided to tell them first. I called Peter Parr straight away. He gave me a spray but also understood that I was defending a girl.

I later found out the bloke I had the fight with was a professional boxer. His name was Josh King, and he would go on to win the World Boxing Foundation lightweight title.

I was a little nervous when I bumped into him a few months later, now that I knew I must have landed a lucky punch.

'Remember me?' he asked, pushing his way past a group of people to confront me at the bar.

'Umm,' I replied. 'Should I?'

'Yes,' he replied. 'You fucking knocked my teeth out.'

I thought it was going to be on again.

'Can I buy you a beer?' he asked. 'Sorry, I was out of line that night. I was being a cock and I deserved what I got.'

Phew ...

I also became a nude model during my bachelor years. Yep. I stripped starkers for a photo shoot in 2006. In a moment of madness I agreed to go nude for a charity.

'It's for a good cause,' said my manager Sam Ayoub. 'You'll be raising money for charity. Nobody will give you any grief.'

Well, he was wrong. I still get ribbed about it today. All my teammates have taken great pleasure in finding that picture and sticking it on the dressing room wall. It has been a great source of amusement for many a Cowboy.

I still remember the shoot. It was for the National Breast Cancer Foundation and was used in the 'Naked Rugby League' calendar, marketed as 'the most provocative calendar ever released by an Australian football code'.

We went out on a boat and there were five people watching as I stripped. They then rubbed oil all over me and gave me a rope.

'Use that to cover yourself,' the photographer said.

'You got a bigger rope?' I asked.

He laughed. All jokes aside, I was more than happy to cop a bit of flak and get my kit off for a good cause. I ended up getting naked again for another calendar in 2009.

I was also a Cleo Bachelor of the Year contestant in 2006. That was all a bit of fun and I met some great people. I hung out with some of my fellow contestants, including V8 driver Rick Kelly, surfer Koby Abberton, and comedian and eventual Cleo Bachelor of the Year Andy Lee.

My biggest public disgrace came in 2010. What started with a pie and a play wrestle ended with a police cell.

'What are you doing?' a man yelled. 'Stop!'

I ignored both the question and the command and went about wrestling my mate. Full of piss and starving after a night out at the Treasury Casino in Brisbane, we had stopped at a 7-Eleven in Brisbane Mall on our way home. We bought pies and sausage rolls, chicken wings and that crappy convenience-store microwaved pizza. We devoured it on the street. My mate may have thrown some food at me. Maybe it was me who threw the food at him? Anyway, we started play wrestling.

'Stop now!' came another order.

I turned to tell the person to fuck off. I stopped myself when I saw it was a cop.

'We're mates,' I pleaded. 'We're just mucking around.'

The officer closed in. 'It doesn't look like mucking around to me,' he said before pointing towards a nearby wall. 'Get over there. Get over there now.'

I looked him up and down. 'Ah, get off ya high horse,' I said. 'We aren't doing anything wrong.'

I ended up giving him some lip. I can't recall exactly what else I said but I can tell you the copper didn't like it one bit. Moments later there were police everywhere, sirens, cars and handcuffs.

I was thrown into the back of a paddy wagon.

'Really?' I shouted as they locked me in. 'Is this really happening?'

I was soon in a single-person jail cell – it was small, sterile and completely surreal.

Really? Jail? Are they fucking serious? For what?

I had been charged with being a public nuisance. I couldn't believe that I was now sitting in a cell, a tiny box with nothing but a plastic bench built into the wall. I looked out the window, a little Perspex square in the door.

'Come on?' I pleaded. 'This has got to be a joke?'

No one came. I was soon freezing. I didn't have a jumper and the cell wasn't heated. There wasn't a blanket or anything that I could use to get warm. I started doing push-ups. Ha! That would have been some sight.

The door opened the next morning.

'Righto,' an officer said. 'We're letting you out.'

I was processed back at the counter.

'Do you want to accept the charge, pay your bail and go now?' the officer said. 'Or do you want us to take you court?'

I handed over the cash, wanting it to be all over. In hindsight, I wish I hadn't paid the bail. I wish I'd gone to court and fought the charge, because my only crime was being a smartarse.

'OK,' the officer said, 'I'll let you out the back entrance. There are a few cameras waiting for you out front.'

'Cameras?' I asked.

'Yeah,' the copper said. 'Everyone knows you're here. I'll take you out the back way so you can avoid them.'

I was filthy. The police arrested me over nothing. They had also told the press. I took the elevator downstairs, thinking the officer was going to help me avoid the reporters.

Ding!

The elevator door opened.

Click! Click! Click! Click! Click!

Cameras were being fired like machine guns, a posse of press waiting outside the lift.

'Yeah, you're a good bloke, aren't you, mate?' I said to the officer who had led me straight to the flashes and unfriendly fire.

He shrugged.

'Come on, face the music, JT,' a reporter said. 'Come out and face up to what you've done. What do you have to say?'

I stared daggers before pushing my way out of the station. My teammate Matt Scott and Brisbane-based player agent Jim

Bannigan, who was also a long-time team manager with the Maroons, had come to pick me up. A car was waiting, engine running, ready to roll.

'Go,' I said as I slammed the door shut. 'Get me out of here.'

I thought that would be the end of it, given that I had done little wrong – but I was soon summoned to face the Cowboys board. The press had claimed that I was kicked out of the casino. My memory was a little clouded because of the alcohol but I didn't recall doing anything wrong while at the Treasury. I decided to hire a private investigator to get all the facts before going before the Cowboys board.

The investigator did his thing and as I suspected I had not been kicked out of the casino. I had done nothing at all wrong at the Treasury. Everyone he interviewed said I was polite and generous with my time.

The board agreed that I should not have been arrested – but they found me guilty of committing a bullshit offence all the same. Unable to get me for anything else, they charged me with drinking while injured.

'Really?' I said. 'But the season is over. Surely that rule doesn't apply in the off-season?'

I was so pissed off over the treatment I received from both the police and my club. Yes, I gave the officer a bit of lip, but I think he arrested me because of who I was and not what I had done.

I suspect the club came down hard on me because of the pressure exerted by the press. They wanted to look like they were being firm, and came up with a charge to appease the media.

*

'I'll have you one day,' I said to the woman after she knocked me back. 'You'll see. You'll crack eventually.'

She nodded and laughed. 'Yeah, right,' she said.

But I had the last laugh because that woman is now my wife.

Samantha Lynch (Sam) started working for the Cowboys in 2006. Following a 10-year stint working for Coca-Cola, she had moved to North Queensland to become the club's sponsorship manager.

I didn't meet her until 2007 – on Valentine's Day as fate would have it. I was at the Heritage Bar in Townsville when I saw a girl I knew from the Cowboys. Sam was sitting next to her, sipping on a drink.

'G'day,' I said. 'I'm JT.'

Sam introduced herself.

She's not bad. A bit of a sort. Maybe later ...

I went back to my mates and being the gentlemen I am, or maybe a cunning pick-up merchant, I sent a bottle of a wine over to her table. Unfortunately it didn't work out so well – she knocked me back a few hours later.

Ha! Ha!

So I told her she would one day be mine – little did I know she would become the love of my life and the mother of my three girls. And it all began with a bottle of wine and a lame pick-up line.

First we were friends. I ended up having a lot to do with Sam at the club. In 2007, I started doing a lot more corporate work with the club's partners. As sponsorship manager, Sam looked after the Toyota account – the principal sponsor of the Cowboys – and the car-manufacturing giant became one of my personal sponsors. As part of that deal I had to visit Toyota dealers around North Queensland, and more often than not Sam would accompany me on those trips. We spent a lot of time together and became good friends.

I started making random trips to Sam's office at the stadium – telling her about all my problems, mostly complaining about the girls I was dating. I would go and see her most days when I had time between training sessions. At first, I would find an excuse to see her.

'Can you read this paperwork for me?' I would say. 'I don't understand it.'

Sam was very different from most of the girls I was chasing around Townsville at the time. She was mature – a few years older than me – intelligent and a high achiever.

Growing up in Brisbane, Sam started working at McDonald's when she was a teenager and went on to manage a couple of stores. She studied at university before going on to work with Coca-Cola Australia. Thankfully she ended up at the Cowboys – and in the sights of a relentless No. 7.

Knock! Knock!

'Shit,' Sam said. 'You can't answer that.'

We were both in my hotel room, under the sheets.

Knock! KNOCK!

'JT,' said the knocker, a Cowboys employee trying to wake me for an out-of-town appearance at a shopping centre. 'Time to go.'

'What do I do?' I asked Sam.

'Nothing,' she said. 'No one can know.'

So we waited, waited and waited some more.

Sam and I first hooked up in 2008, a year or so after we met, in a hotel room while on a sponsorship trip with the Cowboys. We were having a few drinks the night before and it just ended up happening.

Knock! KNOCK!

Sam had planned to go back to her room in the early hours of the morning but we had slept through the alarm. We ended up being late to the shopping centre visit but our secret was safe.

There was no awkwardness following the encounter, and our friendship became stronger. We decided to continue seeing each other in secret. Problem was, Sam lived with a girl who also worked for the Cowboys, so we couldn't be together at her place. And she couldn't risk being seen anywhere near my unit, located on the Strand, a bustling part of Townsville.

We came up with a solution – hotels.

I spent a bloody fortune over the next few months. We booked rooms all over Townsville – and eventually Magnetic Island too – as we met in secret.

'This is ridiculous,' Sam eventually said. 'You're spending a fortune on hotels. We just have to face up to this.'

It wasn't the money I cared about, it was the stress of trying to keep our relationship a secret. Townsville is a bloody small place, and every time we met we ran the risk of being spotted by someone we knew. As I said, we hung out in the same circle of friends, so it got really awkward when we were out with our mates. They must have thought we hated each other because we ignored one another most of the time, not wanting anyone to catch on.

We both walked into Peter Parr's office after deciding to confess our love. We were shaking and sweating.

'We have something to tell you, Parrie,' Sam said to the Cowboys CEO. 'JT and I are in a relationship. We've been keeping it a secret but we thought it was time to tell you because it's going to continue.'

Parrie just shook his head. 'Do you think I was born yesterday,' he laughed. 'I know what you two have been up to. Hell, everyone in Townsville knows. You're probably both on Magnetic Island postcards by now.'

Ha! Ha! And we thought we had been as sneaky as secret agents.

'Look, I have no problem as long as you two keep it professional around here,' Parr continued. 'So far it hasn't affected either of your roles with the Cowboys, so I'm good with it.'

And with that I was officially off the market. My bad-boy bachelor days were all but over. Sam and I wouldn't get married until 2015, but we were very much a couple from that moment on. There were ups and downs, trials and tribulations, and eventually children.

A MELBOURNE MIRACLE

CHAPTER 19

QUEENSLAND WERE UNDER THE PUMP coming into the 2006 State of Origin series. We were facing humiliation. We were on the verge of becoming the first Queensland team to lose four State of Origin series in a row. We would be the biggest embarrassment in Maroons history if we couldn't find a way to beat New South Wales.

Few rugby league followers gave us hope, but we felt New South Wales were vulnerable, especially in the halves. Andrew Johns and Trent Barrett had retired from representative football. Craig Gower was injured, so too was Matt Orford. We didn't know who was going to be their halfback, and for a while neither did they. They eventually brought in Brett Finch to play alongside Braith Anasta in the first match, which was played at Telstra Stadium in Sydney.

I can't recall much about the game except for the end. Down 14–0 after Willie Mason steamrolled his way through the middle to score in the 21st minute, we mounted a comeback. Starting in the 53rd minute when Greg Inglis powered his way over Mark Gasnier to score a powerful try on debut, it continued when Brett Hodgson fumbled the ball in the 72nd to hand Greg a State of Origin double.

Steve Bell scored in the corner two minutes later to give me a shot at levelling the match. Clock ticking, my team two points behind, I lined up my first big State of Origin kick. The boos were deafening as I placed the ball on the tee, only inches from the sideline.

I blocked it all out.

Whooosh!

I nailed it. 16–all. Three minutes to go.

'We got this, boys, ' Lockyer screamed. 'This is all us.'

We were ready to create Origin folklore. Unfortunately, so was Brett Finch.

In a famous NSW moment, the last-minute NSW call-up took the ball and nailed a 40-metre field goal to win the match for the Blues. With a 79th-minute screamer, he leant back, booted the ball and sent it straight between the sticks.

I couldn't believe it. I was sure we were going to win. Just the set before, I was getting myself prepared to take a shot at landing the winning field goal myself. We were charging down the field, play by play, setting it up. But we bombed a play to surrender our shot.

Finch ensured we would not get another.

We were left reeling. Everyone in Queensland was filthy. Everyone in New South Wales was laughing at us. The media were saying we might even kill Origin. Apparently people were losing interest because it was all so one-sided.

We copped a hammering in the press. The papers were brutal, going after our leadership group. They were demanding the heads of our senior players: Lockyer, Price and Petero Civoniceva. They were saying it was their fault and they should be sacked. These guys were Queensland legends. Heart-and-soul players.

And boy, did the sacking calls fire us up.

Under the pump, knives in our backs, sides and fronts, in Game II we came out and belted the Blues 30–6 in a record State of Origin flogging. We gave it to them. And we did it amid a shocking injury toll that forced us to play with a side that everyone had claimed would be embarrassed. Karmichael Hunt, Adam Mogg, Tonie Carroll, Carl Webb and Chris Flannery were all parachuted into the side to cover for injury in that make-or-break clash. The critics expected them to choke.

Mogg, who came in for the injured Inglis, copped heaps before the match. People said he was barely good enough for the NRL, let alone Origin. But just like Inglis, he scored two tries on debut as we flogged the Blues.

Still no one gave us a chance of winning Game III. Of stopping the Blues from creating history by becoming the first side to win four in a row. And the press turned up the heat by calling for our captain's head.

In a completely unfair attack, they said Locky was too old. They said he was too slow and that he could no longer defend.

'I want to say a few words,' Lockyer said on the night before the match, to be played at the Telstra Dome in Melbourne.

He had invited us all into his hotel room. Players only, we huddled around him, hanging for what was to come.

'We've copped a hammering. No one gives us a hope. Most of it has been about me and I apologise for that. I can see that it's been affecting you. I can't do anything about what's been said, but I can do something about what will happen on the field tomorrow night.

'I'm going to go out there and be the best player on the field. I'm going to win you guys this match. And I want every one of you to go in thinking the same way as I am. Think that you'll be the best on the field. Think that it will be you that wins us the game. If we all do that then we can't lose.'

We ran out knowing it was do-or-die for our captain and for the dignity of our state.

Locky's message was ringing in my ear. *Be the best player on the field. Win the match for your side.*

The game started well, with Mogg continuing his try-scoring form to land the first four-pointer of the night. In a freakish effort from the winger after I had put a kick across, he planted the ball in the corner after plucking it from the air. Mogg looked certain to be pushed out when Grothe steamed across to put a shot on him. His whole body was out over the touch-in-goal line when he put the ball down. I don't know how he managed to stay in to give us a 4–0 lead.

Then I fucked up.

Going for the throat in the 25th minute, out to bury the Blues, I threw a Hail Mary pass to Adam Mogg in an attempt to send him over for his second. I saw that he was unmarked, but I didn't see Eric Grothe flying through.

Fuck. No. No. No.

I turned and chased, cursing myself as I ran. Eric Grothe was sprinting down the line after plucking the miscued pass from the air. There was no catching the NSW winger, who ran almost 100 metres to score.

Fuck. Shit. Fuck.

You won't see that on my Origin highlights reel.

Locked at 4–all at the break, New South Wales stole the lead in the 46th minute when Matt King touched down to make it 10–4 following the conversion. And then came the controversy – Grothe going in again to score after Brett Hodgson knocked the ball on. The decision was sent up to the video referee and we were certain the try would not be awarded. The ball, sent into the air by Craig Gower, had bounced forward off Hodgson's chest and then arm before Steve Menzies pounced to scoop it up to send Grothe over.

I was standing right next to the fullback when he dropped it. I even pulled my hands out of the way to make sure that I didn't make it a double knock-on.

TRY!

We were shocked when the decision came through, the green light flashing on the big screen. New South Wales celebrated like they had already won the game.

'This is bullshit,' I said to Lockyer as we gathered behind the posts before the conversion attempt. 'This isn't our night.'

Locky shook his head and pulled us all in. 'We can still do this,' he shouted. 'We are Queensland. Remember what the men who came before you have done in this jersey. We'll do it too.'

We were down 14–4 when we went about making a miracle.

In the 71st minute, clock ticking, Blues on the verge of the record-creating win, Clinton Schifcofske threw me the ball. He had been swung in the tackle and instinctively chucked it out the back. I was on my own 10-metre line when I caught it. I looked up and saw a bit of space, so I took it. I stepped back off my right foot and went through the line. I darted 20 metres before I saw Brent Tate (Tatey) on my outside. I threw the ball right and it stuck. He ran 60 metres to score under the posts.

We can do this.

We had seven minutes to save our state – we only needed one minute. In a moment of madness from Brett Hodgson, which would deliver us a dynasty, the fullback went into dummy half and threw a long ball. He missed his mark, the ball bouncing on the ground. And the man who made the pre-game promise to win us the game delivered on his word. Locky charged through and pounced on the ball before running 15 metres to score.

We held on for the last five minutes to win 16–14. A miracle in Melbourne.

It was the greatest feeling of my life. Pure elation. Electric. It was a whole new level from the 2004 grand final win.

And the celebration was huge. We went nuts in the sheds, Alfie leading the charge. We drank until sun-up, and that was just a warm-up.

'Boys, we'll have a proper celebration at the end of the year,' Mal said. 'I'll let you know where and when.'

That celebration, the 'proper' one, rolled around soon enough. The Origin fellas from the Cowboys flew into Brisbane. There was a car waiting for us at the airport. We were driven to a pub at Hope Island, where we met the rest of the boys. We were into our first few beers when we looked out and saw a helicopter land.

'That's us, boys,' someone from management said.

Are you serious?

He was. We were flown into the Gold Coast hinterland, to a massive property in the middle of nowhere. It was huge. A mansion with food and drinks waiting. There was a golf driving range on the property. There were swimming pools and pool tables.

We spoke about the personal efforts of that series as we sucked back beer. The so-called no-names who earned their place in State of Origin. Steven Bell, Adam Mogg, David Stagg, Dallas Johnson and Chris Flannery were apparently nobodies, selected out of desperation and supposedly not good enough for rugby league's biggest stage. Ha. That jersey was all they needed to be their best.

Queensland has its legends, including Arthur Beetson, Wally Lewis, Mal Meninga, Allan Langer, Darren Lockyer, Cameron Smith, Greg Inglis. They are the stars a side is built around. And then it has the blokes who just go out and do a job, including Paul Hauff, Adrian Brunker, Darren Fritz, Chris Beattie, David Stagg, Adam Mogg and Tim Glasby.

They are equally as important as the legends, and the job they do is what being a Queenslander is all about. The guys who play one to a handful of games and rise to the occasion are our real heroes.

We ripped into the food and drink until the helicopter came back. We thought the party was over – it had only just begun. The helicopter took us to Hope Island, where a gigantic yacht was waiting. It was loaded with even more food and drinks than the last place. We cruised from Hope Island and into Surfers to hit the nightclubs.

The rest is a blur.

Yep, it was a celebration. A proper celebration. Shots. Clubs. Dance floors. Mal had done it all in rugby league and he understood what we needed and when we needed it. What would get us up for the game. Sometimes that was having a drink. It brought us together.

Mal wanted us to relax and enjoy ourselves away from training. At training he wanted our maximum effort.

We would sit back and laugh at all the controversy New South Wales had over their bonding sessions. There always seemed to be a scandal. One year they would be bagged for cancelling, the next they would get caned for putting it back on. Their players always got caught out doing something wrong.

We were always pretty good at ours because the coaching staff would always be with us to the very end.

What came next was a State of Origin dynasty.

THE DYNASTY

CHAPTER 20

IT TOOK JUST FOUR HOURS to sell out Suncorp Stadium for our triumphant State of Origin return to Queensland. The first 10,000 tickets were snapped up in just seven minutes, the rest all gone a few hours later.

A huge crowd, 52,498 screaming fans, mostly Queenslanders, were at the ground formerly known as Lang Park to give us a heroes' welcome as we ran out on the field to face the Blues in the first match of the 2007 State of Origin series. They would all become witnesses to rugby league history.

Soon we would become the first Maroons side since 1995 to win three consecutive State of Origin matches. Later we would become the only side in history to win eight series straight. Rugby league's most famous empire was being forged, the greatest dynasty in the game born.

Seems someone forgot to tell Jarryd Hayne.

Down 12–6 and trying to manufacture a half-time mini-miracle, Brent Tate caught the ball on the wing. He then attempted to kick the ball in field after making a half-break.

Siren soon to sound and New South Wales coming off back-to-back tries – from Nathan Hindmarsh and then Matt Cooper – he saw points back on the inside, and Maroons jerseys rushing through the middle.

Tate missed his mark.

Instead of finding a match-levelling try, Tatey kicked it straight into Jarryd Hayne. What came next will be played on highlight reels for rugby league eternity.

Hayne picked the ball up after trapping it with his feet. He looked up only to be confronted by Justin Hodges, the Queensland centre on him in an instant. I thought Hodgo was about to hurl him over the touchline. Pick him up and throw him into row eight.

But that is not what happened. Instead Hayne, playing in his first ever State of Origin match, stuck his right hand into Hodgo and pushed him off.

Whack!

And then he was off. Beginning his run on the 50-metre line, Hayne tiptoed his way down the sideline as we gave chase. Slater closed, the speedster mowing him down. Again I thought it was over. But this time, instead of a palm it was a kick, Hayne attempting an audacious grubber.

And it came off.

Sealing one of the greatest ever Origin tries, Hayne regathered the ball and crashed over to send the Blues into half-time with an 18–6 lead.

Forget a dynasty, our run looked over after just one year. After bolting to a 6–0 lead, when I chipped into the corner for Inglis to score, we had conceded 18 points straight, to put not just the match but the series in doubt. Few come back from a Game I home defeat.

The comeback mission began in the 50th minute, when Greg Inglis went in over the corner to score another State of Origin double. I kicked the conversion from the touchline to narrow the gap to six. We were on level terms eight minutes later, when I made it three from three with the boot after Pricey crashed over for our third try. And we were in front when Darren Lockyer touched down in the 61st minute to further his State of Origin legend.

We were leading by six, when I slotted a field goal in the 70th minute to make it 25–18. The score remained unchanged and we won after scoring 19 unanswered second-half points to come back from the dead.

Most people remember that match for Hayne's remarkable try. I remember it for two things: winning my first State of Origin man of the match, and it being the comeback that kick-started a dynasty.

After that match we felt invincible. It would never matter what was on the scoreboard: no matter how many points we were down, we always thought we would win. That comeback in Queensland gave us the belief, confidence and shot in the arm that would see us go on to win a record-making eight series in a row.

For the next seven years we would be untouchable. Rather than recount all the games blow by blow – I am sure you have already watched them all – I thought I would tell you a bit about the man who led us to our stunning success before telling you about the plays – and the people behind the plays – that helped make it the magnificent eight.

Respect was the key to Mal's success; people wanted to play for him and they would do anything he asked. I'm not quite sure how to explain it, but he has an aura about him. I guess that comes from who he is and what he has done in the game.

He was never a dictator. He shot straight from the hip and told it how it was, but it was never his way or the highway. Mal was very much an advocate of player power. He always asked for our input and wanted the players to drive the direction of the team.

Mal never worried too much about the game plans and tactics – he left most of that to us. He was more concerned with getting us right mentally. He wanted us in the right headspace.

And he was spot on.

You don't need a coach telling the game's best players how to play. Everyone who is picked to play State of Origin knows their role and what to do on the footy field. A rep coach has to make sure his players are mentally ready to play. He has to be a master at getting them in the mood and ready to rip.

Part of that was making sure we had a good time, and Mal, as you may have picked up in the last chapter, doesn't mind having a good time, sometimes even a little more than us.

'Bed at 10 pm, fellas,' he would say, putting his latest curfew on us.

And then Justin Hodges would give him a red wine. I would give him the next.

'Righto, let's wrap this up at 11 pm, boys,' he would say. 'Big day tomorrow.'

Greg Inglis (GI) would bring him his next red, filled to the brim.

'OK,' he would say. 'Let's make it midnight.'

Hodgo would then break out the scotch.

'Fuck the curfew,' Mal would say. 'Let's have some shots.'

He loved a good time and was always there with us until the death. He even got kicked out of a pub once, security guards throwing him onto the street. We were at the Down Under bar in Brisbane during one of our camps. Unable to get a drink, the hotel packed, Mal thought he would lend the barman a hand. So off he went, behind the bar and to the beer taps. Unfortunately, he didn't get to serve me a drink.

Security pounced on him and turfed him out. He was escorted out, Alfie and me by his side, trying to convince the security guards to let him stay.

'Do you know who that is?' we said. 'That's bloody Mal. You can't kick out Mal. Not in Queensland.'

But they did, so we went down the road to another bar and continued to party. We had a pretty big laugh about it the next day.

Mal wasn't an emotional man, not even when he was getting kicked out of bars. He was always calm. I can't remember him ever losing it at half-time. There were no sprays or dummy spits. Whether we were in front or behind, he would deliver his message at half-time calm and clear.

He was a master in the Origin arena, and just knew what we needed and when we needed it. He was all about taking the pressure off us.

Mal always made sure I was in the right frame of mind. Whatever problems I was facing, whatever was going on away from the football field, whenever I took to the field for State of Origin I was ready to be my best.

Oh, except for that one time I wasn't. That time I was almost sacked ...

*

I went out the Sunday night before the final game of the 2009 State of Origin series. Me and a couple of teammates decided to go out for a quiet beer – all innocent, only intending to be out for an hour. Our team camp was on the Gold Coast, all the glitter and gold of Surfers only a taxi ride away.

'Just a couple,' one of the teammates said.

So I had a beer.

'One more,' another teammate said.

Two soon became 10, my arm did not really need any twisting. Then we started on shots ...

I turned up to training blind drunk. I hadn't slept.

'Yep, mine,' I yelled as Cameron Smith picked up the ball.

He threw it to Locky.

'Yep, hit me,' I said on the next play.

He threw it to Locky.

'My ball,' I said again.

He threw it to Locky.

I walked over to my best mate Cameron.

'What the fuck?' I said.

He turned his back.

Ouch!

Everyone in the team knew I was wasted as soon as they saw me. Stinking of grog, eyes red, stumbling and slurring, I was a disgrace. No one said anything. Not a word. They didn't ask me if I was drunk. They didn't ask me what time I had got home. They didn't call me a dickhead or tell me I had done something wrong.

They simply ignored me, punished me with silence.

I felt pretty good by the time we ran out to face New South Wales in the dead rubber. The players were still a bit off me, but as far as I knew the coaching staff hadn't found out. I thought I would be at my best for the match and that we would go on to claim the clean sweep.

But we were flogged, beaten 28–16 in front of a home crowd of 52,184. I hadn't played well and I felt like shit. I had let my team down. I had let my coach down. I had let my state down. I thought of the 50-odd thousand who had paid their money to see me perform below my best.

Then I thought about my captain – the inspirational player who had saved us back in 2006.

He would never do anything like what I did. Why did you do it? How could you do it?

I picked up the phone and called Locky the day after the game.

'I'm so sorry,' I said.

Locky didn't sugar-coat it. 'You fucked up,' he said. 'And it's unacceptable. I'm willing to forgive you. But can you forgive yourself?'

I didn't know if I could, the gravity of my mistake suddenly clear.

'I don't know what's going to happen, mate,' Locky continued. 'It could be over. This team is more than you. More than all of us. You disrespected the jersey.'

He went silent.

'Locky?' I asked. 'You there?'

'Yeah,' he replied. 'Ring Mal. He's the only one who can help you, but I don't think he will.'

Click …

Oh shit. Mal knows? Shit. Fuck. Shit.

Of course Mal knew. He knew all along. I later found out that he was going to replace me with Cooper Cronk, who he'd brought in as 18th man. He was going to pull me out of the team just before kick-off and hand Coops his debut. Mal only decided not to at the 11th hour, because he didn't want to lie and claim I had been ruled out of the game with injury.

'Yep,' he said, all matter-of-fact, when I finally summoned the courage to call him. 'I know what you did. What do you have to say?'

I think I shat myself.

'I'm sorry,' I said. 'I don't know why I did it, but I feel like shit. Please. This jersey means everything to me.'

Then came the long pause.

'OK,' Mal said. 'You'd better call Boxy and Smithy. You tell them what happened and why. Do that and then we'll have another chat.'

So I did. I made the calls. I phoned both Steve and Cam. I apologised. Mal soon got back to me.

'A part of me says that's it,' Mal said. 'That you're done. How can I condone the disrespect you've shown for the jersey?

'Another part of me says this is JT, a bloke who has shown as much pride in this jersey as anyone. All your teammates know what you did to disrespect this jersey, but they also know everything you've done for his jersey. What should I do?'

I was crying. 'Just let me keep it,' I said. 'Let me show you what it means to me. What I can do in it. What I *will* do in it …'

Again silence.

'OK,' he said. 'But this is your one and only chance. One more fuck-up and you'll never play in this jersey again.'

Phew …

But oh boy, did I feel like shit.

What was I thinking? What did I do? How could I let the boys down?

I wanted to flog myself.

Mal moved our camp away from the Gold Coast to the Sunshine Coast after my disgrace. Away from all the nightclubs and temptation. Away from the bad memories and the moment that almost cost me my Origin career.

Queensland considered going back to the Gold Coast a few years later when their deal to stay on the Sunshine Coast expired. Mal called me and asked me if I would be OK with that.

'I know you have some pretty bad memories of that place,' Mal said. 'Would it affect you if we went back?'

I said it would. I wasn't over it and I may never be. I don't think I will ever forgive myself for what I did. Needless to say, I never fucked up again.

That was my worst State of Origin memory. My worst State of Origin moment. Now to the plays and the players.

I have seen some pretty special things from Queenslanders over the years. I have been a first-hand witness to some of the greatest moments in rugby league history. I'd like to talk about some of them, and tell you a thing or two about the player behind the play.

The Palm: Greg Inglis, Game II, 2008

First he used his speed, skipping to the outside to find space. Next it was pure power.

Whack!

He got rid of Mark Gasnier (Gaz) with a left-hand fend.

WHACK!

Then it was Steve Turner, the same left hand sending the NSW player thundering into the turf.

Again he turned to his speed, powering down the flank. Shoulders back, head held high, he marched towards Kurt Gidley, the NSW fullback.

I loomed up on his inside, thinking I would soon be scoring under the posts. He shaped towards me and I steeled myself to catch. And that is when he showed his sleight of hand, sending the ball to his outside for Darius Boyd to score a classic Origin try.

The player was Greg Inglis of course, and with this play he showed everyone the great State of Origin player he was going to be. Inglis was young and raw back in 2008, yet to establish himself as the player we all know today. But he hinted at the player he would become when he showed what incredible strength and power he possessed in that classic Origin play.

I had never seen a fend like it: *Whack! Whack!* Players sent crashing like skittles. He hit Gaz right in the chest before running him over. He hit Turner with such force that I thought he was going to end up in the grandstand.

It is just awesome seeing that sort of power close up. I was on the inside supporting, so I had a front-row seat. It is one thing watching that great State of Origin moment on TV, it is another to be just a few metres away.

Wow!

I knew Inglis was going to be a superstar from day dot. He didn't need to put on that play to prove anything to me.

I first saw his brilliance when he was playing for the Storm. I am not sure when the match was, but I was playing for the Cowboys in a match against Melbourne not long after Inglis made his NRL debut.

Who the fuck is that? Really? How did he do that?

Inglis had just leapt over the top of me, Gavin Cooper and Josh Hannay to catch a Cooper Cronk bomb and score a try. He had come from nowhere and leapt higher than I thought a human could.

Greg Inglis burst onto the scene in 2005 and made his name by jamming blokes, putting them on their arses. And he isn't strong in the gym. Greg doesn't lift big weights. He doesn't throw them around like some, but he is such a physical man on the footy field.

I have been blessed never to be on the end of one of his fends. I have seen the power and all the destruction it has caused, but I have never felt it. Thank God. I was chasing him one time and he just pointed at me and waved his finger. I was never going to catch him but he was giving me a little warning just in case. 'Don't get too close, JT. You know what is waiting for you. Do you really want me to put my hand in your face?'

He looked after me when he was defending too. He could have absolutely smashed me on several occasions but he always pulled back. In one match he picked me up like a rag doll. I felt every inch of his power as he hoisted me into the air. I was hanging there, helpless and completely vulnerable, waiting to be driven into the ground.

Oh shit. I'm in trouble here.

I braced for impact, waited for his shoulder to drive me into the ground. And then he gently placed me on the grass and gave me a little pat on the head.

What a guy!

And he is a good bloke and a great friend. Whenever you're having a tough time he will reach out and offer help. I have had plenty of calls and texts from Greg during tough times over the years.

GI is the quiet type. Shy. He has never been comfortable with the fame that comes with rugby league, and even in football teams it takes him a while to be himself. He keeps to himself a fair bit and isn't one to open up about anything.

But he is pretty funny when he warms up. He is quick with a joke and loves to gee the boys up.

The Tackle: Billy Slater, Game III, 2010

Never give up. Those were the three words Billy Slater told us were going through his head when Anthony Watmough crashed over the line for what would probably have ended our dream of a rare clean sweep in 2010.

Those three little words inspired this one-time track-work jockey to somehow wedge his slight frame between Watmough and the turf and pull off what could be Origin's greatest ever tackle.

While Billy might be best remembered for his Origin chip and chase on debut in 2004, his tackle on Anthony Watmough to save us from defeat in Game III rates as one of my greatest Origin memories.

'It's about turning up for your teammates,' Slater said after that match. 'We've spoken about it and we did have a call out there, which was never give up. I called it for that tackle and when you call it you never want to let your mate down.

'Even when the ball is going away from you, you want to be moving in case it comes back. That's what never giving up is about.'

And that is what both Billy and Queensland were all about. What made them both so great.

Billy is another once-in-a-lifetime player. His speed is exceptional. Give him space and he's away. Billy is also a great talker and organiser. He orchestrates a lot of plays and puts players where they need to be.

Billy has a few plays he likes to run. When we first started playing together he let me in on all his little secrets and told me about the plays he wanted to put on. He told me how to create space for him.

Billy is also a great defensive fullback. He stopped as many tries as he scored. In my eyes, he is Queensland's greatest ever fullback, and that is a remarkable achievement considering he was dropped in 2005 and wasn't picked again for three years.

I had some great moments with Billy on the football field. In one match he tipped me up for a fifth-tackle play. He told me to go down the short side and kick it back through the middle. So I did. I went towards the sideline and kicked it towards the post, using the outside of my boot. He screamed through to gather the ball and he, of course, scored.

Billy has been a huge part of the Queensland dynasty. I should also mention that he is a pest to play against … well, not to me, but to almost everyone else. He is an A-Grade sledger.

'Hey, mate,' Billy yelled to Te Maire Martin in the 2017 grand final after he ran into the referee. 'Don't go taking a dive. I'm the only one who gets away with that.'

That is just one I recall. Nearly everyone in the NRL has a story about being sledged by Billy. Glad he's my mate.

The Toughness: Dallas Johnson, Game III, 2007

Dallas Johnson copped a knee in the head while making the first tackle in the final dead rubber match of 2007. And he was knocked out. Cold. Gone. Done. He needed three trainers to help him get off the field.

He won't be back. We'll be playing with 16.

I didn't, in my wildest dreams, expect to see Dallas back on the field. But in the second half, after we were ravaged by injury, there he was, back in the defensive line, steeling himself to take another hit. I couldn't believe what I was seeing.

Dallas went on to play the final 35 minutes. He shouldn't have even been allowed back on the field, but he made 25 tackles in a failed bid to save us from defeat. It was the toughest thing I've seen in rugby league.

Dallas was not a big bloke, weighing only 93 kilograms, but he played as hard as any forward in the game. And on that night he showed courage that I thought no man was capable of.

Most remember the flashy moments in Origin. I like to remember the tough ones. And none was tougher than this.

The Courage: Willie Tonga, Game I, 2011

The match had been going for just 17 minutes when Willie Tonga tore apart his shoulder while contesting a high ball with Josh Dugan. He should have left the field. He was in agony. But he refused to leave us short. He played the next 63 minutes with the season-ending injury.

Mal called it the bravest act in Origin history. I can't disagree.

His courage inspired us to a 16–12 win on that night. It has since inspired plenty more. We came up with a call to honour his selfless act after that match. After that night we screamed 'Tong' when we were under pressure. It was a call to arms that got us out of plenty of holes.

The Superman: Israel Folau, Game III, 2008

It was the night I saw a winger turn into Superman. Down 8–4 and trying to claw our way back into the match to make it three series wins in a row, I went to the air. I grabbed the ball and launched a kick into the corner. I still can't believe what came next.

Launching himself into the sky, Israel Folau (Izzy) jumped over the top of Anthony Quinn to make State of Origin's most remarkable catch. He looked like he was flying. His putdown was just as impressive; somehow he held onto the ball and planted it with one hand. It was just a freakish piece of play: skill, ability and athleticism. I watched on from the ground after being taken out by a NSW player.

Israel was a rare talent. He burst onto the scene and got better and better as he emerged from his shell. Izzy was a Mormon with some controversial and well-documented views, but he was just another Queenslander when he was with us. He fit in just fine. It doesn't matter where you come from – religion, race or anything else – when you put on the jersey, you are a Queenslander. We are united and one.

We faced a huge challenge when Darren Lockyer retired from State of Origin at the end of 2011. Locky was a Queensland legend and the heart and soul of our team. He was responsible not only for saving us from crashing to a record four series defeats but for starting the dynasty that would see us win eight series straight.

Locky was sent out a winner in a fitting finale, when we made it six straight by beating New South Wales by 34–24 in a Game III decider. I was happy we sent him out with a victory – but I was shattered to see him go.

I don't think I need to tell you any more about how I feel about Locky, but I probably should talk a little about the player who replaced him – Cooper Cronk.

I had a few issues when Cooper came to start at No. 7 in 2012. Coops was a ready-made replacement for Locky. He was an undisputed talent and had been part of the Queensland team for two years. Coops played off the bench as utility in both 2010 and 2011 while waiting for his chance.

So all should have been well, the winning streak set to continue, when he got the nod – but I had my doubts.

Coops was part of the Storm's 'Big Four', which included Greg Inglis, Cameron Smith and Billy Slater. He had played with them throughout his career and I was wary of being cut out of the play when he became the Queensland No. 7.

My fears were realised after just one training session. Billy was hanging on his side and all the shape was being set off him. I actually went and spoke to Cameron Smith.

'We need to get the balance right, mate,' I said.

I asked Smithy to speak to the both of them and tell them of my concern. I also told him to make sure he gave me the ball when I wanted it.

'I've got GI out with me,' I said. 'We need to make sure we get him some ball.'

There were certainly some teething issues, but we eventually got it right. Cooper ended up playing No. 7 and did a great job of getting the boys around the park. I played No. 6 and put on plays. But I did feel like I was losing control of the team early on.

I never went to Cooper about it because I didn't know him. I really didn't get to know him until later on. Turns out his dad played and coached for my junior club Sunnybank. He also caught the same train as me to school.

We are very different players. He is a very structured player who is a master at executing a game plan. I can play in structure but I much prefer playing instinctively. But that worked when we played together. We complemented each other and Smithy brought us together.

Cooper proved the difference in 2012, the new No. 7 kicking the match-winning Game III field goal that kept our streak alive.

We won our record-making eighth straight series in 2013, when we held on to beat the Blues at ANZ Stadium in a heart-stopping decider. As we went into the match locked on a win each, most commentators were saying New South Wales were 80 minutes away from ending our streak. They said the NSW home crowd would be enough to get them home.

It almost was.

After jumping out to a 12–4 lead in the 61st minute when Justin Hodges scored, the Blues mounted a comeback. The gap was slashed to just two points when Trent Merrin scored under the posts in the 70th minute and James Maloney kicked the conversion. The game would go down to the wire.

I thought we had scored the match-winning try soon after – but we were denied because of interference from a streaker called Wati. Yep. A big fella had ripped his gear off and run the length of the field in the nude before being hammered by security guards. He was tackled in front of me as I was passing to Ashley Harrison, who laid on what should have been the match-winner.

New South Wales got a final shot but we held on to seal the historic win. We had done it: eight in a row. It was a remarkable achievement. Unbelievable. We had gone from being the team that could have lost four in a row to the team that won eight in a row. And it was never easy.

People don't realise how close a lot of those games were. They don't remember the come-from-behind wins or the adversities we faced. New South Wales never went away. They were always a great side and always a chance to beat us. There were games where the Blues were the better team for most of the match. Games they should have won. There was never an easy match. All tough. All brutal.

It was big plays and our never-say-die attitude that got us home. It was errors and lapses that cost them.

I can't see another team repeating what we did. I don't think it will happen again.

GREEN AND GOLD

CHAPTER 21

LET'S BACK IT UP A bit, rewind to 2008. The Rugby League World Cup, being held in Australia and New Zealand, is in full swing. I'm sitting on the Kangaroos team bus, clad in the green and gold of Australia, training singlet sweat-soaked and covered in dirt.

Darren Lockyer is sitting behind me, Greg Inglis in front. I look around and see my mate Smithy; head resting against the glass, deep in contemplation. Behind him Petero Civoniceva is chatting to Israel Folau, the odd couple having a laugh.

How good is this?

I'm riding with rugby league royalty. And now, two years after making my debut for the Kangaroos, I feel like I belong. I'm no longer a rookie and I've earned my spot.

We have just finished training. The bus is rattling back towards our team hotel. We are well prepared to play Fiji in the semi-final of the World Cup in a couple of days in Sydney.

We are one win away from competing for international rugby league's greatest prize. And after we kicked off our campaign with a 30–6 win over New Zealand at the Sydney Football Stadium before flogging England 52–4 at Telstra Dome in Melbourne, I am sure the World Cup will be ours. I am on top of the world.

'Hey, Sam,' I say as I answer the phone.

'How are you?' she asks. 'What are you doing?'

I know something isn't quite right. Her voice …

'What is it?' I ask. 'Don't worry about me. Is something wrong? Has something happened?'

And then my world, all perfect – World Cup wins and rugby league royalty – comes crashing down.

'It's your uncle,' Sam says. 'It's Uncle Richard. He's been bashed. He's dead. He was murdered.'

I'm not sure how I responded to Sam. I'm not sure that I responded at all. Soon I was squeezing my mobile phone, call over and bus bouncing down the road. I stared out the window. Silent. Still. But soon I sobbed. I did my best not to cry, wary of making a scene in front of the boys, but the tears came.

'What is it, mate?' Locky asked, my childhood hero turned mate putting his arm around me after moving up a seat. 'What's happened?'

I told him my uncle had been murdered. Bashed to death.

'Oh fuck,' Locky said. He gave me a hug and I cried some more. We stayed in that embrace for the rest of the ride.

'Let's go and see Ricky, mate,' he said when we arrived back at the hotel.

I shook my head. 'No,' I said. 'I'll keep it to myself.'

I didn't want to be a distraction. I didn't want to ruin our World Cup campaign.

'Na, mate,' Locky said. 'Put yourself first. We'll be right.'

Locky ended up convincing me that the team wouldn't suffer and that Sticky would help. He was right on both fronts.

Ricky gave me both comfort and support. He told me that I had to put myself first and the team second. He told me I could leave camp and travel back to Brisbane to be with my family.

'No,' I said. 'I want to play. That's what my uncle would have wanted. I'll play this game for him and for my family.'

I knew the best thing for both me and them was to play that weekend. I had good support around me in the coaching staff and the playing group. I wanted to play the match for my family. I wanted to dedicate the game to my uncle. I wanted to give my family a bright moment to light up a very dark time.

'OK,' Ricky said. 'Are you sure?'

I thought I was.

I tried to put it all out of my mind so I could focus on the game. But all alone in my hotel room, I couldn't stop thinking about my uncle. About what had happened to him.

I called a good mate who lived in Sydney. 'You free?' I asked. 'Want to hang out?'

We met up an hour or so later. I didn't tell him what had happened. I didn't want to talk about it. I didn't even want to think about it. But by the time he dropped me back to the hotel it was all over the news. I quickly learned the full details of what had happened.

Eight men had beaten my uncle, Richard Saunders, to death in Ewing Park, Woodridge, a suburb of Logan City in Brisbane.

My uncle had been drinking with some mates when an argument broke out with a group of teenagers who were passing through the park. The teenagers left – only to come back with another four men 10 minutes later. They bashed my uncle with a hammer, a fence paling, their fists and their feet. He was dead when they left.

Eight men, aged 16 to 26, were arrested.

It was horrific and confronting. *Belted to death? Richard? My uncle?* I could not comprehend it. I knew the area he lived in had some problems. He was from a tough neighbourhood where a lot of people were struggling to make ends meet. But I had no idea that anyone from that neighbourhood was capable of such violence. Of murder.

I was stunned.

My whole attitude to violence and community changed after that shocking moment. I think I realised that a lot of people were really struggling out there and that they needed help.

I work in disadvantaged communities as often as I can. I don't want to see another family left without a husband, a father, a brother, a son ... an uncle, because of a senseless act of violence.

Of course I can't stop things like this from happening, but I hope I can help ease a bit of community tension and stress, which contributed to my uncle's death.

I dedicated my next game, the match against Fiji, to my family. To my uncle. And I played one of my best games for the Kangaroos. I scored three tries and kicked six goals for a personal haul of 24 points in our 52–0 win over Fiji. I was awarded man of the match.

That award, a gold medal, now sits alongside my first Dally M. It means as much to me as any trophy I have ever won.

*

The pain of losing the World Cup final to New Zealand a week later was lessened by what I had just been through. What I was still going through. The 34–20 shock loss wasn't all that shocking following my uncle's murder.

Regardless, the Suncorp Stadium defeat should not have been so unexpected given New Zealand were always a formidable opponent in the end-of-year tournaments. While I would only ever play in one losing Anzac Test team – we went down 26–12 in 2015 – Australia suffered their fair share of loses to the Kiwis in end-of-year competitions. New Zealand won both the 2010 and 2014 Four Nations tournaments.

I loved playing New Zealand, and one of my green and gold highlights came in 2006 when we played the Kiwis in the final of the 2006 Tri-Nations tournament in Australia. It was a classic. With the scores locked at 12–12 after a ferocious 79 minutes of brutal rugby league, I had a chance to win the match with a field-goal attempt. I missed.

Bodies battered, the boys busted and bruised, we went into extra time. The game would be won – or lost – with a single play.

I grabbed the ball, Smithy picking me up off the back of a lead runner. On my own 30-metre line, I looked to the support on my outside.

Whack!

I stepped back inside, ignoring the support, after throwing a dummy. There was space, not much, but I tried to take it. David Kidwell went to tackle me.

Whack!

This time it was a palm. Kidwell fell to the ground.

Really?

I couldn't believe it because Kidwell was a giant of a man, an enforcer who always bullied me on the football field. My left hand had sent him crashing to the turf.

Ha. Finally got one back!

I was now in the clear.

Run! Run! Run!

I pinned my shoulders back and launched my way down the field. I could feel the chasers, black jerseys gaining. I knew I didn't have the speed to go all the way. I turned to my right.

Tatey ...

Australian centre Brent Tate was flying. He had the pace to get there – and a clear run. I angled toward him.

'Yep,' came the cry on my inside, the voice familiar. And with that I ignored Brent Tate and threw the ball back to my left. I hit Darren Lockyer with a perfect pass – the Australian captain did the rest.

Locky ran 30 metres to score one of the great Test match tries. It was some moment. And to be the one that set up the match-winner was a great feeling. You don't get too many moments like that in your career. We won the match 16–12 and took home the Tri-Nations Cup. I also remember that game for another reason – I threw my one and only rugby league punch.

In a 'What was I thinking?' moment I hit giant Kiwi centre Sia Soliola in the face with a right. Soliola, who later became a prop, had put a late shot on Locky and a bit of a scuffle broke out. I was overcome by rage and ran in and decided to unleash a punch.

Whoops!

I knew I was in trouble a moment after I had hit him in the face. I connected, hit him flush and as hard as I could, but he didn't flinch.

Shit!

I ran and hid behind Petero. Yep, I got out of there and stood behind my biggest teammate. I reckon big Sia would have destroyed me had he got hold of me; seriously, my punch didn't even move him an inch.

I decided that fighting wasn't my go after that. I haven't thrown a punch since.

Another standout match in the green and gold of Australia came in 2012 when I replaced Darren Lockyer as the Kangaroos No. 6. The game was played in Eden Park, New Zealand, in the Anzac Test match on 19 April. There are only a couple of games where I can remember being nervous before a match – this was one of them.

I felt a ton of pressure before this game because I was going to wear a jersey that had belonged not only to a legend but also to one of my heroes. I guess I felt I had to do it justice.

Playing five-eighth for Australia was a big job in itself. But to do it after Lockyer? Yep, I felt like the weight of the world was on my shoulders – again. I guess it was a similar feeling to when I was being compared to Andrew Johns a few years earlier. And just as before that game against the Knights, I was overwhelmed. I didn't sleep heading into the match. I tossed and turned, thinking of failure instead of success.

Don't fuck up. Don't fuck this. Don't embarrass Locky. Don't embarrass yourself.

I thought I had to be as good as him.

I was lucky that I was comfortable playing alongside my teammates. Cooper Cronk came in to partner me in the halves. I had played plenty of footy with Coops by this time, so he made my transition to No. 6 easier than it could have been.

Smithy was also there of course, at No. 9 – steering the ship. Smithy replaced Darren Lockyer as the captain of Australia, and it was a seamless transition. He was the obvious choice, having already captained the Queensland Origin team. Smithy was just like Locky in that you thought you would never lose when he was in your team. He gave us all confidence that we would prevail, no matter what.

I never got to captain Australia – or Queensland – and that might have bothered me had it not been for Cameron Smith. He was always the best person for the job. Anyway, I wasn't thinking about the captaincy before the Eden Park match.

Don't fuck up! That was all I could think.

And I didn't. I went on to play one of my best matches for Australia, putting in a man-of-the-match performance in a comfortable win. I was in my element as soon as I took to the field. I scored a try and ended up forgetting all about the pressure.

The trainer, being directed by the coach, actually tried to get me to come off towards the end of the game. Daly Cherry-Evans was on the bench and they wanted to bring him on.

'No,' I screamed. 'No way.'

I was going to finish the game. I told them they would have to drag me off. I had put myself through the wringer that week and there was no way I was going to give up that jersey now that I had it. It has always been in the back of my mind that any game could be my last for Australia; an injury could end my career or for whatever ever reason I might not be selected again.

I wanted every minute I could get. That is an attitude I kept to the end. I always fought with the trainers when they asked me to come off, and I always asked to play when the coach offered to rest me for a game.

Anyway, I got my way and they left me on. I walked off the field – after 80 minutes – happy with both the team's performance and my own. I didn't think I was any Darren Lockyer, but I certainly hadn't embarrassed myself or him. I didn't shed any tears after the game like I did after playing Andrew Johns, but I certainly felt a similar type of relief.

Phew!

Now to some green and gold fun: let's get to the 2013 World Cup tour in the UK, all beers, dishing out beltings and the bloke with the golden balls.

I always roomed with Sam Thaiday during representative camps. Only the team captain gets a hotel room of his own when we go away, so the rest of us have to share with a teammate.

Sammy and I teamed up early on. I think we first roomed together during a Queensland development squad and we hit it off right away. We are very similar people, both relaxed, and we like the same sort of things, so we decided we would be 'roomies' whenever we were in the same team.

Fortunately, we were in the same team at representative level more often than not – both of us having long careers for both Queensland and Australia. At the start of every tour they would ask you if you had a preference and we would make it known that it was 'me and him'.

There was never a dull moment with Sam. He was a character but I recall him mostly for ice-creams and coffee. After the afternoon team meetings or training sessions, Sammy and I would try to track down the best coffee in town. Sometimes we would succeed, sometimes we would fail – but every time we would retreat to our room with a tub of ice-cream.

I reckon Sammy and I have watched a thousand movies together, spoons in hand, ice-cream in laps. Quite romantic, really! But Sam was at his best on the dance floor.

Going out in the UK was always a blast because you could let your hair down. People didn't recognise you so you didn't have to worry about being caught out doing something silly. People didn't harass you or try to stir you up. We had a fair crack on the drink during that tour. We didn't do a lot of sightseeing but we did a heap of drinking. We made a ritual of going to a place in London called the Church. It was open from midday until 4 pm and you would get in free if you were dressed up. The place was a massive warehouse full of people and booze. For 10 pounds you got four UDL-style drinks in a bag. We would dress up in all sorts of shit and we would play cricket inside the bar, pelting leather cricket balls and smacking them for six.

Sam was a skipping expert. We perfected a game of phantom jump-rope. With two of us heaving an invisible rope, Sam would jump in and out, up and down, and enthral the crowd by impersonating a bouncing, limber and impossibly plausible schoolgirl. He was also a mean breakdancer.

We would walk out of there thinking it was 4 am and it would only be 4 pm. The night was just starting. It was on to a hotel called Walkabout. I can't remember what went on there, given how much we drank at the other joint.

We had plenty of fun on the football field too. The good times didn't stop us from performing – if anything they helped. We were untouchable; we only conceded 22 points during the entire tour.

It was an old-school style of tour where we had plenty of good times and played plenty of good football. The side itself was awesome. We had superstars like Smithy, Inglis, Boyd, Cronk and Matt Scott all playing in their prime. Hayne and Brett Morris both scored four tries each in our 62–0 quarter final win over the USA.

The World Cup final, played at Old Trafford, wasn't even close – the Kiwis were never in it. We belted them 34–2 in one of the most lopsided matches I can remember against New Zealand.

The whole week I could tell we would win. Our preparation was perfect and everyone in the team was oozing confidence. I was personally in my prime. I got the man-of-the-match award in the four games that I played.

Tim Sheens was the coach of Australia for that tour and also a lot of my career as a Kangaroo – he was the national coach from 2009 until 2015. Sheens was a different coach from Mal. He was very tactical and drove the style of football we played. He had strict rules for all his sets and made it very clear what he wanted. We had different sets for different parts of the field. He has a very good football brain and his style obviously worked at that level. Occasionally we wouldn't agree with something and he would change things if the playing group made a case.

The only thing we didn't like about Sheensy was that he was a little strict when it came to us socialising. We actually had a word to him at the start of that tour because he wanted to apply the handbrake to our drinking schedule. Sheensy put curfews in place and wanted us in our rooms by midnight every night. The leadership group made a case and we ended up getting our way. We were going to be there for two months and we needed to have some fun.

And we did.

I was in a taxi in Dublin, going back to the hotel after a night out, when a teammate pulled out the seat's headrest. He started hitting me in the head with it. I just laughed, mostly because of how drunk he was. The cabbie didn't find it as amusing as I did.

'Do it again and I'll kick you out,' the cabbie screamed.

Sure enough he hit me again. The taxi driver booted us out of the cab and onto the street. The next second taxis were pulling up left, right and centre until a posse of pissed-off cab drivers had us surrounded. They were all screaming and I thought we were going to be in for a fight.

'Just give him 100 euros,' one of the drivers said. 'Do that and we'll leave you be.'

So my teammate pulled out a 100 euro note. 'Here's your 100 euro,' he screamed as he ripped the note in half. 'Now fuck off.'

I'm not sure how we got home but I had breakfast with the same teammate the next morning.

'My shout,' he said when we were done, bacon, eggs and coffee demolished.

He pulled out a 100 euro note – held together by sticky tape – and paid the bill. I pissed myself laughing.

I have heard some pretty good stories about boys getting into strife during past Kangaroo tours. Some stories are legendary and part of Kangaroo folklore.

My favourite involves Mark Geyer (MG). Mal sat us down one night and told us the story of the former Panther and the fire hydrant.

'We were having a floor party in our hotel,' Mal said. 'It got pretty wild and the hotel manager came down to tell us to wrap it up.'

Enter MG.

'He was holding a fire hydrant,' Mal said. 'The type that sprays foam. Well, MG gave it to him. He chased him all the way back into the elevator.'

The manager never came back. They partied all night.

Mal also told us about his career as a 'dodgem'-car driver. He said that they would all buy bombs from a UK car dealer whenever they travelled to England and take them racing. They would get the local cops to close the streets and move parked cars. Apparently it was more about smashing into each other than going fast.

We didn't go as crazy as they did in the past, but we still managed to have a bloody good time. We also managed to win the World Cup!

Manchester United, arguably the greatest soccer club in the world, invited me, Smithy and Paul Gallen (Gal) to tour their ground and training facility – Old Trafford in Manchester – during the 2013 World Cup.

English legends Rio Ferdinand, Michael Carrick and Ryan Giggs were waiting for us when we arrived.

'How good is this?' Smithy said. 'You know how famous these blokes are?'

I nodded.

Ferdinand was earning $300,000 a week, Carrick and Giggs not too far behind. They were three of the biggest names in world sport.

'Yeah, they ain't going to know us,' I said. 'Who are we in England?'

Now Smithy was nodding.

'JT,' Giggs said, rushing forward to shake my hand. 'How good was that try you scored in State of Origin?'

I was stunned. *Really? You saw that?*

Turns out Manchester United had attended the 2013 State of Origin decider at ANZ Stadium earlier that year, when I scored under the posts in our 12–10 win.

'Yeah, I liked that try,' Giggs said.

I went red, completely chuffed.

We exchanged jerseys and had a chat before he led us on a tour of the famous facility. And wow! What a facility it was. They had recovery centres, gyms and cinema rooms. Spas, saunas and chefs. They even had a bloke washing the players' cars – Bentleys, Ferraris and Lamborghinis – in the car park.

'Reckon I could get someone to Dairy Farmers Stadium to wash my Toyota?' I said to Smithy.

We were soon looking at their practise pitch.

'Really,' I said. 'A training field.'

The ground was perfect, the greenest grass I had ever seen. And the field was surrounded by stands that were bigger than we have at some NRL grounds. 'What about all the other fields?' I asked, pointing to the other playing pitches. There were at least another 10.

'Oh, they're for all the junior teams,' Giggs said. 'The one furthest away is for the Under 8s academy team. The closest is for our second team.'

Giggs pointed. 'I think Beckham is over there somewhere watching his son train,' he said.

Beckham? What? Really?

David Beckham was one of the biggest stars in the world in 2013. He was a household name across the globe.

'You're geeing me up, right?' I asked.

Turns out he wasn't.

'FUCK!' Smithy shouted. 'Is that David Beckham?'

'No way,' I replied. I looked out the window of the bus, our tour of Old Trafford over. 'Is it?' I said as I jumped up. 'It is. Stop the bus.' I bolted down the aisle before hurtling out the door. 'Becks,' I screamed and I sprinted. 'BECKS!'

He was about 100 metres away and I was closing fast.

'Becks,' I shouted again.

He stopped and turned. He looked terrified, seeing a crazy fella rushing towards him. I realised he thought I was a lunatic. I didn't care.

'Sir,' I said, being unable to think of anything better to say. 'Sir. SIR. S.I.R.'

He stopped and waited.

'Sir,' I said again, puffing and panting when I finally reached him. 'I'm sorry but I just had to meet you. I'm on a tour with the Australian rugby league team and I saw you.'

He nodded.

'I understand if you say no, but is there any chance I can get a picture with you?'

He nodded again. 'Yeah, of course,' Beckham said.

It was then I realised I had no one to take the photo. It was going to have to be my first ever selfie.

'JT,' Smithy said, appearing from nowhere. 'I'll take it.'

Smithy and Gal had chased down Beckham too. We were all starstruck, mouths open, legs shaking. Beckham had no idea who we were but he stood around chatting with us all the same. He was a bloody legend and it was some moment. He was a rockstar, all cool and looking mint. We eventually made it back to the bus. I was stoked; apparently Smithy was too.

'Geez, he smelt good,' Smithy said. 'Didn't he smell unbelievable?'

I pissed myself laughing. 'Smelt good?' I said. 'You're a fucking weirdo, Smithy.' Ha! Ha!

I still can't believe Smithy was smelling Becks – and loving it! And I can't believe I haven't bought him a bottle of Beckham's signature cologne yet ...

I never considered playing in the Super League. While I had some attractive offers over the years, I was driven to win a premiership with the Cowboys. It was unfinished business.

So let's get back to the Cowboys.

THE COWBOY
WAY
CHAPTER 22

GRAHAM MURRAY WAS AXED AS head coach of the Cowboys in 2008.

'Really?' I said when I was told of the club's decision to end Muzz's North Queensland reign. 'Mid-year? Why?'

Muzz, the man who signed me to my first North Queensland deal, was forced out of the club just ten games into the season. Following a shocking start – just three wins from our first 10 games – he was given an ultimatum: walk or be marched. Muzz chose to keep his dignity.

I was dumbfounded. I always rated Muzz as a coach. He was both a good man manager and a good tactician. Years later, in 2013, I was deeply saddened when I learned of the passing of Graham Murray. He was such a big part of the Cowboys and was responsible for my move north. Muzz will never be forgotten, not by me or the club he helped build. Sam and I are still close to his wife, Amanda and daughter, Cara; they always made sure everyone felt welcome and part of the Cowboys family.

Back in 2008, I certainly didn't blame Muzz for our poor season start. I also thought the decision to axe him mid-year without a proven replacement was a bad move.

'Righto, lads,' said Ian Millward, the Cowboys assistant coach who was appointed to replace Muzz for the rest of the year. 'I've come up with a plan to beat these fellas.'

The former English Super League coach was delivering his game plan for our clash against the ladder-leading Storm. It was his fourth game in charge and we were none from three

'We just need to starve them of the ball,' he continued. 'We need to waste as much time as possible. Let's make the game as short as we can. They'll get frustrated and won't be able to get a roll on. So let's play hurt. Let's kick it dead. Do anything you can to run the clock out.'

Really? OK. You're the coach.

So we went down with a cramp at every scrum. We kicked the ball into touch. We did everything we could to slow the game down and stop Melbourne from getting the ball. It wasn't in the spirit of the game and it felt weird.

'See, it's working,' Millward said when we went into the sheds for half-time leading 16–10.

'Let's j—' He suddenly stopped giving instructions. 'Hear that?' he said.

Melbourne coach Craig Bellamy (Bellyache) was screaming. We could hear his voice booming through the dressing-room walls. Bellyache was tearing strips off his team, tearing paint off the walls too.

'See, we have them rattled,' Millward resumed. 'Hear that? It's working. Keep it up.'

That was the full extent of his half-time speech.

We lost 48–20.

Playing for your country is always a great honour. I made my Test debut in 2006, but this photo was taken a few years later, at the Four Nations Final in the UK on 14 November 2009. The Kangaroos thrashed England 16–46, and I was Man of the Match as well as top scorer for the series.
(MATTHEW LEWIS/GETTY IMAGES)

Top Left: Rugby league is full of highs and lows. The friendships formed are right up there with the best of the best. This is me with my mate Cameron Smith – giving me a hand even though our teams were battling it out that night. (ROBB COX/NRL PHOTOS)

Insert Right: In 2008 my bachelor days were over. Here's me and Sam snapping a selfie in the back of a New York cab. (THURSTON FAMILY COLLECTION)

Bottom Left: Injuries are a low. Over my career I have broken my leg, damaged my ankle syndesmosis, and needed three shoulder reconstructions. Here I've suffered a medial ligament strain and dislocated kneecap in a 2006 game over the Brisbane Broncos – but at least we won 26–10! (CAMERON LAIRD/NEWSPIX)

Bottom Right: One man and a sea of blue. State of Origin Game I, 2008. (MARK NOLAN/ GETTY IMAGES)

Captaining the Cowboys was definitely a high. I first had the honour in 2007.
(CAMERON LAIRD/NEWSPIX)

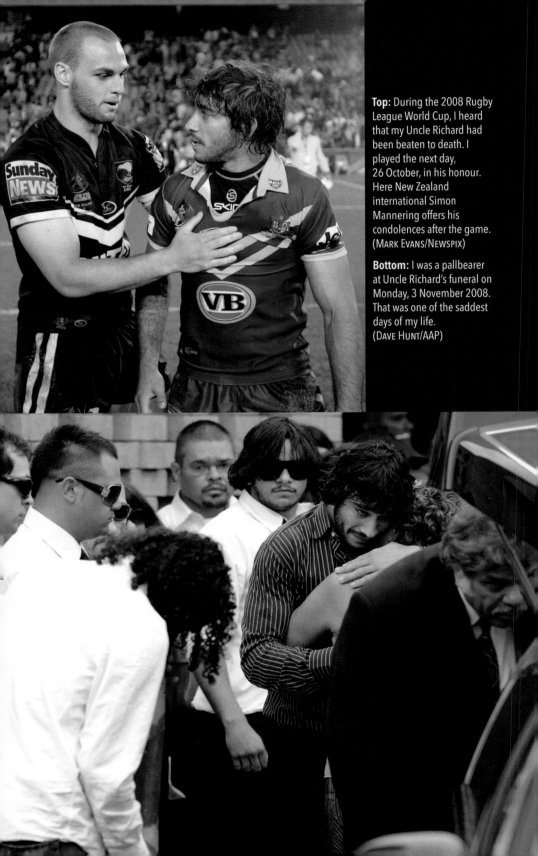

Top: During the 2008 Rugby League World Cup, I heard that my Uncle Richard had been beaten to death. I played the next day, 26 October, in his honour. Here New Zealand international Simon Mannering offers his condolences after the game. (MARK EVANS/NEWSPIX)

Bottom: I was a pallbearer at Uncle Richard's funeral on Monday, 3 November 2008. That was one of the saddest days of my life. (DAVE HUNT/AAP)

Top: Since 2010, the NRL pre-season has included an Indigenous All Stars vs NRL All Stars game, the winning team taking home a trophy named after the first Indigenous Australian to captain a national team, Arthur Beetson. Here's me with the trophy in 2015, when the Indigenous All Stars won 20-6. (GRANT TROUVILLE/NRL PHOTOS)

Bottom Left: Facing the cameras as I leave the Brisbane City Watchhouse after being arrested for drunk and disorderly behaviour in Brisbane's CBD in 2010. (PETRINA BERRY/AAP IMAGE)

Bottom Right: I love to see a kid smile. I've been giving away my headgear since 2006 – this photo was taken after the Cowboys beat the Canberra Raiders at Dairy Farmers Stadium in Townsville on 16 April 2011. (IAN HITCHCOCK/GETTY IMAGES)

Top: No getting away from the press … in 2012 my agent Sam Ayoub (right) and I had 'secret' discussions with the Canterbury Bulldogs. Nothing came of it, except for this snap in the *Daily Telegraph*. (CRAIG GREENHILL/NEWSPIX)

Bottom: Sidestepping Simon Mannering of New Zealand during the Rugby League World Cup Final at Old Trafford, Manchester, on 30 November 2013. We thumped the Kiwis 2–24 – and I was Man of the Match. (MICHAEL STEELE/GETTY IMAGES)

One of the top moments of the 2013 RLWC tour was meeting David Beckham. What a great guy. (CAMERON SMITH/THURSTON FAMILY COLLECTION)

Above: I won my fourth Dally M Medal in September 2015. You could say I got a bit emotional at the press conference afterwards … (GRANT TROUVILLE/NRL PHOTOS)

Below: A perfect finish to a perfect year. I married my beautiful Sam in a secret ceremony on Hamilton Island at the end of 2015. Our parents were the only guests – as well as Frankie and Charlie, of course! (HAMILTON ISLAND PHOTOGRAPHY)

One conversion kick away from delivering the Cowboys the premiership at ANZ Stadium in Sydney on 4 October 2015 – and I missed it. They could probably hear me yelling in Townsville. (CAMERON SPENCER/GETTY IMAGES)

Right: And what a feeling … with Lachlan Coote after I kicked the golden point extra time field goal that gave us a 16–17 win over the Brisbane Broncos. (CAMERON SPENCER/GETTY IMAGES)

Below: With my mate Justin Hodges, Brisbane Broncos captain, after the game. For the first time, two Indigenous captains led the grand final teams, and I know Hodgo was happy for me, much as he wanted the win himself. (ADAM HEAD/NEWSPIX)

Top: I've been lucky enough to win the Golden Boot award for most outstanding rugby league player in the world three times, in 2011, 2013 and 2015. (SCOTT RADFORD-CHISHOLM/NEWSPIX)

Middle: What a moment when my junior club, the Souths Sunnybank Rugby League Club, decided to name a field after me in 2014. Souths Sunnybank is where I learned the basics of rugby league and began to love the game. (SARAH KEAYES/NEWSPIX)

Johnathan **THURSTON** Field

James Cook University awarded me an honorary doctorate in 2015, for my charity and community work. Of course I was proud as punch, though you won't hear me calling myself 'Doctor Thurston' any time soon. Ha! Ha! (JCU MEDIA/RICHARD DAVIS)

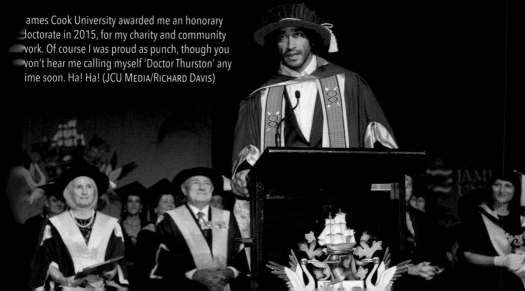

Above: I'm an ambassador for the Deadly Kindies program, which aims to boost the number of Indigenous children receiving early childhood education. Here I am in 2017, injured shoulder and arm in a sling, at the C&K Koobara Aboriginal and Torres Strait Islander Kindergarten in Brisbane. (Darren England/AAP)

Below Left: Me with Queensland Premier Annastacia Palaszczuk, on the night I was awarded 2018 Queensland Australian of the Year for my work with organisations like Achieving Results Through Indigenous Education, the Apunipima Cape York Health Council's anti-ice campaign and the Queensland Reconciliation Awards. (Jono Searle/AAP)

Below Right: I got emotional when I received the Australian Human Rights Medal in 2017, for my work in Indigenous education. In my speech I said, 'You may know that I'm passionate about my sport, my club, my state and my country. But what I'm most passionate about is my culture. (Australian Human Rights Commission (CC BY 2.0) via Flickr)

Main: I made the match-winning conversion in Origin Game II at the ANZ Stadium in Sydney on 21 June 2017 – but it proved to be my last-ever Origin match. An injured shoulder put an end to my season. (Cameron Spencer/ Getty)

Inset: The Maroons went on to win the series at Suncorp Stadium in Brisbane on 12 July, and my good mate Cameron Smith called me up to claim the shield with him. (Mark Kolbe/Getty)

Above: In February 2018 I launched the Johnathan Thurston Academy, to provide education, employment and well being opportunites for young people. Here's the JT Academy Team (left to right): Cameron Hockaday (Director), Samantha Johnson (General Manager), me, Samantha Thurston (Brand Executive), Sam Ayoub (Director). (JOHNATHAN THURSTON ACADEMY)

Right: It was a real bonus that students from my old school, St Mary's College, Toowoomba, came to the launch. Here I am with (left to right): Luke Cesari, Brian Pearson, Zac Brown, Logan Weribone and Peter Weatherall. (JOHNATHAN THURSTON ACADEMY)

Below: The completed family – or so we thought. Sam and I at home with Frankie, Lillie and Charlie in July 2018. (ADAM HEAD/NEWSPIX)

Above: These two legends have always been there for me – my brothers Shane (left) and Robert (right). (THURSTON FAMILY COLLECTION)

Below: Before my final NRL game at Cbus Super Stadium on the Gold Coast, 1 September 2018, with Sam, Lillie, Charlie, Frankie, Dad and Mum. (CHRIS HYDE/GETTY)

Top: I'm going to miss these guys. North Queensland Cowboys players and staff, after my final game at Cbus Super Stadium on the Gold Coast, 1 September 2018. (GRANT TROUVILLE/ NRL PHOTOS)

Middle: Charging down the field, during our 30-26 win over the Titans. (GRANT TROUVILLE/NRL PHOTOS)

Bottom: And so goodbye. Game won, season over, I leave the field for the last time. (SCOTT DAVIS/NRL PHOTOS)

Millward was a champion bloke and a good rugby league man – but he was never going to be our long-term replacement for Muzz.

'Na, don't worry about that bollocks,' he said when one of the boys asked him where our recovery session would be the day after the game. 'Go have a beer and I'll just see yas on Monday.'

We only won another two games that year and ended up tying with the Bulldogs for last place. Only a superior for-and-against spared us from taking home our first wooden spoon since 2000.

Canberra coach Neil Henry – a former Cowboys assistant – was appointed as Murray's full-time and long-term replacement, his contract beginning in 2009.

I recall a conversation I had with a Raiders player shortly before Henry returned to North Queensland.

'Really?' I said after the Canberra player bagged the man who was about to become my new boss. 'That doesn't sound like Neil. Not at all.'

The Canberra player told me that few at Canberra liked Henry. He said they were all glad Henry was leaving. I just shrugged, figuring the player I was talking to had an axe to grind.

I knew Henry well. He had been an assistant coach at the Cowboys from 2002 until 2006 under Muzz before he moved to Canberra to get his NRL start. I thought he was a top bloke. He was – and still is – the best assistant coach I have ever had.

'Na, he's one of the boys,' I told the Canberra player. 'You have him wrong. He loves a beer. He loves having a joke.'

Henry arrived back in North Queensland a stranger, completely different from the person I remembered. I actually found dealing with him quite difficult, and that wasn't a good thing considering I was now the captain of the club, having been appointed by Muzz back in 2007.

I had a well-documented 'blow-up' with Henry later that year.

'Have a few days off, boys,' he told me and the rest of the North Queensland players when we returned from playing the State of Origin series in 2009. 'Go and freshen up.'

Sweet!

It was lunchtime, a warm afternoon in North Queensland, so I headed to the pub with Queensland and Cowboys teammate Willie Tonga. We ordered steaks, bought beers and went out to the courtyard to sit in the sun. A little later, as we sat with beer in hand, steak on the grill, Henry stormed in, assistant coach Dean Lance by his side.

'What are you two doing?' he said. 'This isn't what I meant. What do you both have to say?' Henry had got word that we were at the pub. He had fired his way into the hotel courtyard to give us a spray.

'Fuck, we're just having lunch,' I said.

Henry suggested we were going to go out on a bender and he was trying to stop us before we got started.

'Righto,' I said. 'Fine.' I walked up to the bar, cancelled the steaks, slammed my schooner down and walked home.

The press got a hold of the story and turned it into a big deal. They alleged that I had fallen out with Henry during the State of Origin series; Henry was also the assistant coach of Queensland. The reports said I was considering quitting the Cowboys after being confronted by Henry several times during Origin camp over my drinking.

It wasn't true. While I indeed had a couple of blues with Henry earlier that year – and yes, mostly over alcohol – nothing had happened during the Origin campaign. And I certainly wasn't considering quitting my deal. I had a year to run – I was coming off-contract at the end of 2010 – and I was going to see it out. In fact, I was already discussing a new long-term deal.

My biggest disappointment with Henry came early that year when he fined me $20,000 for repeated indiscretions. I thought it was totally unfair and unwarranted; I still do. Anyway, both Henry and I had got over it. I just wanted to play football and I wanted my team to win. Unfortunately, we lost more than we won in 2009, finishing twelfth with 11 wins from our 24 games, making it another year to forget.

Dr Chris Sarra sat us down in a room in the lead-up to the first ever NRL All Stars clash in 2010. The famous Indigenous rights and education campaigner had been brought in to talk to the Indigenous All Stars team about what it meant to be Aboriginal.

'So who are you?' Dr Sarra asked. 'And where do you come from?'

I shrugged. I wasn't alone.

'No, really,' he continued. 'What do you know about your family? About your past? Who are your ancestors? What did they do and how did they help you become the person you are today?'

Again I shrugged, giving him a blank look.

'Go and stand on that side of the room if you can answer those questions,' he continued. 'Stay where you are if you can't.'

I stood completely still.

All I knew was that I considered myself to be Aboriginal. I didn't know about my family or their history. I didn't know how my ancestors helped me become the person who was standing in that room on that day. And I was a little bit embarrassed. I had been selected to play in the Indigenous All Stars team that would take on the NRL All Stars and I knew little of what it meant to be Indigenous.

'Mum, I need to know more about our family,' I said to my mother after I returned home from the match.

I had just won the first ever Preston Campbell medal for man of the match during our 16–12 win over the NRL All Stars on the Gold Coast.

'Can you tell me about our family. About our history?'

Mum smiled. 'I'll do better than that,' she replied. 'You can go see it yourself.'

So with that Mum organised for me to travel back to where she grew up. She gave my Uncle Mark a call and asked him to take me out to Mitchell in the Western Downs district of the Maranoa Region, Queensland.

Uncle Mark was the most knowledgeable when it came to my family history and culture. He was more than happy to take me back to Mitchell and introduce me to all my relatives who still lived there.

So we hired a mini van, uncles and cousins piling in, and made the six-hour trip from Brisbane.

Mitchell is a sheep and cattle town with a population of just over 1000. I spent the weekend there, staying with family

I had never met. I had cousins, aunties and uncles everywhere. Uncle Mark showed us the old watering holes that he and my mum used to swim in as kids and the fields where they would play. I saw their school and the house where they were raised.

I remember having a conversation with my mother when I got back. 'I feel like I've been there before,' I said. 'It all seemed so familiar. I was relaxed as soon as I got there. At peace.'

And I was. I had a real connection with Mitchell and it was quite an emotional experience going there. I found out a lot of my history and I felt a better connection with my past.

Mostly I remember little stories about my family. Not struggles or life-changing stuff, but tidbits that told me a bit about who they were. Like the story about my pop and how he got the nickname 'Finnegan'. Apparently Pop was always following an Irish bloke called Finnegan around, because he played a musical instrument. Pop loved music and was always around him trying to learn how to play. So they started calling him Finnegan. I like that story because it told me a little bit about who my pop was.

I came back from the trip a different person. After hearing stories about my family I decided I needed to make some stories of my own. I knew I had to do more with my life in terms of making a difference. I wanted to make sure I did all I could to be remembered for the right reasons.

I walked into Samantha's office at the beginning of 2010 with an email I had received from my manager. By now people were used to seeing me in Sam's office; our relationship was well and truly out in the open. They weren't used to me storming into the room, gigantic grin on my face.

'Take a look at this!' I said. I showed her the email, printed out on A4 paper. 'It's an offer from a French rugby club,' I continued. 'Check out how much it's for.'

The offer was for almost $800,000 a year.

Apart from my visit to Mitchell, I remember 2010 for being all about contracts and cash. For being a circus. I was to be a free agent the following year and I was getting offers from everywhere. The media had a field day. These were just a selection of headlines from that year:

JT headlines list of off-contract stars.
Thurston considering quitting NRL to join
overseas exodus.
JT could be first $1 million man.

I have to say the money being offered, especially from French and Japanese rugby clubs, was tempting. But Samantha told me my career was more important than cash.

'You haven't done your job here, Johnathan,' she said. 'You won't be remembered as a legend of the game if you leave the NRL now. You'll never be an immortal. You'll be forgotten. And you haven't won that premiership you've always said you have to win for the Cowboys.'

She was right. I loved Townsville. I loved the Cowboys. And I had an unquenched thirst to bring North Queensland their first ever title. The thought of leaving the Cowboys, walking out without winning a premiership, was too much to contemplate.

I soon signed a deal to stay in North Queensland till the end of 2013. I was back in Sam's office regretting my decision later that year. The season was over – we had finished second last – and I had just fronted the Cowboys board and been demoted to co-captain after being found guilty of drinking while injured during my Brisbane arrest.

'Did I do the right thing?' I said. 'Should I have looked a bit harder at those other offers?'

Sam, still working for the club as a sponsorship executive, told me that some people on the board wanted to sack me. One of them, who I won't name, called me 'a stain on the club'.

'This is how they repay me for my loyalty?' I said.

Samantha ended up taking me to Peter Parr's office.

'Look, you did the wrong thing,' Parrie said. 'Yeah, you're only guilty of being a smartarse but you did get arrested and you did spend the night in jail.' Parrie was all serious. 'You didn't get sacked,' he continued. 'And while you might have been demoted to co-captain, nothing else has changed. Sometimes you just have to eat a shit sandwich.'

I burst out laughing. 'Ha,' I started. 'Ha! Ha! Ha! What the hell? A shit sandwich?'

Parrie shook his head. 'What are you on about?'

I laughed again. 'A shit sandwich?' I asked. 'Why would anyone have to eat a shit sandwich? That is hilarious.' I had never heard anyone use that expression before. I laughed some more.

Parrie deadpanned. 'It wasn't a joke,' he said. 'It's like saying sometimes you have to take your medicine.'

I just kept on laughing. 'Shit sandwich,' I said as I left his office. 'I'm going to use that one.'

At the beginning of 2018, I read a newspaper report that said Parrie and Cowboys chairman Laurence Lancini had saved me from being sacked. Apparently the board had voted to sack me following my arrest. The only reason they didn't tear up my contract was because both Parrie and Laurence said they would quit if they followed through and terminated my deal.

I wiped my lips and got on with the job in 2011. I had forgotten about the arrest drama but not about finishing second last. The previous year had been a horror show on the field. We won just five games, and would have collected the wooden spoon had it not been for the Melbourne Storm being caught out in the biggest salary cap scandal in the history of rugby league.

'Coops,' I said as I shook his hand. ''Bout time you came back.' I gave my old mate Gavin Cooper a hug, and smiled ear to ear.

I was stoked when the Cowboys signed Coops for 2011. And I was a kid in a candy shop when he finally turned up in Townsville. Gavin Cooper is my biggest partner in rugby league crime and one of my best mates. I met Coops in 2005 when we were both recruited by the Cowboys. He was one of my first friends in Townsville and we stayed close even when he left to join the Titans at the end of 2006.

'Yeah, bra,' he said when we were reunited as Cowboys. 'Let's go and win you that premiership you're always talkin' about.'

I nodded. 'Shit yeah,' I said.

Little did I know that he would help deliver me my dream just a few short years later – or that we would form one of the most potent partnerships in the NRL.

Coops returned to the Cowboys as a right-edge back-rower. I was on the left. It was only when Scott Bolton was injured that we were put together on the football field. We immediately clicked and went on to form an on-field partnership that would endure and thrive right up until my very last game. I would put him over for 29 tries over the next eight years. Our friendship will last forever.

Coops knows me better than anyone, both on and off the football field. He can see when I am struggling with something and he knows what to say to pick me up. He is also one of the only people who can read my body language on the football field.

'Pick ya lip up,' he says when he senses that I am frustrated. 'Get on with it.'

Coops is a potent attacking player. He is fast, big and knows how to hit a hole. The big fella has always been my go-to man in attack. And Coops is much more than a big frame – he is also tactically smart. If we are running a shape, or he sees a weakness in a defence line, he will come up with a plan to exploit it.

Coops was my saviour in defence. I am not the biggest bloke in the world, and opposition teams target me when I am defending. Rival teams send all their biggest players at me and Coops is the guy in my team who protects me. He will get ahead of the line when a runner tries to isolate me, his big right shoulder forcing the attackers back.

Coops also double-defended for me, which means he would come in when an attacker singled me out, to make it a two-man tackle.

Phil Gould (Gus) came into my life in 2011 when he was hired as consultant to our coach Neil Henry. Gus was only with us a short time but he left a hell of an impression.

'How do you want to be remembered?' he asked me. 'What is your rugby league legacy going to be? Do you want to be a good player? Or do you want to be a great player?'

I couldn't answer.

We had a heart-to-heart and he told me that I had the potential to one day become one of rugby league's great players. He told me I was good enough.

'But it's what you do from now until the end of your career that will determine your legacy,' he said.

I have never forgotten those words.

Unfortunately, Gus didn't stick around long. I think he made a couple of trips to Townsville before ending his role with the club. But I would soon see him again.

The 2011 season ended up being a much better year for us, both on and off the field. We won 14 games to storm into the finals for the first time since 2007. Unfortunately, we got pumped in our sudden-death semi, losing to Manly 42–8. I wasn't happy with the finals defeat, but there were certainly positive signs after four very tough years.

The contract circus started again in 2012. My deal with the Cowboys didn't finish until the end of 2013 – but that didn't stop the media speculation. It was relentless. These were just a selection of the headlines in major newspapers:

> *Thurston non-committal over Cowboys contract.*
> *Thurston set to sign NRL's biggest deal.*
> *Thurston NRL's hottest off-contract commodity.*

'Has all this started again?' I asked my manager. 'Didn't we just sign a deal?'

'Mate, that is just the start,' Sammy said. 'You're the biggest name on the market, and clubs have been calling me since you signed your last deal. This is also something you have to take seriously because the next contract could set you up for life. It will be the most important piece of paper you ever sign.'

Pressure much? I just wanted to play football.

'Mate, I just want to stay at the Cowboys,' I said. 'I don't want to go through all of this again.'

'If you want to get what you're worth then we have to test the market,' Sam said.

Sammy was right. I had done the hard yards and had put myself in a good position. I was established and in career-best form. My next contract was going to be the biggest contract – in terms of value and importance – of my career. I owed it to myself to find out what I was worth.

I asked Sammy to deal with it all behind the scenes until the season was over, and again our year was over earlier than I would have liked.

It was another year of improvement. Beating the Broncos 33–16 in the preliminary final – and watching on as a young bloke named Michael Morgan scored a hat-trick – was a season highlight. But we ultimately crashed out in the second week of the finals, losing to Manly in a 22–12 defeat.

The headlines started again almost as soon as our season ended.

Des Hasler has lured Johnathan Thurston back to Belmore in an after-dark bid for the North Queensland Superstar.

The *Daily Telegraph* in Sydney had a picture of me on its back page, making a secret trip to Belmore at the end of 2012.

Busted!

Yep. I indeed went back to my old club at the end of the season to discuss the possibility of a return. Again I wanted to stay at the Cowboys, but my manager had convinced me it was in my best interests to have a look around. And if I were to leave North Queensland, the Bulldogs would be the first club I was going to talk to.

After all, I started my career at the Bulldogs and I did have some interest in going back there to finish my career. So I made the night trip to my former home.

'Wow,' I said as I walked into Belmore Sports Ground for the first time since 2004. 'Is this the same place?'

I hardly recognised my first NRL home. The training facility had gone from a sweat-stained dungeon to all modern and state-of-the-art. Everything was brand new, shiny and first class. There was an indoor running track, a theatre and even sleeping pods.

I was particularly impressed with the theatre room, given we used to do our video review on a 68-centimetre television that was wheeled around on a stand.

'This must have cost a bit,' I said.

I was impressed by the tour, and my meeting with Bulldogs coach Des Hasler, but I'm not sure if they felt the same way about me because they never made an offer.

Another club soon did.

I burst through my front door, back home in Townsville after a whirlwind trip to Western Sydney. Samantha greeted me.

'We're moving to Penrith,' I blasted. 'I just agreed to a three-year deal with the Panthers.'

It was now 2013 and I had just said I'd join Penrith from 2014, a deal worth more than $3 million.

I had been bursting to tell Sam that we were going to be rich – and moving to Sydney – but I waited until I got home. Finally, I would get to see the look on her face.

'Like hell you have,' Samantha said with a snarl. 'We're not moving to Penrith. I hope you can get out of it or you'll be living in Sydney on your own.'

Oh crap.

I had only hours before agreed to make the biggest move of my career, after touring the Panthers facility in Western Sydney and meeting with Gus, now the Penrith boss. I thought it was a done deal.

Gus had laid out his plan for me at Penrith, making me an offer worth over $1 million a year. It wasn't exactly a spur-of-the-moment decision, given I had stayed in contact with Gus ever since he had come up to North Queensland as a consultant to Neil Henry. But I wasn't certain I wanted to make the big move until I met Gus, and senior executives from Channel 9, in Sydney.

Gus's offer for me was outstanding, and a big part of why I wanted to go to Penrith had nothing to do with football. Gus had a plan for me to become a leader in the Western Sydney community, and he had designed and developed an Indigenous program for me to spearhead.

Gus, also a Channel 9 commentator, had been working closely with executives at the television network to formalise and develop a post-rugby league television career for me.

And it all made sense. I had already started doing some work with Channel 9, but I was a long way from being a polished TV product. I needed plenty of grooming.

It was going to take time and I would only get better with practice and experience. The Channel 9 head office was in

Sydney, so making the move south would allow me to work closely with the network until I retired.

Penrith was also building towards something special on the football field. Gus had worked hard to give the club one of the NRL's best junior pathways, and I knew they would soon be having on-field success. There was the money too – their offer would make me the NRL's first $1 million-a-year man.

'Do the deal,' I told my manager Sammy before I boarded my flight back to Townsville. 'I want to go to Penrith. Go and get it done.'

Then I walked in my front door, expecting Samantha to meet me with hugs and kisses.

'Sydney,' she said later, the conversation moving to the dinner table. 'We can't move. Our life is here.'

Samantha was pregnant with our first child. I'll get into that in detail a little later on, but I'll mention it here because it played a major part in her not wanting to move.

'I'm pregnant,' Samantha said. 'We're about to have our first child. Everyone is here, Johnathan, all our family, our friends. Do you expect me to leave my entire support network so I can raise a baby alone in Sydney?

'There's no way I'm going to Penrith. If you want to then that's fine, but you'll be going by yourself. I'll come and visit but I can't live there. I need to be here in Townsville.'

I told her I couldn't go back on my word. 'My word is all I have,' I said. 'I can't renege on a deal, and especially not with Gus. You know how much respect I have for him.'

Sam wasn't only worried about moving to Sydney. 'And what about your legacy?' she said. 'You haven't won a premiership with Cowboys. And even though you played for the Bulldogs, you're largely thought of as a one-club man.

You'll always have opportunities here in North Queensland if you finish your career here. You need to think about the big picture. We had this chat last time you came off contract.'

I went and had a talk to my mate Jamie Fitzpatrick. Fitzy would become the godfather to my children and is one of my best mates. I met him as soon as I moved to Townsville and he has always looked after me.

He is the bloke I talk to when things get tough. Fitzy has always had my best interests at heart and tells it to me straight. I go to him whenever I have to make a big decision – and this one was huge.

Fitzy told me the pros and cons of both leaving and staying. I didn't sleep that night.

I called Sammy Ayoub the next morning and told him that I would be moving to Sydney on my own. He laughed before he spoke.

'I haven't done the deal, you idiot,' Sam said. 'I haven't even spoken to Gus. I thought you were a bit quick to make a decision and I thought Samantha might want some input, so decided to let you sleep on it. I also had a big chat to Fitzy last night so I know where your head is at.'

Phew!

I would have stuck to my word if the deal had been done. I would not have disrespected Gus or my word. Instead, Sammy and I went to the Cowboys and told them to stop mucking around and get it done. They had put an offer in but it was nowhere near the level of the Penrith deal.

'Leave it with me,' Parrie said.

I soon had a new and revised deal sitting in front of me. I signed on the dotted line. I was labelled a trailblazer after signing that deal with the Cowboys. It was reported that it had made me rugby league's first $1 million-a-year man. The media wrote plenty about the value of the deal. That did not concern me. What did was the responsibility that came with earning that type of money – both on and off the field.

On the field I had to deliver. I had to play like a $1 million footballer. I knew I would be crucified if I didn't perform. I also wanted to repay the club for the investment. Off the field I would have to work for the money. Part of being a marquee signing is becoming an ambassador, a spokesman and a role model for the club. You have to work for sponsors, become a media go-to man, and play a leading role for the club in the community. In short, you have to work for every cent.

A lot of players struggle with money when they suddenly sign a big deal. We have all heard the horror stories of players left with nothing. Thankfully my manager has always looked after me when it comes to my money. Sammy put me in front of a financial advisor way back when I was at the Bulldogs, even though I was earning next to nothing. And he put me on a weekly allowance as soon as I moved to North Queensland. The rest of my money was put into building a property portfolio.

I could easily be in a sad situation now had it not been for the good people around me.

I was hoping to concentrate on football once I signed the four-year deal that would almost make me a Cowboy for life – but 2013 was going to be another difficult year.

We spent most of the season dealing with speculation surrounding the future of our coach, Neil Henry. The press labelled him a dead man walking after we crashed to our ninth loss of the year in round 13 – and by July he was indeed told his contract would not be renewed.

I always found Henry to be a difficult coach. While he was a tactical master, I don't think he was particularly good at managing players as men. He became hard to talk to in 2013 when things weren't going well. He wasn't very approachable and not even I, as club captain, felt comfortable talking to him. Still, nobody likes to see a person lose their job. Henry was a good bloke and will always be a mate. We had plenty more good times than bad and he was a big part of my rugby league journey.

We made the finals in 2013, finishing eighth, but we were knocked out by Cronulla 20–18 in the first week of the finals. It was a game that will be remembered for the Sharks having seven tackles in a set.

The year finished well for me personally with the Rugby League International Federation (RLIF) presenting me with my second Golden Boot for best player in the world.

I had no input into the club's decision to appoint Paul Green as Neil Henry's replacement. I saw his name tossed around and spoke to some people about him.

'Oh, he's an angry ant,' someone said.

Ha! Ha!

I thought that was pretty funny.

I didn't know a lot about Greeny until he arrived. A former Cowboys player, he had coached Wynnum Manly to consecutive premierships in the Intrust Super Cup before joining Trent Robinson as an assistant at the Roosters.

I first met him at the Dally Ms in 2013. He hadn't been announced as coach but he had been appointed. He introduced himself and we had a bit of a chat. He asked me for my thoughts on the club, where we were at and what needed to be done. I was pretty excited after that chat.

Greeny changed so much in such a short time. He came to Townsville and put a broom through the club.

'You can't win away from home,' he said during an honesty session, conducted on a pre-season camp on the Gold Coast. 'You can't win without JT. You have a soft underbelly. You are not a serious footy team. That is how everyone on the outside perceives this club.'

Greeny asked us what we would like to be known for. How we would like people outside the club to think of us. We came up with our answers and they became our goals and mission statement. I won't reveal what they were because they are still used by the club today.

Personally I knew Greeny would get the best out of me. He pulled me aside early on and gave me permission to play anywhere I saw fit on the football field. Previously I had been locked on an edge. I could now play on both sides of the ruck.

Greeny brought to the club a training style that I had never seen before. It appeared casual, but the intensity that was required when he meant business was next level. And he didn't just work with the best 13.

Greeny did so much work with the blokes from 13 to 24 to bring them up to the required level. He trained smarter – not necessarily harder. He had a big emphasis on skill – it was at a higher intensity than we had ever done before.

From the day he arrived, I knew we would win a premiership under him. It didn't happen in 2014 – we finished the regular season in fifth before going down to the Roosters by one point in a 31–30 semi-final heartbreak.

But we all know what happened in 2015 …

*

Our season looked like going from bad to worse. We had lost our first three games and now my good mate Cameron Smith was intent on making it four.

'Jeez,' Smithy yelled after the Storm kicked a field goal at 1300SMILES Stadium to put us behind 17–4. 'It's a bit hot up here, boys. You guys really struggle in the heat, don't ya? Thought you fellas would be used to it. You look a bit tired, JT.'

There were 18 minutes left on the clock and Smithy thought we were down and out. He was trying to kill off any chance of a comeback by getting in our heads. But it only fired us up.

Antonio Winterstein went over in the corner soon after Smithy ran his mouth, to make it 17–10 after I kicked the conversion.

And then, with just a few minutes left on the clock, Winterstein scored another, also in the corner, to give us hope. Now we were just three behind, the score 17–14. I grabbed the ball and looked at the clock. It was the 77th minute.

Tick. Tock. Tick. Tock.

I had to make the sideline conversion for us to have any hope. I also had to kick as fast as I could.

Tick. Tock. Tick. Tock.

There were exactly two minutes left when I placed the ball on the tee.

Tick. Tock. Tick. Tock.

One minute forty-one remaining when I struck the ball.

Tick. Tock. Tick. Tock.

One minute thirty-eight to go when it went over.

Now 17–16, we had a little more than a minute and a half to go the length of the field to save the game.

Tick. Tock. Tick. Tock.

A penalty off the restart put us in the attacking zone. The clock continued its relentless march. We got through two plays and I looked up at the clock. There were 39 seconds left in the match.

Tick. Tock. Tick. Tock.

I demanded the ball and I took my shot.

I nailed it!

The 79th-minute field goal sent the game into golden point extra time. And I kicked my second clutch field goal in the 84th minute of the match to win the game.

'Yeah, it was a bit hot tonight,' I said to Smithy as I shook his hand. 'We really struggle in the heat. We should be used it by now.'

Ha! Ha!

That was the back-from-the-dead win that kick-started our season. We went on to win our next 11 games and record the biggest winning streak in the club's history.

Nothing could stop us.

We got behind in a lot of those games but we always found a way out. We had that belief that we could win no matter what. We didn't look at the clock. We didn't look at the score. We mounted our biggest ever comeback to beat the Eels 36–30 in round 13, and we beat the Raiders with a field goal on the buzzer in a round 15 classic. None of those games were easy – but we just did whatever it took to win.

I knew it was our year.

We were in that magical place they call the 'zone'. All the boys were at another level that year. Michael Morgan

(Morgo), Lachlan Coote (Cootey), Jake Granville (Jakey), Jason Taumalolo (Jase), Gavin Cooper (Coops), Matt Scott (Thumper), James Tamou, Kyle Feldt (Feldty), Justin O'Neill (Juzzy) – they were all at their best.

I personally was at the peak of my powers. I ended up winning my fourth Dally M by 11 points. I had some great years – winning the Golden Boot in 2011 and 2013, and the Dally M in 2005, 2007 and 2014 – but 2015 was my most complete.

In 2015 I excelled both at club level and on the representative stage. Honestly, I can't even remember winning my third Dally M award in 2014 but I can certainly remember my fourth.

After becoming the only player in history to win four Dally Ms, my life changed to the extent that I couldn't go out in public without being mobbed. It became ridiculous. I couldn't work it out. I already had three Dally Ms but for some reason that fourth made me super-famous. I wouldn't say I struggled with it, but the intensity of public scrutiny just took off.

And that went up again after the premiership. We, of course, combined to deliver North Queensland the title when we beat the Broncos by 17–16 in my golden point field goal fairy tale.

I was awarded the Golden Boot at the end of 2015 to cap off the best year of my life.

Looking back now, almost leaving North Queensland to join Penrith was a sliding-doors moment. Had my manager told Gus that I had agreed to go to the Panthers I wouldn't have won the premiership with the Cowboys in 2015.

Who knows what would have happened with the Panthers?

But it is a fact that I would not have kicked a field goal in extra time to deliver North Queensland their first ever title.

That was the defining moment of my career. It was my legacy, that thing Gus had told me about back in 2010.

I was brought to the Cowboys in 2005 to win the club a premiership and I got to be a part of that in 2015.

It was the best moment of my career and a part of rugby league history that can never be erased. I am happy for that game and the match-winning moment to define my career. And not just for me or because of me, more because of what it meant for my club, my teammates, my coaching staff and most importantly the Cowboys fans.

'JT, have you got a moment?' said Karen Filby, a Toyota representative and a good family friend. 'Someone is here to see you.'

I was in Bowen for a Toyota visit, standing on a junior football field, handing out headgear to kids.

'Sure,' I said. 'In a minute. I'll just finish here.'

'I think you might want to come now,' Karen said. 'It's Hugh Jackman.'

What? Hugh Jackman! THE WOLVERINE!

'You got to be kidding me?' I said. 'Hugh Jackman out here in the middle of nowhere. Wants to meet me? Ha.'

But sure enough Hugh Jackman, the Hollywood movie star, was standing in front of me a few minutes later. He had his children, Oscar and Ava, by his side.

'Hi, JT,' he said. 'We're in the area filming a movie called *Australia*. We're big fans, so when I heard you were here I thought we'd come down and try to meet you. Can we get a photo?'

I was starstruck. 'Ummm,' I mumbled. 'Sure. Only if I can get one too. I'm a big fan of yours.'

And I was. I love Wolverine. I love the X-Men. I love Hugh. Ha. I guess you get the picture – I am a bit of a Hugh Jackman fanboy. He ended up sending me the picture, signed and all.

I never thought football would have me mixing with Hollywood movie stars, or standing on stage with an Aussie rock legend when I come to think of it.

'We have a special guest,' said Jimmy Barnes during a 2015 Cold Chisel concert at 1300SMILES Stadium in Townsville. 'Get out here, JT.'

I had earlier that day called Paul Green, my Cowboys coach, and asked him if he had any spare tickets to the concert. I had two but had invited three mates!

'Yeah, I have four but I only need two,' Greeny said. 'You take mine and give me yours.'

Turned out to be quite the swap, because my tickets were in the bleachers and his were in the second row.

'Score,' I said when we got there. 'How good is this? We'll be able to reach out and touch them.'

A bloke in a black band shirt was soon talking to my good mate Jamie Fitzpatrick. Turns out Fitzy knew the bloke, who just happened to be the concert promoter.

'Why don't you boys come backstage and meet Jimmy, Mossy [Ian Moss] and the boys?' he said.

Shit yeah!

Soon I was shaking hands with Barnesy.

'Where are you sitting, lads?' he asked.

'Somewhere near the front,' I replied.

'Na,' Jimmy said. 'That won't do. You can come and watch from the side of the stage. I'll get you some backstage passes.'

And not too long after that, show started, Jimmy rocking out, Mossy wailing on his guitar, Barnesy invited me on stage with Cold Chisel. I ran out and I danced like an idiot. I didn't dare grab the microphone and try to sing, I was embarrassing myself enough as it was. I jumped up and down in a lame attempt to dance as Cold Chisel belted out a tune. I looked out into the heaving crowd.

Is that Greeny?

I thought I could see him in the crowd. Way up the back.

Yep. That's Greeny. Wow. Shit seats.

He didn't look impressed.

Ha. Ha.

MAL, KEVIE AND QUEENSLAND

CHAPTER 23

I WENT INTO THE 2014 State of Origin series expecting our record-making run of eight to become nine. With only one change to the team that did the job in 2013 – Aidan Guerra coming in for the injured Sam Thaiday – and two of the three matches to be played in Queensland, I was sure we would win. The dynasty would continue.

But it didn't.

New South Wales came out swinging in the opener and beat us 12–8 in a Suncorp Stadium shock. After Darius Boyd went over in the corner to score the first try, the Blues went in twice – first Brett Morris and then Jarryd Hayne – to leave us trailing by 10–4 at half-time.

Trent Hodkinson kicked a penalty goal in the 42nd minute to extend New South Wales' lead to 8 – and that would be enough for the Blues to win.

We mounted a comeback, of course, Boyd scoring again in the 56th minute to make it 12–8. We went close in the 74th – but Brett Morris denied Boyd his third. We went close in the 78th – but Hayne denied Chris McQueen. And we went close in the 79th – but Daly Cherry-Evans was stopped three metres short. We lost.

I didn't see the defeat coming. I didn't think we were vulnerable heading into the series. I didn't think the Blues had a better team.

We went to Sydney on a mission to save the series – we failed, the record-breaking run over after a gut-wrenching two-point loss.

In a 6–4 win to New South Wales that was hailed in the press as the beginning of a Blues era, New South Wales defeated us to win their first State of Origin series in nine years. It was a game I would like to forget. We got out to a 4–0 lead when I kicked my second penalty goal of the night to surpass Mal Meninga as the Maroons' highest ever State of Origin point scorer with 162 points. And then Thaiday crashed over in the 51st minute for what we thought was the match-winning try. Referee Ben Cummins had other ideas, sending the decision to the video referee. Our celebration stopped when the replays showed Thaiday had lost the ball, Hayne stripping the footy to stop Sam.

The Blues finally cracked us in the 71st minute, when Trent Hodkinson sliced through to make it 4–4. The NSW No. 7 then converted his own try to give New South Wales a two-point lead. That ended up being enough for New South Wales to break our record run.

I didn't like losing too much. It was a shitty feeling. Only three or four of us in the team had ever lost a series before. It was new and shattering for everyone else. It was certainly hard to take after what we had done the year before.

But full credit to New South Wales – they won by executing their big plays. That proved the difference. The difference between winning and losing in Origin is taking your chances.

Paul Gallen was the captain who led New South Wales to the series win. He tried and failed so many times and finally got to lift the shield. Whilst I wasn't happy for him, not one bit, I know what it must have meant to him. He was a tough opponent and always gave his all; I respect that.

Gal is the captain of the Sharks – a team I have always hated. Their fans always gave it to me, as did their players. They are a very tough footy club to play against and a very tough footy club to like.

Gal was also a player we would always target in State of Origin. We often tried to expose him when he was defending, always trying to find him out on the defensive line. But on this occasion he had the goods, so well done. Gal earned his place in Origin history as the NSW captain who finally broke the drought.

I put Josh Reynolds on my shitlist after that match too. I was put on report late in the match following a confrontation with the NSW upstart.

'Show some respect, you fuckwit,' I screamed as I tapped him with my head. 'You've been around for five minutes. Who the fuck do you think you are?'

Reynolds, who had made his State of Origin debut the year before, had been hitting me late, pushing me around and verballing me all match. He was being a grub, basically. I ended up losing my cool.

'Show some fucking respect,' I screamed again before I was dragged away.

I can't remember being more pissed off on a football field. I just remember thinking, *Who are you and what have you done?* You don't earn respect on a football field by hitting blokes late or verballing them. You have to bide your time and prove yourself. I have never disrespected a senior player.

So yeah, I was pissed off after the game. We all were. We came together, a tight huddle, and spoke about not wanting to feel the heartbreak of a series loss again. We vowed to make up for it, both in Game III and then the following year. The media was claiming the dynasty was over, that the Blues would now go on a record-breaking run.

But while our unbroken streak of eight was officially over, we were far from a fading force. We proved as much when we blitzed the Blues by 32–8 in Game III, before going on to reclaim the series in 2015. We won Game I by a single point before New South Wales forced it to a third match by beating us in Game II. We then went on to demolish the Blues with a record-breaking 52–6 romp in the decider. I kicked a record-making nine goals from nine attempts.

That game was the only Origin match I can say was easy. It was the only Origin game where I always felt in control. That was some freakish performance. It was also the end of an era.

Mal had always wanted to coach the Kangaroos. I'm told he went for the job in 2009, only to be beaten to the role by Tim Sheens. So it came as no surprise to me when he put his hand up to coach Australia when the chance came again at the end of 2015.

Mal loves a challenge. After taking us to eight straight series wins he probably needed something new. We didn't want him to leave, but we didn't say a word, because he had well and truly made up his mind. I don't think it will be a long-term thing. I reckon he will go out and achieve whatever it is he has set out to do and then move on to something else. Only time will tell.

Mal's current challenge is to make Test football a better product. Mal knows how big Origin is. He also knows how big international football should be. I admire his bid to install the Kangaroo jersey as the most prized possession in rugby league. If anyone can do that, it will be him.

Mal played in some of the great Kangaroos teams. He scored Australia's most famous try. Yeah, you know it. Ricky Stuart runs 80 metres before turning it back inside to Mal to win the second Test against Great Britain in 1990.

I think McDonald's even made cups to commemorate the moment!

And that is what Mal wants again – not the cups but the famous moments that will never be forgotten. He wants Australian rugby league to capture the public's attention like it used to.

I always thought Kevin Walters (Kevie) was the right man to take over from Mal. He appeared to be part of the succession plan and was very much the natural choice. Kevie had been Mal's assistant for years. He had also been involved in the system for a long time, as both a player and an official. I don't think anyone in the team even considered another option.

And then my Cowboys coach Paul Green came and saw me.

'I've been offered the Queensland job,' he said. 'And I think I'm going to do it.'

I was shocked. 'What?' I said. 'You're quitting the Cowboys?'

He shook his head.

'No,' Green said. 'I'm going to do both.'

I was still shocked. I wasn't sure how he was going to do both. I was also upset for Kevie – a mate, who I thought had earned his shot. I have a great relationship with Kevie, and I knew how much the Maroons job meant to him. I would have been shattered for him had he missed out.

I also had a personal interest, given Green was my coach at the Cowboys. Greeny assured me that the Cowboys would not be affected should he take on the Queensland role. He told me he had the systems to ensure we wouldn't suffer while he was with the Queensland team.

Personally, I wanted him to keep his entire focus on the Cowboys. While I knew he could have been great in the Queensland role, I didn't see how it would help us at club level. His tactics and trick plays would have won the Maroons matches, but what would his absences have done to the Cowboys?

The Cowboys obviously thought they knew the answer – and it probably wasn't the response Greeny was hoping for. I don't know the content of his conversations with the club but he ended up turning down the Origin gig.

So Kevie got the Origin job. His first order of business as coach was to motivate us and instil his passion for the jersey in each and every player. Kevie is a very emotional man. He loves Queensland and went about inspiring us through his words and actions. As a tactical coach, he was very much in the Mal mould. He was happy for the playing group to take control and ownership of what we did on the field. He let the senior players look after the structures.

I considered him a perfect fit. Even though he is emotional – you can see it whenever he speaks – he also knows when to relax and give us space. He made a point of making sure we were calm and did not play the game out in our head.

Kevie and Mal are not the only two men who helped build the Maroons. We have had some of the best minds – and personalities – in rugby league quietly contributing in the background. Men like Neil Henry, Michael Hagan, Alfie, Trevor Gillmeister and Anthony Seibold have all done their bit.

With Kevie at the helm, in 2015 we went on to make it 10 series wins in 11 years. We won Games I and II, to prove we were far from that spent force the press had suggested when the Blues got us in 2014.

THE FAMILY MAN

CHAPTER 24

'JOHNATHAN,' SAM SAID. 'LET'S HAVE a baby.' They were words that would forever change my life.

'Really?' I said. 'A baby? Now?' I didn't know if I was ready to be a father. 'A dad?' I asked. 'Me. Ha! Ha! Ha! I can't even look after myself.'

I had always wanted children. I wanted to end up having lots. But back in 2011, when Sam told me she wanted to have a child, I didn't think I was ready. I was living large and carefree – the world was at my feet. I was at the height of my power on the football field and I could do whatever I wanted away from it. I was going on trips: New York, Hawaii and Las Vegas. I didn't have a mortgage or a lawn to mow. I had no responsibilities and I was enjoying my life, just me and Sam. I wasn't ready to grow up.

'I'm being serious, Johnathan,' Sam said. 'I'm not getting any younger. We need to start thinking about this now.'

I was 29 at the time – Sam was 36.

'I don't know if I'm ready,' I said again. 'Let me think about it.'

And I did. I had always imagined doing the children thing the 'proper' way: getting engaged, married, moving into a house and then filling it with kids. I also thought that would all come when I had finished my football career.

Well, I didn't need to put a ring on Sam's finger to know I loved her and she was the only one for me. But we couldn't wait until I retired from rugby league to start a family with time running down on Sam's biological clock.

You're just being selfish. Grow up. Think of Sam.

'OK,' I said to Sam a little while later. 'I love my life the way it is with you now and I don't really want it to change. But I want children one day and if you think it has to be now, let's do it.'

So how do you make a baby?

Our Hawaii holiday suddenly turned horrible.

'What is it, babe?' I asked, rushing into the bathroom.

Sam was crying, out of the blue and seemingly over nothing.

'Tell me,' I said as she continued to sob. 'What's wrong?'

She eventually composed herself enough to talk. 'I think I've just had a miscarriage,' she said.

Sam had her first miscarriage while we were holidaying in Hawaii at the end of 2011. She didn't even know she was pregnant until she lost the baby. She was shattered. Samantha hardly talked for the next four days. She blamed herself because we had gone skydiving the day before.

'Don't be stupid, babe,' I said. 'You didn't even know you were pregnant. And you don't know if the skydive had anything to do with the miscarriage.'

Nothing I said helped – she was broken. Sam didn't leave the hotel room until it was time to go home. We cancelled all the tours and activities that we had planned and sat in the dark.

The second miscarriage was worse.

'We are going to have to break up,' she said after miscarriage number two. 'If I can't give you a family then you should just leave me. You need to find someone else who can give you what I can't.'

I signed the papers and was given a cup. Next I was handed a key.

'Your room number is on the key ring,' said the nurse. 'Go and let yourself in whenever you feel you're ready.'

I was as ready as I was ever going to be. I walked down the hallway and found the door with the number that corresponded to my key. I let myself in. The room wasn't much bigger than a cupboard, containing only a chair, a TV and an assortment of pornographic magazines.

I gave sperm at two different clinics after Sam and I decided to try IVF – and it was terrifying. I sat in a little waiting room, on a bench with a few strange blokes, before I was called and given the cup. Afterwards I took the contents to a closed window in the same room. I pressed a little button and the shutter came up. I was a little surprised to find a laboratory on the other side, full of scientists and doctors wearing white.

One of them came over and took my cup. 'Thank you,' he said. 'You're done.'

It was a bloody awkward experience, made no less so by my teammates. The boys found out I was going to give sperm and on the day of the deed I woke up to a selection of picture messages.

My good mate Glenn Hall took a photo of himself, naked in the shower, and sent it to me. 'Something to help get you in the mood, big boy,' the accompanying message said.

The messages and photos from the other lads were in the same vein. They might have had a bit of a laugh but it was serious for both Sam and me.

Upon medical advice, we turned to IVF after the two miscarriages. We did all the tests, Sam took the injections and I, of course, gave my sperm. Sam had almost lost hope after three embryos, implanted in Townsville, failed to take.

My heart broke for Sam. I watched her take the daily injections, saw her get her hopes up every time an embryo was implanted, and was there for the tears when she was told it hadn't worked.

She again told me I should find a woman who could give me a child.

'Never say that again,' I said. 'I'm in love with you. No matter how much I want children, I want to spend my life with you more.'

We decided to give it one last try – this time at an IVF clinic in Sydney, even though we had lost a little hope.

Frankie Louise Thurston was born nine months later.

'It's a girl?' I asked. 'Are you serious?'

Yep. They were the first words that came out of my mouth when I met the next love of my life ...

Seven months earlier we were sitting in an obstetrician's room waiting to see if the latest IVF had worked. Sam was shaking as the doctor rolled the ultrasound scanner over her belly. We both looked at the green-and-black screen, hoping and praying for a heartbeat.

'It's a perfect baby,' the obstetrician said.

We both beamed, our smiles saying more than words. We didn't speak until we left the room

'Did you see that?' Sam asked. 'Did you see it too?'

I knew exactly what she was talking about. 'Yep,' I said. 'A doodle. I saw it too.'

I gave Sam a hug and shed a tear. I had refused to get my hopes up – as did she – until we'd had that test. After two miscarriages and three failed attempts at IVF, we dared not dream.

But now we could celebrate. We were going to have a little boy – or so we thought. We also had to prepare.

We were living in a three-bedroom unit when we learned we would finally become parents. We thought we would be OK for a while, at least a year. There was a park across the road and the unit was pretty big. Then, a few months before the baby was due, Fitzy called and told me he had found me the perfect house.

He was right. It was in the part of Townsville where we planned to live and was priced to sell. We bought it a week later. The house needed some work so we got builders in to do the renovations. All was planned to be finished the day the baby was due.

Sam and I spent most of our time preparing the baby's room. We loaded the wardrobe full of clothes – all blue – assembled the cot, and laid out the toys. It was a time of excitement, wonder and anticipation. I was also nervous.

A dad? A family? A house?

At least I wouldn't have a lawn to mow – I made the builders rip out all the grass and replace it with a synthetic lawn. Have I told you I am lazy? Ha.

The moment finally arrived. I drove Sam to hospital a day after playing for Queensland in the 2013 State of Origin opener, a 14–6 loss to New South Wales.

I was holding my baby the next day.

'A girl?' I asked. I looked down to Sam. 'It's a girl,' I said. 'We have a little girl!'

We named her Frankie and I was in love straight away.

Frankie is the best thing that has ever happened to me. She changed my life. I looked down at her, all big eyes and beautiful face, and made a vow to become a family man. I was going to be the best dad that I could be. I couldn't believe that I wasn't sure about having a kid when Sam told me she wanted to try for a baby.

The drive home from the hospital was surreal. I strapped Frankie into the baby capsule.

'Have I done it right?' I asked Sam. 'Is it tight enough?'

I then jumped behind the wheel.

'Why are you driving like an old person, Johnathan?' Sam asked. 'The speed limit isn't 20 kilometres per hour.'

I had never driven that slow in my life. 'Shhh,' I said. 'Don't distract me. I'm not letting anything happen to Frankie.' What should have been a 10-minute drive took almost half an hour.

We then spent our first night in our first house. I went to sleep with a smile on my face. I had my Frankie. I had my family.

Frankie is a dream. More Sam than me, she is creative, cute and full of endless energy. Her imagination both astounds and entertains me. She likes to tell me stories. I like to listen. Every day she takes me somewhere, far away, off to a magical place she has created in her brilliant little mind, and I am content.

She creates characters, places and stories that leave me in awe. I am not one bit creative. I don't have an imagination and my dreams have always been about football. So I love letting Frankie tell me about fairies and monsters. I also reckon she is smarter than me. She knew her alphabet before she could walk and every day she will tell me something I don't know.

She is also a perfectionist; maybe that is a bit of me. But every time I look at her I just see Sam. I loved her from the moment she was born.

'So when can we have another one?' I asked Sam a couple of months after Frankie came home. 'We can't stop at one.'

'How many do you want?' Sam asked.

'As many as you can give me,' I replied.

Charlie Grace Thurston was born in 2015. I was hoping for another girl when Sam told me she was pregnant with our second. I wanted Frankie to have a sister. We had some friends who had girls, and I used to watch how close they were and I wanted that for Frankie.

'It's a girl,' the doctor said when he delivered Charlie. 'A perfect, healthy girl.'

She was beautiful. I was stoked. He handed her to me.

'Oh no,' I said. 'She has Daddy's ears.'

I laughed when I said it but deep down I was concerned. She was gorgeous, a stunner, but there was no denying that she had inherited my big ears. And I was worried for her. I haven't spoken about this but I've copped heaps because of my ears. I was bullied as a child and teased as a teenager. I have always worn my hair long in an attempt to hide them. My parents got so concerned because of the bullying that they asked me if

I wanted to have surgery to pin them back. I think I was just too scared to get it done.

Anyway, that's enough about ears.

Charlie was the next greatest love of my life. While Frankie is like Sam, Charlie is like me. Sometimes it is like looking in a mirror. Charlie does the opposite of whatever you tell her. She gets that from me. And I reckon I am harder on her than I am on Frankie because I can see so much of myself in her. I want her to be better than me – not the same.

She has already broken my heart. I used to put her to bed every night. I would give her the bottle, rock her in my arms, and then tuck her in. I did that for the first few years of her life.

'No,' she said when I returned home from an Australian tour. 'Mum. Not you.'

Suddenly she wouldn't let me tuck her in. I tried again the next night and got the same response.

I was devastated. Crushed. 'She's forgotten me,' I said to Sam, tears in my eyes. 'She doesn't know who I am.'

Sam shook her head. 'No, she's angry that you left her,' she said. 'And she's holding a grudge. Remind you of someone you know?'

Yep. She is stubborn. Just like her dad. She still won't let me tuck her in. And it still makes me sad. Putting her to bed was my thing. And that was taken away from me, a sacrifice I made for rugby league.

Little Miss Perfect was born two years after Charlie. We called her Lillie Rose Thurston. Little Lillie has been a dream. She is the most chilled of all the girls. Seriously, nothing fazes her.

I could have another ten Lillies. She has only recently begun to walk, and we are learning more about her every day, but already we know she loves her big sisters. She hangs on their every word and follows them everywhere.

My girls have grown up with Australia watching on. They have become public figures because of who I am, and it has presented some difficulties, especially with Frankie.

My firstborn has always had people in her life. From the day she was born people would approach her on the street. They would walk over to her at cafés, in shopping centres and at the park. They would know her name and they would say hello. They would want pictures.

Frankie is very outgoing because of all that attention. She loves people and wants to interact with everyone. And while we have always taught her to be polite, we have also had to warn her to be careful of danger. She will talk to anyone. She thinks everyone is a friend.

It has been difficult to deal with as a parent. As a father I don't want anyone I don't know near her. But I also understand that she is going to grow up in the public eye and that most people's intentions are good. It is something I am still learning to deal with – and something the girls will have to cope with throughout their lives.

My biggest hope for our daughters is that they grow up happy. As a parent I just want to be able to give them every opportunity to do whatever it is that they want to do with their lives. I plan on giving them plenty of love and support, and advice when they want it.

I married the love of my life in a very private ceremony after the 2015 grand final. In a spur-of-the-moment decision, we decided to get married. Only our parents attended the ceremony, which was just six weeks in the planning. And it was perfect: bride beautiful, sky blue and sun shining. Turns out doing the whole life back-to-front thing also had an upside – Frankie and Charlie were there to watch their parents get married.

I walked in the door, training over – every inch an ordinary day.

'What?' I said, confronted by Sam in the kitchen. 'What are you doing standing there?'

She pulled her hand from behind her back. She was holding a little white stick with a couple of pink lines on it.

'I'm pregnant,' she said.

I almost fell over.

'What?' I said. 'How? When? Why?'

She shook her head.

Lillie was going to be our last child. We were happy with three and not intending to have another baby. I had my family.

Sam told me she was pregnant with our fourth child, four games out from my rugby league retirement. I was shocked – after having to have our first three through IVF, she finally fell pregnant naturally, aged 43.

Sam wasn't sure she could handle another pregnancy. 'I'm too old,' she said. 'I don't know if I can do it.'

I was adamant we could. 'We can do this, babe,' I said. 'I'll be there for you. We all will.'

You'd think I would be desperate for my next bub to be a boy – I'm not. I'm glad I ended up with three girls and I am hoping for another one. I can't imagine what sort of life a boy would have with me as his dad. The amount of pressure he would be under to live up to the Thurston name would be unbearable. Imagine if he was no good at sport?

So yeah, I love kids. Always have. And that is probably why I have spent a good part of my career doing whatever I can to help the little ones out. I think I gave away my first headgear in 2006.

'Hey, JT,' said a kid as I left the field. 'Give us ya headgear.'

I shrugged. 'Yeah, sweet,' I said as a chucked it to him.

And then he smiled. It was priceless.

I called Madison Sport – one of my oldest sponsors – the next day.

'Hey, do you reckon I would be able to get a few more headgear pieces this year?' I asked.

They wanted to know how many.

'One for every game,' I said.

Now they wanted to know why.

'I gave one away to a kid at the game last night,' I said. 'And you should have seen the look on his face. I want to make a kid smile like that every week.'

A box, chock-full of Madisons, arrived that week. And so it began. I was soon back on the phone to my sponsor.

'Hey, do you reckon I could get two for every game?' I asked.

Again they wanted to know why.

'Two halves,' I said. 'Two headgear pieces. I can make two kids happy instead of one.'

Another box soon arrived and I was tripping over headgear. I am not sure if Madison knew what they were getting themselves into back then, because I must have given away almost 1000 headgear pieces since that day the kid asked me to throw it over the fence. It must have cost them a fortune.

And I have to thank them, because I get a bigger kick out of it than the kids. To see their eyes light up when I put it in their hands, the smiles before they hug their mum or dad, well it means just as much to me as it does for them.

And most of the time I get to relive that feeling, with the majority of recipients sending me photos and letters of thanks. Most of the kids would end up going home and sleeping in the headgear, all game-worn and sweaty, refusing to take it off and demanding it never be washed.

Occasionally it backfired.

I walked into the bowels of Parramatta Stadium to face the press following a match against the Eels. I sat down and steeled myself for the first question.

Fire away.

'That kid obviously wasn't a JT fan,' a reporter said.

What? Sorry? I don't know what you mean?

'You didn't see it?' he continued.

I shook my head.

'That kid you gave your headgear to,' the reporter said. 'The Eels supporter. He threw the headgear back at you. He either doesn't like the Cowboys or he hates you.'

Everyone in the room laughed. I did too.

'No, I missed that one,' I said. 'But that's Eels fans for you.'

Turns out the kid was afraid of germs. His father contacted the club the week after the match and explained his son suffered from a severe phobia and freaked out when I put a sweat-soaked, dirt-covered piece of game-worn playing gear in his spotless little hand.

Whoops!

The father explained that he was indeed a big fan of mine. That he meant no disrespect and felt terrible for throwing it back. I tracked the kid down the following week when we played at Penrith. I met him and gave him a new – and spanking clean – jersey.

It's not just headgear I have given away. Throughout my career I have given away shorts and socks, boots and jerseys. I have been left walking around the dressing room wearing nothing but my underwear after some games. I have rarely refused a request.

THE LEGEND

PART FOUR

MAROONED

CHAPTER 25

SEASON 2017 COULD NOT HAVE started better. After opening with a win against the Raiders at home, we travelled to Brisbane to face the Broncos in the all-important Queensland derby.

And at Suncorp Stadium, in front of 47,703 people, I scored my 2000th point in the NRL before going on to kick a golden point field goal to seal a dramatic 21–20 win.

And then it all went to shit.

I picked up a calf injury when the Tigers beat us at home in round 6. It wasn't a particularly bad injury, but I was told I would miss a few games.

'Will I be back for the Anzac Test?' I asked.

'Yeah, you should be right,' said the Cowboys' physiotherapist.

The Anzac clash against New Zealand was looming, and it was a game I didn't want to miss. I had already made the decision, albeit reluctantly, to retire from representative football at the end of the year, and I didn't want to miss one of my final chances to play for Australia. While there was a World Cup coming up late in 2017, this would certainly be my last Anzac clash.

So I got stuck into my rehab work and declared myself fit on the eve of the game. The critics questioned my decision to return, claiming I wasn't back to 100 per cent and risked further injury. I was fine, at least until I went chasing Roger Tuivasa-Sheck (RTS).

With the crowd roaring, adrenaline pumping and the Anzac trophy on the line, I got straight back into the groove. I took hold of the ball and booted it to the corner, looking to pin New Zealand in. It was a perfect kick and the ball beat RTS and found the in-goal. I turned on the afterburners, as there was a chance to trap him behind his try line and force a repeat set.

Well, RTS has one of the best steps I have ever seen, and with a jink and shuffle he left me lunging at nothing but air. I dived in a desperate bid to grab him but he was gone. I ended up crashing into the dirt, shoulder first.

Whoops. This isn't good.

I was immediately in pain, not crippling 'Oh shit' agony like when I broke my leg, but enough for me to know there was something wrong. I pulled myself off the ground and dragged myself back into the defensive line. I had a bit of a feel around my right shoulder and it hurt to touch. I gave it a roll and while it didn't feel right, I thought I could go on. So I ignored it and got stuck in.

A trainer was standing in front of me soon after. 'You hurt?' he asked. 'You don't look right. You want to come off?'

'Na, I'm sweet,' I said. I shook my head and ordered him away. Again I knew something was wrong but I wanted to play on.

*

I went on to finish the game: we won 30–12 and I booted five from five. But I may have made the injury I sustained in the RTS missed tackle worse. I had no problem playing through the pain – it isn't so bad when the blood is pumping around the body and your adrenaline is racing – but when I got back into the sheds I couldn't even lift my arm above my head. Alarm bells were ringing. I asked the medical team to check me out.

'This doesn't feel real good,' I said. 'I can hardly move it now it's cooled down.'

I was told I would need to get a scan the following morning to determine the extent of the injury. Getting scans is never fun. I always expect the worst, and waiting for the results is a punish. Patience is not one of my virtues.

'Come on,' I said to the guy who took the scans. 'You must have some idea? Is it bad?'

He shook his head and I knew I was in the shit.

'No, mate,' he said. 'It doesn't look good. But wait until your doctor has a better look. No point worrying until then.'

Yeah, right. I was shitting myself. I was 34 and just one big injury away from retirement. I tried to lift my arm up again and couldn't.

This could be it. Is this the end?

Horrible thoughts were going through my head.

The doctor gave me some better news. 'I think you're only looking at a couple of weeks,' he said. 'Keep on doing your rehab stuff and you should be OK. You might be able to get away with an operation at the end of the year.'

Thank goodness.

So I went to work on my rehab. I did the hours in the gym, went to the physio, and trained as hard as I could. I was determined to get back for what was going to be my last State of Origin series for Queensland. I didn't want to miss any of the three matches, and I made it my mission to be back for Game I. And I almost was ...

Despite officially being ruled out of Origin I – what the team told the press and public – I was given the all-clear to play. Heading into camp we did some testing and the results that came back were good.

'Yeah, you'll be right for Game I,' I was told.

You beauty.

So I prepared myself for what would be one of my biggest ever games. I ripped into the weights. Hammered myself on the field. And I mentally prepared myself to lead Queensland to a big win over the increasingly confident NSW Blues. I was in a great place, a skip in my step and a smile on my face. And then it all went to hell ...

I was summoned to a meeting with the coaching staff just two days out from the game. I presumed it would be a meeting about tactics and game plans. And then I saw the doctor.

Why is he here?

'What's going on, lads?' I said.

Kevie looked at me, all stern and serious. 'You'd better have a listen to the doc, mate,' he said.

Oh shit ...

'JT, we read the scans wrong,' said the Queensland doctor. 'We just spoke to your club doctor and your shoulder is still no good.'

I shook my head. 'Na, it's fine,' I said. I was matter-of-fact. 'You read them right. I'm ready to go. I am playing.'

'No, you are not,' he said. 'You're not playing. Sorry, but we can't risk your career. This might be your last ever game if you run out. You're still a long way off playing. Sorry, we missed a couple of things and your club doctor has a better handle on it than us. You have to take his advice.'

I looked straight at Kevie. 'I won't let you down,' I said, tears rushing down my face. 'Let me play. I'm fine.'

Kevie shut me down fast. 'You can't, mate,' he said. 'And you won't be letting anybody down. You have nothing to prove to me or to Queensland. You have nothing to prove to anyone. You could never let any of us down. Look, I'd rather you miss the first one and have you back for the next couple than the other way around.'

His kind words did little to cheer me up. I was shattered. I had been preparing to play in this game, a game that was shaping as the biggest of my career. New South Wales had been installed as favourites. Everyone was saying that the Queensland dynasty was over, that we were too old and ripe for the picking.

This was a home clash and one I desperately didn't want to miss. And we needed to win Game I, arguably the most important game of the series. The statistics say that if you win the first game you will almost certainly win the series.

So I cried. I blubbered like a little girl. I was just devastated.

In the end, I'm glad that they took the decision out of my hands, because without a doubt I would have played had it been my choice. And that decision could have cost me my career. I could have smashed my shoulder completely and never played another game of rugby league. Or worse. I might never have been able to pick up my little girls again.

I watched the game from up in the stands and my mood was dark. Seeing that game, the way it went down, and knowing I could have been out there doing something about it was the ultimate frustration. The Blues just beat us up that night. They bashed us, and looking back now I am not sure I would have made a difference. We got beaten 28–4 in front of 50,000 Queensland fans. It was humiliating. I walked out of the ground determined to be there for Game II. I wanted to help my teammates exact revenge.

I was told I could make my return for the Cowboys in our round 14 clash against the Eels at TIO Stadium in Darwin – provided I passed a fitness test.

Fitness test?

That is a fancy word for being able to survive a beating. I was sent out onto a field with two of the biggest blokes I know and told to tackle them. Coen Hess (110 kilograms) and Corey Jensen (104 kilograms) were given the ball and told to run through me. I was told I could play if I could stop them. Yep, not a lot of fun.

Jensen (CJ) charged at me first. He came straight towards my right shoulder and I went in hard. I brought him down.

'Go harder, CJ,' yelled the trainer. 'What the hell was that? Your job is to break him, not give him a hug. Run at full speed this time and go in hard.'

Yeah, thanks.

So he went again, this time charging.

You can hide on a football field if you have to, but there is no disappearing when you're going one on one with a teammate, the coaching staff watching on. CJ ripped in. He came at me bumpers up and full pelt. Again, I got him down.

This went on for another 10 minutes, with both CJ and Hessy lining me up and me bringing them down. It was tough and it hurt – but the shoulder withstood the test.

I was given the all-clear to play in the match.

Some in the media have suggested I rushed myself back into that game so I could prove I was good for Origin II – but I wouldn't have played if it wasn't right. I didn't think I needed to get through a game before playing Origin. I have always been confident in my ability to go into a big game without a warm-up. And I didn't have to play to prove anything to the Queensland selectors, who would still have picked me either way.

Anyway, I got through unscathed. I even scored a try and landed six out of seven with the boot. We won 32–6 and I had some good touches. I certainly got some confidence from the match and proved without a doubt that I was ready for State of Origin. *Or so I thought...*

I was struck down by nerves leading into the game – and that is extremely rare for me. In fact, I had only been seriously nervous twice: before I took on Joey in 2006, after beating him to the Dally M the year before; and the game where I stepped in to replace Darren Lockyer as the Australian No. 6 after he retired.

But here I was, sitting in a hotel room, legs shaking, heart racing and thoughts rushing though my head. *What if you fail? What if you let everyone down? This is all up to you.*

It was the weight of expectation that made me so nervous. Everyone was looking for me to come back and save Queensland, and I didn't want to let anyone down. It was up to me to stand up and deliver and keep the series alive after the Game I thrashing. I had to deliver for myself, my coach, my teammates and the fans. I also had to deliver for anyone who had ever worn the Maroons jersey in the past. This was more than a match. It was a dynasty and my legacy. I didn't want to finish my Origin career as a loser.

I also began to doubt my fitness. I didn't know how the injury would stand up in the toughest arena in rugby league. And I didn't want to be a passenger. It would be selfish to go out there if I thought I wouldn't be at my best. I knew there were other players who could fill my shoes.

So yeah, I was nervous.

I took a deep breath as I put my match-day suit on. I told myself I was ready and raring to go as I put on my tie and tucked in my shirt. And I stood tall as I walked out of the hotel room.

We had a meeting before getting on the bus. Queensland team manager Steve Walters (Boxy) started off by cracking a few jokes to lighten the mood. He certainly knew how to get a laugh. And then Kevie took over, the coach all emotion, passion and intent.

In a stirring motivational speech, Kevie told us how he believed in us. We had all been written off after the Game I belting, but he knew that we were the better team. He brought up all the talk and headlines about us being finished, legacy over, legend done. He also singled me out and told everyone what I went through after being told I would miss Game I. He then said it was up to each and every one of us to prove them all wrong. We got on the bus determined to do just that.

I listened to music as I made my way into ANZ Stadium for what the home crowd was expecting to be a State of Origin decider. I tried to zone out, to ignore everything and everyone. I especially wanted to ignore myself – but I couldn't switch off the voices in my head.

I began worrying that the boys would see my nerves. I looked around the dressing room – headphones now off and jersey going on – to see if anyone was looking at me. I didn't want anyone seeing me panicked. I didn't want them feeding off it.

Snap out of it. You're all good.

I ordered myself to stop with the self-doubt and get rid of the nerves as soon as my jersey was on. It wasn't an easy thing to do, but I was able to reduce the roar in my head to mere butterflies in my stomach. I did that by looking at Cameron Smith.

It is my job to be a leader and remain calm. Guys in the team look to me to settle them. But I also have someone I look to when I need some help, and that is Smithy. Cam is an absolute rock, ice in his veins and steel in his stare. And my butterflies were just about gone after Smithy got up and delivered his pre-game speech. I can't exactly remember what he said, but he spoke with little emotion and broke down what we all had to do, all matter-of-fact. I always know I am going to be OK when Cameron Smith is in my team.

I ran out onto the ground knowing they were coming for me. The Blues had identified my shoulder as a weakness and were going to do everything they could to expose it.

And come for me they did. First it was NSW captain Boyd Cordner, the 105-kilogram back-row forward, hurling his gigantic frame into my body. I went in hard and low, looking for big contact. I wanted to give my shoulder an early test to remove any lingering doubt. And Cordner went down. The shoulder was fine. I knew they would continue to target me. Bring it on ...

Whack!

I went in just as hard in the 15th minute when Tyson Frizell jumped out and ran straight at me. He grabbed the ball on an overs line and came at me like a freight train. I saw Coops was coming across to help but he was never going to get there in time. I was on my own. So I went in high and hard, looking to bring him down, ball and all.

Bang!

He bumped me off and I went crashing into the ground.

Shit!

I hit the ground and shouted in frustration. I was filthy with myself for missing the tackle. I jumped straight up and sprinted back into the defensive line. A play or two later I noticed I had lost some movement in my right arm. And alarm bells rang, loud and clear.

No. Not now. Please.

I ignored the pain and played on. New South Wales had come out all guns blazing and I had to help stop their charge. The Blues were intent on finishing us off. They didn't want to head to Queensland and be forced into a Game III decider at Suncorp.

I felt the game slipping when Mitchell Pearce went over to score NSW's third try. And I had a bit to do with that try being let in. Having not seen James Tedesco (Teddy) lurking for an inside ball, I ordered Tim Glasby to shoot in and put some pressure on Jake Trbojevic, who was set to get the ball. It was a mistake because Teddy was waiting behind the ruck. Tim did his job and went for Jake – but the Blues forward hit Teddy on the inside. Pearce scored untouched when he supported Teddy to take New South Wales out to lead 16–6 after 28 minutes. I would have been able to stop that try if I had spotted Teddy.

My shoulder was getting more painful by the minute. I could still pass. Still tackle. But it wasn't a lot of fun. Frizell came at me again in the first half. Ears pinned backed, chest puffed out, he ran like a raging bull. This time I went low and I made the tackle. It hurt like hell when I drove my shoulder into his leg but I wasn't going to miss twice. I knew I was in real trouble when I rolled off. I was in agony. Still I wasn't about to put my hand up. I ignored the pain and played on.

I thought I had hidden the injury well. I made all my tackles and had resisted the urged to grab at my shoulder or favour my other side. But the doctor fronted me the moment I walked off the field for the half-time break.

'How's your shoulder?' he asked.

I couldn't lie.

'Not good,' I said, shaking my head. 'But I'm going back out. Just give me some pills.'

I needed some relief from the pain. I didn't care about damage done – but I was in agony. I needed some painkillers to get me back on.

The doctor handed me some pills and I threw them down my throat. I sat back and listened to Smithy as I waited for them to kick in. As always he was cool, calm and collected.

'We've got this,' he said. 'We hung in there and almost got them at the end of that half. Our opportunity will come. We just have to stick in there.'

There was no panic. Queensland doesn't panic. That is what makes us a special team. I think that goes back to Darren Lockyer. He is the man who started one of the greatest eras of dominance in Australian sport. Never did you think you were going to lose when Locky was in your side. It didn't matter what the scoreboard said, or what was left on the clock, you knew you were never out of the game.

And it was the same when Smithy was in your team. He took straight over from Locky and had the same calming effect on his players. I really don't know how Smithy remains so calm to deliver his message with precision. He tells us exactly what we need to do and how to do it. And this half-time break was no exception.

We came out firing. Josh Maguire (Moose) made a break almost immediately and Dane Gagai scored midway through the half to put us back in the match. I converted from the sideline to make the score to 16–12 with just 25 minutes left. We had momentum. We had the team. But we were still behind on the scoreboard. And it stayed that way until the 77th minute.

Billy Slater found Michael Morgan, who produced a bit of magic to find Gagai with an inside ball and the winger did the rest. He charged over the line and planted the ball to tie the game at 16–16.

Now it was up to me. Injured shoulder and all, I had a kick to win the game. As usual, it was from the sideline.

'You got this,' said Smithy as he threw me the ball.

I replied with a wink.

I took the ball back to the mark. It was in a very similar position to my previous kick, which made it just inside the post. I made a slight adjustment and lined it up. I was aiming at an 'S' in a New South Wales road safety sign. I took my steps back and I was happy with where the ball was. As always, I wiggled my toes. I looked down to the point of the ball I wanted to strike. Again I imagined the steps: one, two, three, four ... plant, and kick. I then visualised the kick going over. Now time to do it for real.

Whack!

I knew it was over as soon as I hit it. Sometimes you don't even have to look up to know that you have nailed it. This was one of those times.

Oh yeah!

I watched the ball go over and we had won the match. And I had done my bit by kicking the pressure goal. Pulling off a match-winning play is the best feeling you can have as a football player. I will never be able to get enough of that feeling. That is what I play for. I always want the ball in my hands when the match is on the line, and there is no better feeling in rugby league than getting it and doing the business. Whether it is kicking, scoring a try or putting on a play – I want to be the man who decides the match.

It was time to celebrate.

'Ouch,' I yelled as I attempted to raise my arm to salute the crowd.

I couldn't get my arm past horizontal. My shoulder had seized up and I felt only pain. Again I ignored it, this time to celebrate.

I was just so relieved that we had won the game. As I said, I had rarely felt as much pressure as I'd felt coming into the match. It was a game I was desperate to win, so I wasn't going to let pain get in the way of a party. But as the victory sunk in and the celebrations continued, I started thinking about my shoulder. Deep down I knew it was stuffed.

Na. It's right. Don't worry.

But the little voice in my head refused to accept it. I ignored the pain and continued to celebrate. Then I went to take my jersey off. I couldn't.

'Can you help me with this?' I asked a teammate.

He wrestled it off my body – I winced and groaned.

'Shit, you better get that checked out,' he said.

And I did.

'Doesn't look good, JT,' said the doc as he put me through a series of tests. 'But don't worry too much until we get some scans. It might not be as bad as it looks.'

I hoped he was right. I was one game away from playing my 300th NRL game. Yep. It was the very next game. I was also about to play my last ever Origin game.

'Just two more games,' I said to the doctor. 'Just get me through the next two games.'

He gave me a fake smile.

This could be it? It all could be over.

I wanted to cry. 'Just two more games?' I repeated. Then I pleaded. 'Please. Just two.'

That is all I wanted: two lousy games. I didn't care what happened after that. Seriously, I would have been happy to retire after notching up game 300 and playing in a State of Origin series win. But deep down I knew I was done. I was up half the night icing the injury in hope of a miracle. And I woke up in the morning with a sliver of hope when I was able to lift my arm.

Two more. Just two more.

But I wasn't able to hold it there for more than a second.

The press pounced when I walked into the hotel lobby.

'It's a little bit tender, but it's a lot better than I thought it would be,' I lied. 'It's heaps better than when I first did it.

I couldn't lift my arm above my head. I've got a good range (of movement), so that's a positive sign.'

The questions came rapid fire.

'Will you be OK to play in your three-hundredth game against Penrith on Saturday night?'

'How about the Origin decider?'

'I'll reassess when I get back [to Townsville] and talk to my medical staff there,' I replied. 'If they give me the go-ahead, it should be fine. It's too early to call [for Game III]. We'll just wait and see.

'Like I said, I trust our medical staff. They know my body better than anyone. If they give me the green light, then I'm ready to roll.'

Someone pointed out that I had played just my third game in 73 days. Another journo pointed out that it looked like I had played the entire Origin match in pain.

I replied by way of putting on my bravest face.

It was a long plane trip back to Townsville. I couldn't stop thinking about my shoulder. I had been injured before, but I had never had an injury ahead of a milestone game. The thought that I had played my last Origin match was excruciating.

I got off the plane and went straight to the hospital. I got my scans done and went to 1300SMILES Stadium to wait. I walked in and the physio was there, results already in his hand.

'Can we have a bit of privacy, please?' he asked, turning to a few other Cowboys staffers in the room. That is when it finally hit. That little bit of hope I was clinging to was ripped away.

He held the scan up, the light behind revealing the ugly truth. 'It isn't good, JT,' he said. 'Not very good at all.'

'I just want two games,' I said. 'Just two games. Please just give me a couple of games.'

He shook his head. 'You need an operation,' he said. 'You have to have it done now.'

I shook my head. 'No, I can have the surgery after Origin,' I said. 'I can get through another two. I know I can.'

'No, you can't,' he said. 'It's not possible.'

I continued to plead. I asked about needles and strapping.

'You might never play again if you take the field,' he said. 'That is how bad it is. You're finished for the season.'

I kept on pushing.

'You may never be able to pick your kids up again if you play,' he said. 'It's the worst injury of this type I've ever seen.'

And with that I stopped pleading. Yeah, that hit home. So I sat in silence for a few minutes. I couldn't manage a word. Finally I picked myself up and zombie-walked myself to my car. I opened the door, sat down and turned the key to start my Toyota.

I called Samantha as I pulled out of the car park.

'Hello,' she said. 'How is it? How were the scans?'

I couldn't reply.

'Are you there?' she asked. 'What's happening.'

I went to talk, but cried instead.

'Oh,' she said. 'It's OK, honey. It'll be OK.'

She stayed on the line until I finally got home. I didn't say a word the entire trip. I just sobbed and cried. I had tears running down my face. My eyes were red raw.

I pulled into the driveway and all my girls were waiting: Sam, Frankie, Charlie and Lillie. They ran to me as I pulled myself out of the car.

'We love you, Daddy,' Frankie said as she covered me in kisses. 'You can spend some more time with me now.'

I went to hug her – but I couldn't lift my arm.

Despite the endless love from my girls, it was all doom and gloom for days. I put a blanket over my head and surrounded myself in darkness. Things got really bad at night. I can't sleep on my left shoulder because of a previous injury and now I couldn't sleep on my right. I was forced onto my back. I have never been able to get to sleep while lying on my back so I had to take a fistful of pills just to get to sleep.

Soon all the tablets were making me depressed. Sure, they were helping me sleep and relieving a lot of the pain, but they were also driving me deeper into despair.

All of the pills I was taking were 'downers'. And they were taking me down to a place I didn't want to be. But with the pain and not being able to sleep, I was left with little choice.

It was the girls who got me through. I have no idea how I ever got through these things without them. I guess I used to go out and get drunk.

Eventually I was forced to leave my bed and see the surgeon. I was hoping to get the operation after Origin III. I wanted to, at the very least, be able to celebrate with the team. I didn't want to be hobbling around with my freshly cut-up arm in a sling. But he had other ideas. He told me I needed to get it done right away, that it would get worse the longer I left it. I went in for the operation a couple of days later.

'That was the worst shoulder I've ever seen,' he said when I came to. 'It looked like you'd been in a car crash.'

He explained how there are three tendons that hold your shoulder together. 'All three of yours were damaged,' he said. 'But the middle tendon was four centimetres back from where it should have been. It looked like it had exploded. The other two were frayed but the middle one was completely shredded.'

He went on to tell me that he had to pull the bottom half of the tendon out and stitch it back to the top half, before anchoring it into holes he drilled into my shoulder bone.

'At least you didn't break any of my drill bits this time,' he said. 'You snapped two last time you were in here.'

I left for Origin camp nine days after the operation.

'What the hell is that?' a teammate asked after bursting into my hotel room.

I laughed. 'It's my bed,' I said.

I had borrowed a huge recliner from a nursing home. I knew I wasn't going to be able to sleep in a bed so I got hold of this big old chair that came from a retirement village.

Word soon got around about the 'old person's chair', and the boys got stuck into me. They thought it was hilarious. It was the biggest source of amusement for them heading into Game III. But the laugh was on them because the chair was the most comfortable thing in the world. So much so that I had it shipped from the Gold Coast to Brisbane when we shifted camp.

More laughs were to come when they found out I had taken it with me. They gave me heaps but it was a beauty.

We had a team meeting on the Sunday before the game. A few guys were making their debuts that week so I walked in expecting the meeting to be about them. It wasn't. Boxy was crying.

Oh. They are all here for me.

Boxy never gets emotional, so I knew something was going on. And he was looking straight at me. I started crying too, an outright mess before I even took my seat.

Boxy stood up and confirmed that this meeting had been called to honour me. He said the upcoming game had been dedicated to me after injury had robbed me of a true farewell. I blubbered and cried some more.

Smithy spoke too, and I cried even more. I was a wreck. And I started to panic because I hadn't prepared anything to say. Then they played a video with messages from past players, my parents, my wife and my girls. It blew me away. I tried hard to keep it together but it was too much.

Next, they gave me the ball that I kicked the goal with in Game II, framed with photos. They also gave me a picture of Frankie and me walking hand in hand after a game. I've used that photo on the back cover of this book because it is my favourite photo of all time.

Yeah. It was emotional. I got up and gave the worst speech of my life. I struggled to get a word out.

I left the room glad that it was out of the way. It was smart of the coaching staff to address my farewell early.

I had spoken to Kevie and Smithy before we went into camp and told them I didn't want to be a distraction. I even offered to stay away from the team. But they assured me that the boys wanted me in camp and that my presence would be a positive not a negative.

Still, I had been concerned about the looming emotional farewell, and what effect it would have on the team, but now it was out of the way.

My head was in the right space come Monday. While I wasn't playing, the coaching staff had asked me to help out with the left edge in a coaching role. And I enjoyed the job immediately. For the first time since getting injured I had something to do apart from worry about my shoulder. I had a new focus and I enjoyed the week almost as much as I would have had I been playing.

I was still emotional come game day, knowing my last Origin campaign was about to end.

The Queensland Rugby League and Channel 9 had organised a presentation for me on the field and I'm sure it would have been too much had I not already got that emotion out the week before. So I was able to contain my feelings when I was called up on stage before the game.

I walked up to the coaches' box ready for the game. And what a game it was. With Valentine Holmes scoring in the 15th minute, the game was never in doubt. I knew we had it won by the time we went 12–0 up. Our back five were outstanding. Some of the work they did was just freakish. And our guys in the middle were relentless.

It was a dominant performance. I was particularly impressed with our left edge: Gavin Cooper, Cameron Munster, Michael Morgan and Holmes. Between them they had only played a handful of Origin games, and they went up against a very experienced NSW right edge, which included Mitchell Pearce, Boyd Cordner and Blake Ferguson. And they smashed them up to leave me full of pride.

Smithy called me up on stage after he collected the State of Origin shield. 'I'm supposed to go and lift the shield up now,' Smith said. 'But I'm going to invite my little mate Johnny Thurston up here. We've had our own presentation and functions around his last Origin game, which was Game II, and it was unfortunate that he couldn't finish here tonight in front of his beloved Queensland fans.

'I have to tell you, I don't think I've ever come across a more passionate Queenslander, and mate, for what you've done for this jersey, I don't think we can ever thank you enough. I know there's been plenty said but mate, you're the greatest player and person to have ever pulled on this jersey. I just want to thank you on behalf of the team and everyone here for everything you've done.'

Wow. I was stunned. I walked up and hoisted the trophy with Smithy in one of my proudest moments yet. I will never forget that night, or that moment. I was so proud of the boys. It ended up being a great way to go out. While you live to play in those games, the feeling the boys gave me was the next best thing. Thanks, fellas. I love you all.

FIRING UP THE FELLAS

CHAPTER 26

ONE DAY IN SEPTEMBER 2017, I grabbed the newspaper and bolted to the field.

'Hey Jase,' I yelled. 'Come and have a look at this.'

I stuck the back page of the *Daily Telegraph* in front of his smiling-like-always face. The headline read:

Roosters' Jared Waerea-Hargreaves lays down a challenge to Cowboys wrecking ball Jason Taumalolo.

Jason Taumalolo stopped, stared and then he read.

Jase and Roosters giant Waerea-Hargreaves had had a colossal collision in round 21, when Waerea-Hargreaves was penalised for a late shot on Taumalolo. That was a killer game – we went down 22–16 – and even Greeny admitted the Roosters won on the back of their physicality.

There had been no apologies from Waerea-Hargreaves, and I could tell the *Telegraph* article was reminding Jase all about it. You might even say that steam was coming out his ears as he read.

> 'He went to pass the ball and I committed – Bob's your uncle,' Waerea-Hargreaves said. 'You say "bring it on", he says "OK". That's footy. That's what we're meant to do. That's what you want – your best players going at each other.'

The Cowboys were due to play the Roosters in the preliminary final that Saturday – 23 September – and now Waerea-Hargreaves was again telling Jase, 'Bring it on'. The *Tele* was predicting a '229kg smash-up'.

Jase was no longer smiling when he looked up.

'Yeah, he is going to smash you,' I said. 'Get a load of this shit. He thinks you are soft, mate. He owned you last time.'

Jase, a happy-go-lucky gentle giant when not on the field, knocked the paper out of my hand.

'Yeah well let's see what happens this time,' he said. And with that he stormed off.

I unofficially became a part of the Cowboys coaching staff when I returned from Origin, and I made it my job to fire up a few of the fellas. I singled out Jason Taumalolo during the finals and gave him an almighty poking. And it had a devastating effect. We will get to that soon.

My first priority when I came back from Origin was to get my shoulder right. I was ready to get stuck into the rehab and determined to get back onto the field as fast as I could. And it wasn't easy. Rehab is repetitive and boring. Sometimes you feel like it isn't getting any better and you struggle to see the light at the end of the tunnel.

The first part of rehab is all about trying to get some motion into the injury. I had to get some movement into my shoulder because if it stiffens up you are screwed. I had done it all before and I knew what I was in for, but that didn't make it any better. It was just hours and hours of rubber bands, tiny dumbbells and mindless movements.

It was a rollercoaster. Some days it sucked and I hated the world. Other days I made progress and smiled. Unfortunately, there were more bad days than good.

I began worrying about what my moods were doing to the team. I wasn't training with the boys but I would see them before and after sessions. Mostly when I bumped into them I had the shits.

It got to a stage where I felt my moods were rubbing off on them. And that is when I had to stop and take a good hard look at myself. I didn't want to bring them down just because I was in a tough spot. So I decided I would go in acting happy even if I wasn't. It didn't make the rehab any easier. After six weeks of torturous monotony I was over it.

'How did I ever rehab two shoulders at once?' I asked the physio, referring to 2007 when I had reconstructive surgery on both my shoulders.

He simply shook his head.

Every morning I considered turning the car around and going home. I didn't want to go to training. I didn't want to be around people. I just wanted to be by myself.

The only good thing about that period was getting the chance to spend more time with my family.

'Hey, Daddy, you can pick me up from school now,' Frankie said.

Oh yeah. That would be pretty cool.

And it was. I had never been able to drop off or pick up my girls from kindy. But with a more flexible schedule I was able to become a bigger part of their little lives. It was a big thing for me to be able to walk them into kindy every day, holding hands before kissing them goodbye. And I always had a smile on my face when I would go to pick them up, knowing they would run out to me shouting my name. I was covered in hugs and kisses without fail. And boy, did I need them.

Soon I realised that I was getting moments I would never have again. Moments I would have been denied if not for the injury. And that is when I decided I was OK.

I took every opportunity I could to hang out with the girls. I went to singing classes and dancing lessons, to the park and to the pool. It was brilliant. Frankie really enjoyed it because she was old enough to realise what the time meant. She was already noticing how much I was away before the injury.

'Don't go to the airport, Dad,' she would say. 'Not another trip. Can't you just stay home and watch the footy with me?'

So yeah, there was a silver lining.

The Cowboys were doing OK. They went on to win three on the trot after my surgery. *Johnathan who?* Ha. But a long line of injuries finally caught up with them, and they went on to lose five out of their last six. And no wonder, this was our list of injured heading into round 24: Justin O'Neill (elbow), Lachlan Coote (ankle), Shaun Fensom (knee), Michael Morgan (concussion), Te Maire Martin (knee), Matthew Scott (ACL), Gavin Cooper (calf), Antonio Winterstein (hamstring), Patrick

Kaufusi (foot), Ben Spina (biceps), Josh Chudleigh (ACL) and of course me.

With such a horror injury list, the boys were doing well just to compete in games. We had players playing out of position, and guys playing more minutes than they should have. At times they looked completely spent.

We had team meeting after team meeting and I did my best to pick them up. The message we kept on giving them was that it didn't matter who came into the team, anyone in this squad could do the job.

Greeny had got the team to a point where everyone could slot in and perform in any given role. His message was to believe they could beat any team no matter who took the field. I thought they could. Did they? I am not sure.

But they soon would.

We headed into the final game of the regular season needing a win to guarantee us a spot in the top eight. And we were beaten 20–10 by our staunch rivals the Broncos. Most people thought our season was over. Some of us did too. Our hopes of making the finals came down to the last clash of the round. We needed the Bulldogs to beat the Dragons. And it was a long shot.

The Dragons were red-hot favourites. A win would guarantee them a spot in the finals. The Bulldogs were playing for nothing. It had been a horror year for my old club. They had drama both on and off the field, and they headed into the final clash of the year with talk that their coach, Des Hasler, was about to be sacked. So the Bulldogs were struggling. They were also our only hope.

I went to a Father's Day barbecue at a friend's house on the day of the game.

'Don't you want to go in and watch the footy?' my friend asked when the game started.

'Na, all good,' I said.

I was happy to keep it on in the background, walking in occasionally, hoping for a miracle. It was 6–6 when I went home to put the girls to bed. I forgot the game was even on after I bathed them and tucked them in.

And then the texts started coming.

Are you watching this? You seen the score? Go, Doggies.

I flicked the TV on and the Bulldogs were leading 14–6. Still I didn't want to get my hopes up. But the texts didn't stop and I kept watching. We set up a group chat and the boys were riding the Bulldogs hard.

'Na, they'll still win,' one of the boys wrote when the Dragons scored to make it 14–12.

Not everyone was so confident when the Dragons finally hit the front. Matt Dufty strolled his way over the line to make it 18–14 after the conversion kick.

'OK, what are we doing for Mad Monday?' one of the boys asked.

Shit! Mad Monday.

It was my job to organise our end-of-season drinks. I'd got so caught up in the game that I forgot all about it. Matt Scott was helping with the party planning. I buzzed him.

'We'd better work out what we're doing,' I said. 'We should probably start straight after this game.'

I was in the kitchen when the texts started again.

'Doggies, bra,' someone wrote. 'They're coming back.'

I went back to the TV and it was locked up at 20–20. So then, for the first time since 2004, I sat back and cheered for the Bulldogs.

'Woohooo,' I screamed as Michael Lichaa scored in the 73rd minute to save our season. I jumped off the lounge and punched the air. And then I cancelled Mad Monday.

Season resurrected and the Cowboys back from the dead, I rocked up to training the next day and the boys looked brand new – fresh, with a bounce and spring that I hadn't seen since the start of the year.

And I felt pretty good too. I was finally out of my shoulder sling and it felt like we had just started a new season. In short, we were pumped. We had gone from limping out of the comp to steaming into the finals.

Something was brewing.

We went into the first game of the finals facing zero pressure. We believed we could win but no one else did. Apparently, we shouldn't even have been in the finals. We were the easybeats according to everyone, and that suited us fine.

It was during that week that I remembered a chat I'd had with Greeny mid-year.

'We only need a game plan to beat Melbourne,' he said. 'If we can do that we can win the comp.'

Greeny believed that we could beat everyone on our day except Melbourne. And now so did I. Yep. We only needed to beat Melbourne once to win the comp. None of the other teams worried me. And apparently the rest of the team felt the same way.

Greeny had another chat with me that week and told me I could have as much input as I wanted. I had been helping out with the team throughout the year and had become comfortable with the role. He told me he would like me to continue throughout the finals and contribute where I could.

I actually forgot I was injured that week. I felt like I was a part of the team. So much so that I almost ran out onto the field with them for the first finals match against the Sharks.

I stopped at the last minute and headed up to the coaches' box instead. Damn, I wanted to play. I sucked in a big breath and resigned myself to watching instead of playing. And what a game it was to watch.

Our season looked dead and buried until the 74th minute, when Ethan Lowe nailed a penalty goal to lock the scores up at 14–14. After a game where we were never in front but always in the match, Michael Morgan kicked an extra time field goal that proved the match-winner in a 15–14 epic.

It was some game and it wasn't without controversy. Some people said the referees robbed the Sharks. No doubt they had some calls go against them, but that is rugby league. They had other chances to win the game but didn't. They came out trying to blow us off the park and it backfired because we were prepared to play an 80-minute grind – or 90 minutes as it turned out.

We completed our sets and forced them to make errors. No one gave us any credit for the win but we didn't care: we were off to face the Eels in another sudden-death, all-or-nothing clash.

I was into Jase for the first time in the lead up to the match against the Parramatta Eels. He's a pretty shy bloke and I thought he needed some more firing up.

'Geez, that Nathan Brown is tough,' I said. 'And this week I reckon he's coming after you.'

I had his attention. 'What?' he asked. 'Nathan Brown?'

I nodded and did my best to keep a straight face. I continued to push and poke.

'Didn't you see the paper yesterday?' I said.

He shook his massive head.

'Well, there was a story that compared him to you,' I said. 'They had both your stats lined up and his looked pretty good. Apparently he's in the same class as you, Jase.'

'He hasn't played for his country,' Taumalolo said.

Again I did my best not to laugh. 'Yeah but you only play for New Zealand,' I said.

He gritted his teeth and stormed off.

I cut the story out of the paper that night and put it on my bedside table. I took it to training the next day.

'See, look at this,' I said. 'Here it is.'

'Yeah, let's see his stats after the game,' Jase said.

I folded up the article and put it in my pocket. I carried it around all week, pulling it out and waving it in front of Jase's face every time we crossed paths. I gave him a final look just before he ran onto the field. And for once in his life he looked angry.

He went out and destroyed not only Nathan Brown but also the Eels. He was an absolute powerhouse as we went on to win 24–16, against the odds, of course.

I had turned poor Jase into a killer by the time we took on the Roosters in the grand final qualifier. Before this game I made JWH his target. Well, JWH made himself the target all on his own.

Bring it on.

That is what the headline screamed in the *Daily Telegraph* with JWH urging Jase to come and get him, the one I told you about at the start of this chapter.

You fucking beauty.

I was so stoked. I didn't have to do a thing. But I did anyway. I carried that bit of newspaper around with me all week. And the result was brutal. Jase walked all over Jared. He just destroyed him. To be blunt it was embarrassing for JWH. He failed to deliver after putting his team under huge pressure by playing soft. I would have been filthy with him if he was in my team.

'You owned him,' I said to Jase after the game. 'Congratulations.'

I meant it. Season 2017 was when the other JT came of age. And he wasn't the only one to announce himself as a force. Scott Bolton was another guy who really stepped up in 2017. With James Tamou leaving and Matt Scott injured, Bolts led from the front and became a premier prop. Bolts has always been a reluctant leader, so it made me really proud to see him take on the role when injury ended my year.

And then there is Michael Morgan, the player who I have no doubt will become my successor for both the Cowboys and Queensland. Morgs became a genuine top-class playmaker following my injury. He went from outstanding running half to the complete package.

I helped him where I could but I can't take credit for his transformation. He did that on his own. Morgs was reluctant to take control of the team at first. He is naturally a laid-back guy and he didn't feel comfortable issuing orders on every play. Just like me when I got to the Cowboys, he didn't have the game-management skills you need to be a dominant half. But he does now.

Morgo learned how to control a game in 2017. He became comfortable ordering the team around to particular parts of the ground and being responsible for every play. He also stepped up his kicking game. I personally saw the work he did behind the scenes, and his kicking game came on in leaps and bounds. He worked out the right areas of the field to kick to and really began to isolate opposition back threes with his precision. He also found the right kick at the right time.

Everyone at the Cowboys has always known that Morgs was going to be a star, even if he didn't. As I said, he is a really humble guy who doesn't put himself out there. It was a highlight of my season to watch him turn into the player I knew he could be.

So did we come up with that game plan to beat Melbourne? Well, we thought we had – but unfortunately we hadn't. We went into the grand final full of confidence, with a game plan we thought would deliver us the premiership. But Melbourne just didn't allow us to execute that plan.

Against most teams, all you have to do to win is be 5 per cent better than them. Against Melbourne you have to be perfect just to stand a chance. And we were far from perfect on that Sunday night.

Losing Shaun Fensom just three minutes into the game certainly didn't help. In fact it was a major blow. Along with Jake Granville, Shaun was a big part of our defensive plan. He is a workaholic who keeps the middle clean. And beating Melbourne with just 16 men was always going to be tough.

We were never really in the match. The boys gave it their all, but Melbourne were just a class above.

Still, we held on until the 20th minute when Josh Addo-Carr went in to score. But 17 minutes later the game was all but lost when Billy Slater went over to make it 18–0 at the break.

We scored first in the second half to gain some hope, but Dale Finucane crashed over in the 64th minute to kill us off. I think we were a far better team than indicated by the final score line – 34–6.

And don't think we weren't gutted by the defeat. While some commentators thought we should just have been happy to be in the finals – let alone the grand final – we genuinely went into the match believing we could deliver North Queensland their second NRL premiership. While it didn't hurt as much for me personally as the 2005 grand final loss against the Tigers, no doubt because I wasn't playing, it rocked every Cowboy who took the field that night to the core.

I walked out onto the field after the match and looked them all in the eye.

'This feeling will never go away,' I said. 'It will burn, hurt and twist in the pit of your stomach for the rest of your life. The only thing you can do to ease the pain is go out and win the premiership next year.'

I also told them I would be out on the field, alongside them, doing everything I could to make it happen.

I wanted to go out with a fairy tale.

FAREWELL

CHAPTER 27

I WANTED TO RUN A victory lap with my mates. I wanted to hoist the Provan-Summons Trophy into the night air. I wanted to find my wife – ANZ Stadium a sea of blue, yellow and white – and kiss her before hugging my girls, Frankie, Charlie and Lillie.

I wanted to end my career with a premiership, a kiss and three hugs – but my final season in the NRL ended up being one of the most difficult years in my 17 NRL seasons.

Let's start with the footy. I set the bar high when I began my final pre-season. Shoulder strong, body fresh, I thought I could turn back the clock and be at my best. I never once considered that my body would fail me.

I signed my final contract at the beginning of 2017 – a one-year deal – and I was adamant that I would be in my prime. I was comfortable with my decision both to play in 2018, and to retire at the end of that year. And I was planning on going out with a bang. I'd had a good look at the Cowboys NRL roster before agreeing to the deal.

'What a team,' I thought. 'Have a look at these names.'

We had retained all our senior players, guys like Matt Scott, Gavin Cooper, Coen Hess, Michael Morgan and Jason Taumalolo. We had also recruited Australian Test prop Jordan McLean.

I was confident we had a premiership-winning team when I signed the deal, and almost certain we could win the competition when I started my final pre-season. I looked at all the men on the training field – sunburnt backs, sweat-soaked singlets – and thought I was going to finish with a fairy tale.

We had basically the same team that had shocked rugby league by making the grand final in 2017. The only difference was me and Matty Scott – two players with Test experience – would be back from injury, and as I said Jordan McLean – the incumbent Kangaroos prop – had joined us fresh from his premiership win with the Storm. We were installed as pre-season favourites to win our second title.

Yep. Things were looking good.

The season started with a celebration: a round 1 win in my 300th game. With my family and friends in the stands, I celebrated my milestone with a 20–14 win over the Sharks.

I don't often think about records or numbers, but this one was very important to me. Not too many players get to 300 – in fact, only 31 players in the history of the game. Of all the things I have achieved in rugby league, this is the number that makes me really proud, because as a kid I would have been happy just to play *one* NRL match.

Too skinny. Too small. He'll never make it.

I thought of all the knockers and knock-backs when I played my 300th game. I thought of all the trials and tribulations. I thought of those tracksuits I was never given and sweeping the floor in the butcher's shop.

Wow. 300? Who would have thought?

Terry Lamb, Steve Menzies, Cliff Lyons, Andrew Ettingshausen, Paul Langmack ... suddenly my name was alongside some of the toughest and most enduring players to have ever strapped on a boot. Any player who makes the NRL is good. Well, not just good, but outstanding. And of those who do end up making it into the top grade, the average length of a career in the NRL is just 43 games. So to make the 300 club was both an honour and a privilege.

I was also relieved, given that I'd feared I would be stuck on 299 forever after my shocking shoulder injury.

I celebrated with family and friends after the game before making a vow to get on with the year. I wasn't going to think about milestones or the fact it was my final season – my focus was to be solely on the Cowboys, and leading them to a premiership. I didn't want to be distracted – or to be a distraction – from leading North Queensland to NRL wins.

At least that was the plan.

We lost our next five games – beginning with a 24–20 heartbreaker to the Broncos – to put a huge dent in our premiership credentials. Our 27–10 loss to the Bulldogs at home in round 6 was particularly hard to take, given my old club were struggling and tipped for a tough year.

The rugby league critics were beginning to doubt we were the real deal, and the losses had certainly put us on the back foot. Injuries to Jordan McLean, Javid Bowen and Kane Linnett were also a cause for concern.

I left no stone unturned trying to help my team break out of our slump. Personally I wasn't happy with my form, and I trained as hard as I could and remained positive in a bid to lift the team.

Our second win of the year came in round 7, when we beat the Titans 26–14 at home. We made it three in round 9 by beating the Panthers by six in Bathurst. But then we dropped back-to-back games to all but end our season.

A heartbreaking one-point loss to Souths at home in round 11 meant that we would need a miracle to make the finals. Still I hadn't given up hope, but I knew we would probably be playing the rest of the season for pride.

I went into our round 12 clash against the Melbourne Storm knowing it was probably going to be the last time I ever played against my great mate Cameron Smith. The 1300SMILES Stadium clash was our only match against the Storm in 2018, and it would be the last time I took to the field with Smithy unless we made the finals.

I have mentioned Smithy a few times already but I haven't really gone into too much detail. So time to tell you a bit more about him. My rugby league rivalry with Smithy began way back when we were 13 and it ended in Townsville when we clashed for the 23rd and final time. I was always out to get one over Smithy, but more often than not, and especially later in my career, he had the last laugh. And our rivalry officially finished with the Storm beating us 7–6 in another deathblow to our season. Yep, he got the final word. He won our last fight by a point.

It was weird after that game, walking off with my mate, knowing that we would never be on the same rugby league field again. To be honest, I tried not to think about it. I don't think we even mentioned the end. We just hugged and peeled off to the sheds like it was any other game.

It was strange for Smithy to be so quiet because he is never short of a word. While Locky wasn't the chirpy type on the footy field, Smithy, well he would never shut up. He was always in your ear, trying to put you off your game. Not a lot of players can get away with talking so much, but Smithy is not a lot of players. He is a one-off.

Smithy is the best rugby league player I have played with or against. I've never seen him get flustered on the field and he is an out-and-out match winner.

So what makes Smithy so good? Let's start with the tough stuff.

Smithy does a lot of the hard work that few people see, the unfashionable stuff that few are willing to do, but the stuff that needs to be done. He is always the third man into a tackle. He is always the player who takes the ballcarrier to the ground. Smithy is also a master at slowing down the ruck. All these qualities make him the best defensive player in rugby league.

And attack? Yep. He can do that too.

Smithy, in fact, singlehandedly redefined the way No. 9 is played. He changed the role of the hooker by being the first to play like a half, both creating and controlling shape. Smithy has dictated the attack of all the teams he has played for. He is the one picking up the runners and sending them on their way. Most hookers play like this now – but before Smithy, all the attack came off the halves.

Smithy is smart, his football brain unmatched. He knows how to swing momentum and come up with the right play at the right time. You very rarely see him take a wrong option. Locky played four or five sets ahead of the game. Smithy plays eight sets ahead.

Yep. He is that good.

Add to that a flawless passing game, a kicking game as good as any half and defence as good as any forward, and you have a once-in-a-lifetime player.

Losing my last match to Smithy was tough because it was a continuation of a terrible year, but I still believed in my team and clung to hope. I prayed for my latest rugby league miracle as my first season as a State of Origin spectator rolled around.

My year went from bad to worse when Queensland lost the State of Origin series to New South Wales. After going down to the Blues 22–12 at the MCG in Game I, the Maroons surrendered the shield for just the second time in 13 years when they lost to New South Wales by four points at ANZ Stadium in Game II.

I found watching the second game, from the Channel 9 box where I was working as a guest commentator, particularly difficult, because I thought it was a game we should have won. I don't want to sound arrogant, but I am certain we would have won if myself, Cameron Smith or Cooper Cronk were on the field. So yes. It was very frustrating to be up in the commentary box.

I thought New South Wales had a foot in the grave at half-time and Queensland just needed to be more composed and play smart for 40 minutes. They had such a good opportunity to win that match. They blew it.

And I think if Queensland had won Game II, they would have gone on to win the series.

I was pretty brutal after the game and said some harsh words about the team on the Channel 9 broadcast, which I now regret. I couldn't fathom some of the things that I saw.

I was highly critical. I didn't think the players in the key positions had connected well enough. They didn't make the right decisions, and it led to the painful defeat.

The day after the game, I felt pretty ordinary about what I'd said. I probably should have used wiser words. I doubt the team were happy with my comments. I didn't mean to be so harsh. I think I was just so frustrated that I had to let it out.

I had very little to do with the team throughout the series. I wanted to phone some of the boys at times and make a contribution – but I also didn't feel it was my place. I had conversations with Kevie about the team – about players and positions – but I didn't go into camp or to any of the training sessions.

I guess part of that was because my decision to step down from Origin was still very raw. I was still processing the fact that I wasn't playing for the first time since 2005. I'm not sure I would have been able to handle going into a camp and knowing that I was only there as a passenger. Ultimately my decision to stay away was about the team and not me. I didn't want the boys picking up on any negativity.

The loss hurt me and it hurt the Maroons – but Queensland have a bright future. Sure there won't be another Cameron Smith, Billy Slater or Cooper Cronk. But there will be new names and new heroes. There will be Cameron Munster, Kalyn Ponga and a bloke called Michael Morgan.

I think Morgo is Queensland's next long-term half. He has a great football brain and knows what the team needs and when. We saw how good he could be during the Cowboys grand final run in 2017. I think he is not only the long-term No. 7 for the Maroons but also the future Queensland captain. I hope – and think – he will go on to become an Origin great.

And how about that kid Ponga?

Wow!

Didn't he show us what a star he is going to be in his State of Origin debut? His attacking performance didn't surprise me because I have watched him come through the grades at the Cowboys. I know what he is capable of with the ball in his hands. I was, however, surprised by his defence. He plays fullback – where he only makes a couple of tackles a match – but Ponga was asked to play in the middle in the toughest game of his life. I thought he would struggle with the defensive load.

He didn't.

Ponga came on and jammed blokes and got through a load of work. He then still had the energy to run with the ball and be his usual threatening self. It was one of the better Origin debuts you will see. I had a little giggle after the game when he did an on-field interview with Locky.

'So what was the difference between that and a club game?' Locky asked.

'Nothing,' Ponga replied.

Ha! Ha! How is that for confidence?

But he might want to go back and look at the tape. I watched him closely and there were a few times he was bent over, sucking the big ones in under the goalposts.

I first saw Ponga play on YouTube. It was shortly after we signed him at the Cowboys and a message lobbed in my inbox.

'You seen this kid play?' asked my mate. 'Check this out. He's going to the Cowboys next year.'

I clicked on the link, all blue and begging to be pressed.

Holy crap!

It was this kid playing club football. He was friggin' unbelievable. It was only schoolboy football but he was so far ahead of the other kids, you could just tell he was special.

I forwarded the link on to Michael Luck, our football manager at the Cowboys in 2015.

'How many more years do I have to play to make sure I get a game with this kid?' I asked.

'He's only young, mate,' Luck replied. 'He's three or four years away. He'll be long past your time.'

I played with Ponga 18 months later, the kid bursting onto the NRL scene with the Cowboys in 2016.

Ponga's talent was on show from the moment he arrived in Townsville. He would come and play against the NRL squad in opposed sessions at training during his first year. He embarrassed us. He was skipping across our line during our defensive sessions and making us look like reserve-graders. He would run the length of the field on kicking chases if we had a staggered line.

'Mate, you're making us look silly,' I said to him one day, pulling him aside after he had torn us apart. 'Go a bit easy, hey?'

So yes, I think Queensland will be OK with guys like Ponga and Morgan coming through. Never write off the Maroons!

Watching Queensland lose to New South Wales was tough – but it was also a distraction. It was back to reality when the State of Origin series was done and dusted.

'You coming for a beer, Johnno?' one of the boys asked after we lost to the Dragons 24–10 at home in round 19.

I simply shook my head.

'Knew you wouldn't,' the teammate continued, 'but thought I'd ask anyway.'

I hadn't been out in public – unless absolutely necessary – since the celebrations that followed my 300th game. I had been hiding at home, too embarrassed by my personal performances to walk out the front door.

The year had begun with the promise of a fairy tale premiership finish and by round 19 we were fighting to avoid the wooden spoon. I really struggled to deal with both my form and the form of the team. I took every loss personally and refused to believe we were out of the premiership hunt until it became a mathematical impossibility.

So I didn't want to be seen in public. Didn't want to front up to the fans and be asked to explain my team. Myself.

I would go so far as to say it was the most challenging season of my football career. We had a team that was capable of winning the competition. I was fit and should have been firing. But for whatever reason the team couldn't put it together – and neither could I.

I went to a dark place.

'Is this how I'm going to finish?' I asked Samantha. 'With a wooden spoon? Is this how I'll be remembered? Is this what my rugby league legacy will be?'

That conversation I had with Gus, all those years ago when he came to the Cowboys as consultant to Neil Henry, was ringing in my head. 'You'll be remembered for the way you finish,' Gus had told me.

So I locked myself inside, such was my embarrassment. I only wanted to be around my family. I got messages from mates asking me to go out.

'No way,' I said.

I couldn't face anyone. I feared my legacy was being ruined and I just wanted to save it.

So I trained as hard as I could and did everything I could to turn it around – but it wasn't to be. Nothing worked. We kept on losing.

I was at training, kicking stones, when one of the boys cracked a joked. I have no idea what it was, but it made me laugh.

Ha! Ha! Ha!

It was then I realised what it was I would miss most about rugby league. I wouldn't wake up in 2019 missing the premiership rings, the Dally Ms or the last-minute wins. I would miss my mates.

I laughed again.

Ha! Ha! Ha!

I was struggling not only with my form and the prospect of ruining my legacy, but also with my looming retirement. I was going to miss rugby league and I didn't know what I would do without football.

So enjoy it while you can.

I decided I would soak it all up. To stop worrying and start savouring. I was going to enjoy the rest of the year with my mates. I was going to laugh and high-five, and above all I was going to smile.

A sellout crowd of 25,095 turned out to 1300SMILES Stadium for my last ever game in North Queensland.

Wow!

I got tingles up and down my spine as I ran out, crowd roaring, flags waving, opposition team lining up to applaud me as I took the field.

Really? They're all here for me?

And then I saw my mum. 'Go get 'em, son,' she said as she embraced me. 'Have a good game.'

The entire week leading into the game had been overwhelming – tributes, fanfare and text messages from family and friends – and now I was hugging my mum on the edge of the field.

'Thanks, Mum,' I said, doing my best not to cry. 'Thanks for everything.'

I shook my head, trying to shake away the emotion. I couldn't think of my friends and family, all in a private box the Cowboys had provided for the game, or the thousands of people in the stands holding JT signs and screaming my name. I had a football game to play.

And it ended up being some game. On a perfect night in Townsville, we destroyed the Eels 44–6. Ben Hampton opened the scoring in the fourth minute when he touched down for a try, and it didn't stop until the 53rd minute when I converted a try scored by Coops to bring up 44. We were on fire. No one would have stopped us.

I had managed to hold back the tears before the match, but there was no controlling myself after the game. Not when Samantha, Frankie and Charlie met me on the field with kisses and cuddles. Not when the full house of Cowboys fans turned the flashes on their mobile phones into 25,000 shimmering stars in the chock-a-block stands. And definitely not when Gavin Cooper and Matt Scott launched me onto their shoulders and chaired me from the ground like a king.

*

It was some farewell from North Queensland – and my rugby league farewell, the week after on the Gold Coast, was every bit as good.

I was already overcome with emotion seeing Samantha, Frankie, Charlie and Lillie all on the field as I ran out for my last NRL game. My mum and dad too. And then there was Smithy; he and his wife Barb had made the trip from Melbourne to be at my last game. He was standing beside Samantha as I ran onto the field; I was humbled and couldn't have felt prouder.

I was then distracted by my teammates running out onto Cbus Super Stadium, all of them wearing headgear in a surprise tribute.

'Ha!' I laughed. 'How good?'

My last game of rugby league was surreal: family, friends, and a sell-out crowd of 26,681 all there to see me go out with a 30–26 win over the Gold Coast Titans. There was also a standing tribute from the Titans in the seventh minute of the match. I managed to compose myself throughout the game – and even after it.

'Thanks to the Titans organisation for allowing me to run out with my family,' I said at my final post-match presentation as a player. 'To have them with me is something that I am extremely grateful and thankful for. To our boys, thank you for all the memories I have with you, both on and off the field. The friendships with you are the things I value the most. Thanks for making this year very enjoyable and easy for me.

'To the fans, it has been very overwhelming and humbling over the last few months and I am extremely grateful for the support. I want to thank you all for watching me, not just this year but throughout my career, and it has been a pleasure to play for the Cowboys and represent the region.'

I was doing well until I looked at my wife.

'To my wife Samantha,' I said, my voice finally cracking. 'I can't thank you enough for everything you have given me in my life. It is no coincidence I am a better person because I have you by my side. My mum and dad, my two brothers and my sister, thanks for your support over the years. I am thankful and grateful for your support, as I am to the rest of my big family.'

And with that I walked off the rugby league field for the final time. I took off my boots, my jersey, my shorts – and I retired. Job done.

Rugby league will always be in my life. Next year I will be part of Channel 9's NRL coverage, working as a commentator. I will be at the footy every week and entrenched in the action, which will help make the transition easier. I can't wait to be reunited with two of my heroes – Darren Lockyer and Andrew Johns. I'll also be working with legends of the game like Peter Sterling, Brad Fittler, Wally Lewis, Paul Vautin and Gus Gould.

I will also be kept busy with business ventures and post-rugby league roles. In February 2018, I proudly launched the Johnathan Thurston Academy. My hope is that the Academy will establish itself as a leading national provider of employment with training programs aimed at health, wellbeing, sport and education across Australia. I am really committed to supporting individuals to reach their personal, educational and career goals.

I am also looking forward to becoming an ambassador for the Cowboys, beginning in 2019.

Finding a competitive fix will be difficult. I hope to do that by playing golf. I love golf and it provides me with a big mental challenge. And judging by the way I hit those golf balls, the challenge will continue.

I won't rule out an NRL coaching career. As I mentioned earlier, during 2017, when I was injured, I got to do a lot of work with Paul Green and the Cowboys coaching staff. I enjoyed that and got to see the amount and type of work they do. To be honest, the hours they put in behind the scenes scared me away a little. Jeez, they work hard. I can't see myself pursuing a role as an assistant or head coach in the near future, but I'm certainly interested in doing some consultancy work.

Facing up to retirement, even though it was well planned, was tough. Things put in place for life after football made it easier, but it was still a daunting prospect. The thought of life without rugby league scares me. It is all I have ever known and the one thing I enjoy above all.

I still don't know who I will be without rugby league. I genuinely love the game. It has been a rollercoaster, with highs and lows, twists and turns, flat-out and a slow climb, and I didn't want to get off.

I will miss that two-minute bell. That moment when the game is about to start and you are looking into the eyes your mates before telling them you are ready to give them all you have.

I will miss being a rugby league warrior. While the NRL will still be a big part of my life, I have fought my last battle. There will be no more wars. No more rivalries. No more teammates.

I am a gladiator gone.

I hope you have enjoyed the ride.

Always, JT.

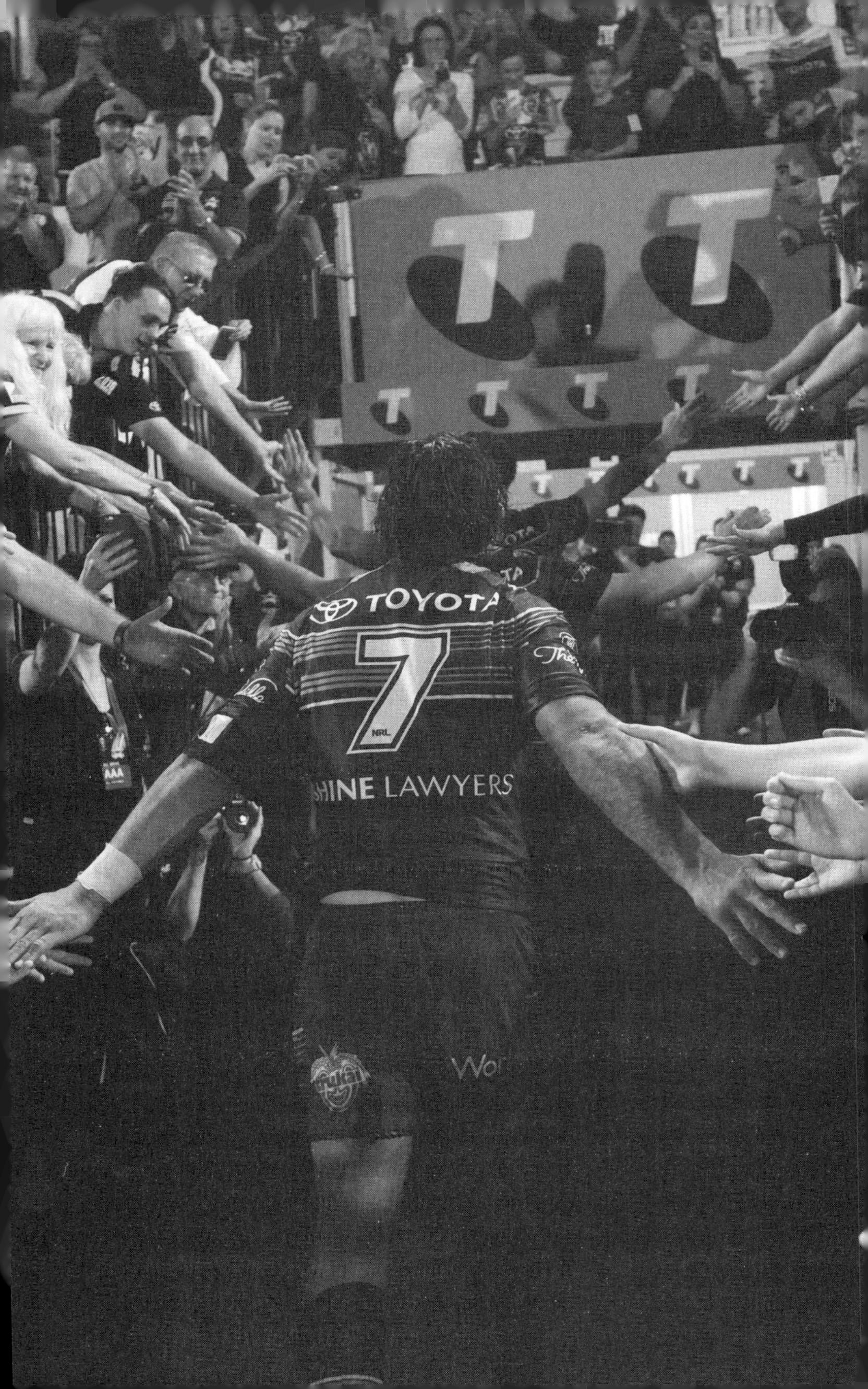

TOYOTA
7
NRL
SHINE LAWYERS

JOHNATHAN THURSTON
THE AUTOBIOGRAPHY

ACKNOWLEDGMENTS

IT'S TIME TO THANK SOME of the people who have played a role in making me both the player I was and the person I am.

I'll start with my mum and dad: Thanks for helping make my dream come true. None of this would have happened without your love, support, encouragement and unwavering belief. I hope I've made you proud.

To my brothers and sister, Robert, Shane, Katrina: I love you all. Thank you for always being there, for your support, your love and your loyalty.

To Uncle Dean: You are my guardian angel. I will be forever thankful to you for always looking after me.

To the rest of my uncles, aunties and cousins, we are forever family. You all played a part in shaping and developing me to the man I am today and for that I am eternally grateful. Your place in my childhood has given me some of my fondest memories. I may not see you often but you are always in my thoughts and forever in my heart.

To Uncle Richard: You are alive in my memory and in my heart.

To Nan and Chops: I think of you often and will love you always. I hope I've made you proud and that you're looking down on me with a smile on your face.

To Sam Ayoub: I might still be playing park football if it wasn't for you and whatever it was you saw in me. I cannot thank you enough for taking a chance with me, for your loyalty and dedication. It has been a hell of a ride and I couldn't think of anyone better to have shared it with.

To Peter Parr and Laurence Lancini: Thanks for convincing me to become a Cowboy. Words cannot do justice to how grateful I am to the both of you; for your loyalty, your advice, support and ultimately your friendship. You've both been there for me when no one else was and I hope in some small way, I've repaid you. You both give everything and expect nothing in return. I have the utmost love and respect for you and look forward to many more years of friendship.

I also have to thank my sponsors, in particular ASICS, Skins, Madison, the Toyota Motor Corporation and the North Queensland Toyota Dealers. Your belief and support allowed me to concentrate on becoming the best footballer I could be. I hope I've lived up to your expectations and look forward to continuing our long-standing relationships. Thanks again.

To Mal Meninga: Thank you for being a mentor and a mate. You weren't afraid to tell me what I needed to hear. You challenged me to be better in every way. Thanks for the lessons, sometimes hard, learned.

To Darren Lockyer, a hero who became a great mate. You're truly an inspiration and I consider myself so fortunate to have spent time with you on and off the field – you had a profound effect on my representative career, so thank you.

To Cameron Smith: Where do I start? My journey would have been nowhere near as enjoyable without you. The best thing about playing football is the mates you make and your friendship is most definitely a testament to that. You're a once-in-a-lifetime footballer and a once-in-a-lifetime friend. You've been a constant source of inspiration, motivation and confidence for me. Samantha and I love your family dearly and look forward to holidays with you, Barb and the kids. Now let's get to that bucket list.

To Gavin Michael Cooper: My roomie! Thanks for the greatest times – both on and off the field. You know me inside out and back to front. You know exactly what to say and when to say it to pick me up and make me laugh. You were my partner in crime. We have shared the highs and lows and your friendship has been a constant in my life. I have so much love and respect for you and can't wait to continue our journey.

To Jamie Fitzpatrick: My confidant! Thanks for your guidance, friendship and loyalty. You've been there for me during the tough times and helped me make some of the biggest decisions in my life. Throughout it all, you've always had my best interests at heart. Who knows where I'd be today without you. Here's to the next chapter!

To all the clubs that honoured me with a farewell presentation, thank you. It was something I never expected and I was honestly humbled. They were moments I very much appreciated and will never forget.

To James Phelps, my publisher Helen Littleton and the team at HarperCollins Publishers Australia: Thanks for all your work on this book. Phelpsy, you've been a mate for a long time and I there could not have been a better writer for this book.

You don't get to where I am in my life without a lot of help from a lot of great people so I'd also like to make mention of: Paul Canning, Gary Reen, Mick Kennedy, Leo Reynolds, the Seddon family, Rob Walmsley and Kate Fahey, Steve Folkes, Ricky Stuart, Steve Price, Willie Tonga, Sam Thaiday, Billy Slater, Steve Walters, Kevin Walters, Allan Langer, Gaz Carden, Kevin Moore, Willie Mason, Graham Murray, Neil Henry, Paul Green, Steve Sartori, Dr Chris Ball, Matt Scott, Michael Morgan, Paul Bowman, Matthew Bowen, Paul Rauhihi, Matt Sing, Mark Fitzgerald, Phil Gould and Denis Handlin.

And most importantly to Sam, Frankie, Charlie and Lillie: You are the loves of my life. I will treasure you and love you until my final breath.

There are so many others who had a lasting impact on me personally and my career; to all of you ... THANK YOU!

JOHNATHAN THURSTON
ACADEMY

JOHNATHAN THURSTON ACADEMY

Inspiring individuals, encouraging education and overall well being.

The JT Academy, established in 2018 with bases in Sydney and Brisbane, aims to be a leading national provider of outstanding employment initiatives, and training programs aimed at health, wellbeing, sport and education across Australia. The academy's key strength is developing and delivering high-quality programs to individuals, equipping them with the right skills, knowledge and attributes to make a significant and positive future impact. Through strong education, community and industry partnerships we are committed to supporting people of all ages to reach their personal, educational and career goals.

JTLEARNING

Through online learning, the Johnathan Thurston Academy is powered by GO1, an online learning platform equipped to facilitate learning for users across a range of topics. Our content is targeted to support children, youth, adults and organisations across all industries to address the changing needs of individuals and organisations.

JTCOMMUNITY

Johnathan Thurston Academy develops and delivers a range of community programs and initiatives focusing on education, employment, health and well being to assist our local communities. Through community consultation our programs are developed to support disadvantaged and marginalised youth and their families through delivery of capacity building programs. Our key programs include: JTBelieve (school engagement) JTWomenToLead (encouraging young women to think big and be bold) and JTSucceed (employment participation).

JTEMPLOYMENT

Johnathan Thurston Academy, with Lendlease as our major employment partner, is a unique collaborative employment zone. The goal and focus is to connect jobseekers to all of our employment partners including (but not limited to) Lendlease projects and communities throughout Queensland, New South Wales and Northern Territory.

We aim to ensure that all opportunities for potential connections are both exhausted and managed in the one zone. We have created a unique and sophisticated platform that streamlines all employment and training opportunities between jobseekers and employers.

The main objective of the Academy is to ensure that locals throughout the regions have access to employment and training opportunities. We will link and connect with local community, government departments, schools, sub-contractors, retailers, project operations, local councils and all key community and industry stakeholders.

The JTJobBoard (jtacademy.com.au) is hot spot for jobs across the nation, with some of Australia's biggest employers using the JTJobBoard to attract jobseekers and increase community workforce participation and engagement.

JTYOUTH

JTYouth zone provides a unique, safe place for young people to learn and engage with positive messaging. Sports, health, education, wellbeing and some creative activities. The JTYouth zone will welcome thousands of young people whom we will engage and provide positive messaging to raise their aspirations and provide them with access to high quality messaging, learning and activities.

For more information: www.jtacademy.com.au